KB055013

한국 인권문제

시민적 · 정치적 권리 국제규약 인권보고서 3

한국 인권문제

시민적 · 정치적 권리 국제규약 인권보고서 3

한국학술정보

| 머리말

일제 강점기 독립운동과 병행되었던 한국의 인권운동은 해방이 되었음에도 큰 결실을 보지 못했다. 1950년대 반공을 앞세운 이승만 정부와 한국전쟁, 역시 경제발전과 반공을 내세우다 유신 체제에 이르렀던 박정희 정권, 쿠데타로 집권한 1980년대 전두환 정권까지, 한국의 인권은 이를 보장해야 할 국가와 정부에 의해 도리어 억압받고 침해되었다. 이런 배경상 근대 한국의 인권운동은 반독재, 민주화운동과 결을 같이했고, 대체로 국외에 본부를 둔 인권 단체나 정치로부터 상대적으로 자유로운 종교 단체에 의해 주도되곤 했다. 이는 1980년 5·18광주민주화운동을 계기로 보다 근적인 변혁을 요구하는 형태로 조직화되었고, 그 활동 영역도 정치를 넘어 노동자, 농민, 빈민 등으로 확대되었다. 이들이 없었다면 한국은 1987년 군부 독재 종식하고 절차적 민주주의를 도입할 수 없었을 것이다. 민주화 이후에도 수많은 어려움이 있었지만, 한국의 인권운동은 점차 전문적이고 독립된 운동으로 분화되며 더 많은 이들의 참여를 이끌어냈고, 지금까지 많은 결실을 맺을 수 있었다.

본 총서는 1980년대 중반부터 1990년대 초반까지, 외교부에서 작성하여 30여 년간 유지했던 한국 인권문제와 관련한 국내외 자료를 담고 있다. 6월 항쟁이 일어나고 민주화 선언이 이뤄지는 등 한국 인권운동에 많은 변화가 있었던 시기다. 당시 인권문제와 관련한 국내외 사안들, 각종 사건에 대한 미국과 우방국, 유엔의 반응, 최초의 한국 인권보고서 제출과 아동의 권리에 관한 협약 과정, 유엔인권위원회 활동, 기타 민주화 관련 자료 등 총 18권으로 구성되었다. 전체 분량은 약 9천여 쪽에 이른다.

2024년 3월

한국학술정보(주)

| 일러두기

· 본 총서에 실린 자료는 2022년 4월과 2023년 4월에 각각 공개한 외교문서 4,827권, 76만 여 쪽 가운데 일부를 발췌한 것이다.

· 각 권의 제목과 순서는 공개된 원본을 최대한 반영하였으나, 주제에 따라 일부는 적절히 변경하였다.

· 원본 자료는 A4 판형에 맞게 축소하거나 원본 비율을 유지한 채 A4 페이지 안에 삽입 하였다. 또한 현재 시점에선 공개되지 않아 '공란'이란 표기만 있는 페이지 역시 그대로 실었다.

· 외교부가 공개한 문서 각 권의 첫 페이지에는 '정리 보존 문서 목록'이란 이름으로 기록물 종류, 일자, 명칭, 간단한 내용 등의 정보가 수록되어 있으며, 이를 기준으로 0001번부터 번호가 매겨져 있다. 이는 삭제하지 않고 총서에 그대로 수록하였다.

· 보고서 내용에 관한 더 자세한 정보가 필요하다면, 외교부가 온라인상에 제공하는 『대한 민국 외교사료요약집』 1991년과 1992년 자료를 참조할 수 있다.

| 차례

정 리 보 존 문 서 목 록

기록물종류	일반공문서철	등록번호	2020110105	등록일자	2020-11-20
분류번호	734.23	국가코드		보존기간	영구
명 칭	시민적.정치적 권리에 관한 국제규약(B규약) 한국 최초 인권보고서 제출 및 심의, 1991-92. 전5권				
생 산 과	국제연합2과	생산년도	1991~1992	담당그룹	
권 차 명	V.5 1992.7.10-10월				
내용목차	* 제45차 인권이사회. Geneva,1992.7.13-31 - 수석대표 : 박수길 주제네바대사 - 한국인권보고서 심의(심의기간:7.13-15) - 심의 후속조치, 평가				

0001

	분류번호	보존기간

발 . 신 전 보

번   호 : ___WGV-1050___ ___920710 1632___ WG종별 : _____

수   신 : 주   제네바   대사. ~~총영사~~

발   신 : 장   관   (연이)

제   목 : 인권이사회 회의 _____   ·····

      1. 표제회의에 참석하는 KNCC 및 민변측 관계자를 파악 보고하고, 이들의 현지활동 상황을 상세 보고바람.

      2. 특히 동 관계자들이 사실무근한 허위사실 유포 등 법에 저촉되는 활동을 하는지에 관해 주시바람. 끝.

                             (국제기구국장 김재섭)

예고 : 92.12.31. 일반

	보안 통제	씨 네

앙 고 재	92 년 7 월 10 일	4 2 과	기안자 성명		과 장	심의관	국 장		차 관	장 관	
			이								

외신과통제

0002

외 무 부

종 별 : 지 급

번 호 : GVW-1378   일 시 : 92 0713 1130

수 신 : 장관(연이)

발 신 : 주 제네바 대사

제 목 : 인권 보고서 심의   — 헌부본은 7,13. 중우과에 기배포됨 —

　　92.7.13. 아국의 최초 보고서 심의시 본직의 기조발언문안을 별첨 송부하니, 참고
바람.

　　첨부: 연설문(영문)

　　(GVW(F)-0432). 끝

　　(대사 박수길-국장)

　　예고: 92.12.31. 까지

국기국

주 제 네 바 대 표 부

번 호 : GVW(F) - 0432   년월일 : 20713   시간 : 1130

수 신 : 장   관 (연이)

발 신 : 주 제 네 바 대 사

제 목 : 첨부

총 14 매 (표지프함)

브 안 동 제	 그
외신과 동 제	

0004

432-147

주 제 네 바 대 표 부

번호 : GVW(F) - 433   년월일 : 20713   시간 : 1230

수신 : 장 관 (연이)

발신 : 주제네바대사

제목 : 연설문 (국문)

총 10 매 (표지 포함)

```
관        안 계   7
종
```
```
외신관
봉      계
```

연이 배포함·

433-10-1   0005

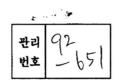

외 무 부

종 별 : 지 급

번 호 : GVW-1386

일 시 : 92 0714 0130

수 신 : 장 관 (연이, 법무부, 기정)

발 신 : 주 제네바 대사

제 목 : 인권 보고서 심의

연 : GVW-1378

1. 45 차 인권 이사회는 금 7.13 (월) 오후 예정대로 아국 최초 보고서 심의를 가졌는 바 요지 아래 보고함.

가. 개요

0 금일 회의는 18 명의 위원중 POCAR 의장 포함 14 명이 참석한 가운데 의장의 대표단 소개에 이어 본직이 연호 내용의 기조 발언을 함.

0 이어서 위원들의 질문이 있었는 바, 8 명의 위원이 질문을 마친 상태에서 종료시간이 되어 명 7.14 (화) 오전 회의를 속개, 나머지 4 명의 질문을 듣기로 함

0 아국 대표단의 답변은 예정대로 7.15 (수) 오후 회의시 있을 예정임

나. 위원들의 주요 질문 내용은 아래와 같음.

1) 국가 보안법 관련

0 개정 국가 보안법 부칙상 소급효 불인정 문제

0 반국가 단체의 개념

0 사형 규정 유형

0 일반 범죄에 비해 구속 시간이 긴 이유

0 금서 목록 존재 여부

2) 기타

0 영장주의 예외가 넓게 인정되는 근거

0 사상 전향 제도

0 법관의 지위 및 독립성 보장

0 군사 법원의 지위, 항소권 보장

0 규약의 유보 조항 철회 가능성

국기국   안기부   법무부

차반. 1차보

PAGE 1

92.07.14   09:03

외신 2과 통제관 FS

0006

O 보안 관찰법 문제

O ILO 가입 계기 노동법 개정 의사 여부

O 기자 및 일부 교사의 정당참여 금지 이유

2. 관찰 및 평가

O 모든 위원들이 질문에 앞서 아국의 최초 보고서에 대하여, 동 보고서가 규약이 정하는 기준에 따라 우리의 인권 관련 법제 및 조치 사항을 성실하게 설명하고 있음을 언급하면서, 특히 보고서와 기조 발언을 통해 설명된 그간의 민주화 진전과 인권 신장 상황을 평가함.

O 대부분의 위원들은 국가 보안법에 대하여 많은 관심을 보였으며, 이밖에 규약과 국내법 관계, 법원의 독립, 규약 유보 문제, 사형 제도등에 관해 주로 질문을 하였는 바, 다수 위원들이 민변의 반박 보고서 및 AI 보고서등을 참고하였으나 국가 보안법에 관한 질문의 수준은 구체적인 사례 제시나 이론적 논리의 전개보다는 용어의 정의등 추상적인 질문이 많았음.

O 금일 회의장에는 김찬국 KNCC 인권 위원장 및 김경남 사무국장, 최영도 변협 인권 위원장, 민변의 천정배, 조용환, 박원순 변호사외에 장의균 후원회 소속 일본인과 아국 유학생이 방청하였는 바 특이 사항은 없었으며, 당지 북한 대표부 박덕훈 참사관도 잠시 회의장에 들렀음. 끝

(대사 박수길-국장)

예고 : 92.12.31. 까지

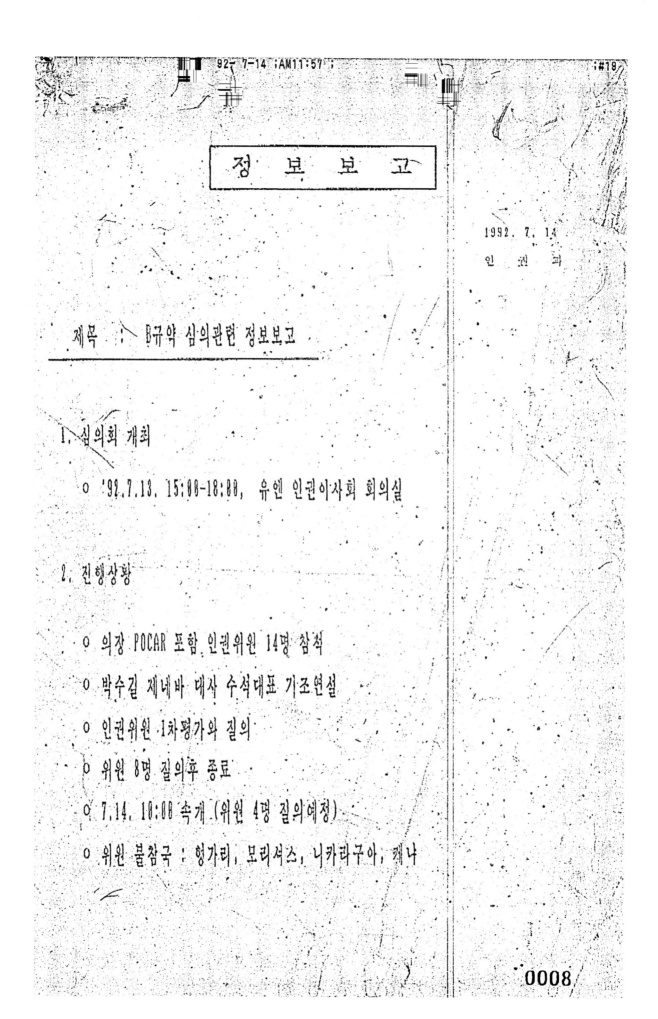

정 보 보 고

1992. 7. 14.
인 권 과

제목 : B규약 심의관련 정보보고

1. 심의회 개최

　o '92.7.13. 15:00-18:00, 유엔 인권이사회 회의실

2. 진행상황

　o 의장 POCAR 포함 인권위원 14명 참석

　o 박수길 제네바 대사 수석대표 기조연설

　o 인권위원 1차평가와 질의

　o 위원 8명 질의후 종료

　o 7.14. 10:00 속개 (위원 4명 질의예정)

　o 위원 불참국 : 헝가리, 모리셔스, 니카라구아, 캐나

0008

3. 수석대표 기조연설 요지

  O 제6공화국하에서 이루어진 인권상황, 민주화 진전상황

  O 보고서 제출후 UN, ILO 가입 등 일련의 진전사항

  O 향후 인권신장을 위한 정부조치 및 계획 설명

4. 위원 개별검토 (individual observation)

  O 정부보고서가 규약이 정하는 기준에 충실, 아국 인권관련 법제 및 조치등을
    체계적으로 설득력있게 설명

  O 제6공 이후 정부의 민주화 개혁조치와 실질적 인권신장 성과 인정, 긍정적 평가

5. 주요 질문사항

  O 국가보안법 관련

    - 개정 국가보안법 부칙상 소급효 불인정 문제

    - 반국가단체 개념

    - 사형규정 유형

    - 일반 범죄에 비해 구속기간이 긴 이유

    - 금서목록 존재여부

0009

O 기 타

  - 성장주의 예외가 널리 인정되는 근거

  - 사상전향제도

  - 법관의 지위 및 독립성 보장

  - 군사법원의 지위, 항소권 보장

  - 규약 유보조항 철회 가능성

  - 보안관찰법 문제

  - ILO가입 계기, 노동법 개정의사 여부

  - 기자 및 일부 교사의 정당참여 금지사유

6. 참고사항

O 금일 회의장에는 김창국(KNCC 인권위원장), 김경남 (KNCC 사무국장),

  최영도(변협 인권위원장), 천정배, 박원순, 조용환 변호사 (민변),

  장의균 후원회 소속 일본인과 아국 유학생 방청

O 특이사항 없으며, 북한 대표부 박덕훈 참사관도 잠시 방문

0010

보도자료   *법무부 발표

유엔 인권이사회 우리의 국제인권규약 보고서 긍정 평가

제45차 유엔 인권이사회는 지난 7.13(월)부터 스위스 제네바의 유엔
회의장에서 정부의 국제인권규약 최초보고서에 관하여 심도있는 검토를 한
결과, 한국정부가 6공화국 출범이후 지속적으로 추진해 온 민주화 및 인권
신장 노력을 높이 평가하고 이에 따른 성과를 매우 고무적인 일로 환영하면서
한국사회가 인권보장에 있어 바람직한 방향으로 가고 있다고 평가를 하였음.
다른 한편 위원들은 위와 같이 괄목할만한 성과에도 불구하고 아국이 국가
보안법의 운용, 규약규정의 구체적 실천문제, 일부 유보의 철회 등 일부
분야에서 아직도 개선해야 할 것이 있음을 지적하고 차기 보고서에서는
개선 노력이 반영되기를 희망하였음.

1. 인권이사회의 보고서 검토 과정

가. 수석대표 기조발언

O 동 인권이사회의 정부보고서 검토는 18명의 인권이사회 위원중 14명이
   참석한 가운데 7.13. 오후 정부 수석대표인 박수길 주제네바 대사의
   기조발언으로 시작되었음. 박수길 수석대표는 기조발언을 통해
   우리의 보고서를 소개하면서 제6공화국 헌법하에서 이루어진 인권
   신장과 민주화 진전, 특히 헌법소원제도의 활발한 운영과 민간차원의
   인권신장 노력 등에 관하여 설명하고 보고서 제출 이후 UN 가입,

0011

ILO 가입, 주요 인권협약 가입, 남.북 교류협력 합의서 체결 등 일련의
진전사항과 아울러 향후 인권신장을 위해 정부가 취할 제반 계획과
조치들을 제시하였음. 그중 특기할 사항으로는 고문방지협약 가입
방침 표명, 형법 및 형사소송법 개정방향, 노동관계법 개정 검토 등임.
이와 함께 박수길 수석대표는 정부가 앞으로도 헌법과 국제규약을
반영하여 국민의 인권신장을 위한 노력을 계속해 나갈 것임을 밝혔음.

나. 인권위원의 논평 및 질의

O 7.13-14. 이틀간 참석위원 14명중 12명만이 우리 보고서에 대한 논평과
   질의 하였으며, 질의는 한반도 분단상황과 인권보장의 장애요인,
   형사사법상의 적법절차, 사형제도, 국가보안법 적용상의 제반문제,
   여성애 대한 평등보장, 아동의 권리보장, 외국인의 권리보호, 인권침해
   예방을 위한 조치 등 인권관련 전 분야를 망라하여 폭넓고 상세하게
   개진되었음.

O 위원들은 정부보고서를 평가함에 있어 특히 한국이 제6공화국 출범이후
   이룩한 성과중에서 헌법 및 각종 인권관련 법령의 개정과 헌법재판소
   신설 등 제도개혁, 사회안전법의 폐지와 집회 및 시위에 관한 법률,
   국가보안법 개정, 지방자치제도의 실시로 인한 국민 참정권 확대,
   언론의 비판과 감시기능의 활성화에 따른 인권침해 예방 등에 긍정적인
   평가를 하면서 한국이 개방적이고 적극적인 인권보장 노력을 기울이고
   있다고 언급하였음.

O 국가보안법에 관하여는 아국의 안보상황에 비추어 국가보안법의
   당위성을 인정하면서도 냉전체제의 몰락, 남북관계의 개선 등에 비추어
   동법 남용 가능성, 특히 개념정의의 모호성, 정치적 소신의 강요
   가능성 등 문제점을 지적하고 그에 대한 설명과 함께 개선노력을 요청
   하였음.

0012

o 한편 여성차별, 신체의 자유, 집회결사의 자유, 재소자 처우 등 기타

　인권 제약요소에 관하여는 국제적 인권보장 기준에 비추어 이러한

　관계 법령의 운용이 어떻게 정당화 될 수 있는지에 관한 질의가 많았음.

다. 상기 위원들의 질의에 대해, 우리 대표는 7.15. 오후 답변하게 되며, 정부의

　인권보장과 관련한 기본입장을 심도있게 설명할 예정임.

2. 의의 및 평가

o 금번 유엔 인권이사회의 정부 최초보고서 평가는 국제무대에서 최초로

　우리의 인권보장제도 및 운용실태에 대하여 원칙적인 면에서 긍정적인

　평가를 받았다는 점에 그 의의가 있으며, 다른 한편 특히 국가보안법의

　남용 가능성이 지적되는 등 인권이사회가 아국의 인권상황을 보는

　시각을 확인하는 계기가 되었음.

o 유엔 인권이사회는 우리 정부의 최초보고서를 검토함에 있어 우리나라가

　국제사회에서 차지하고 있는 위치에 비추어 인권보장에 있어서도 선진국의

　수준과 기준으로 모든 질의와 평가를 개진하였다는 점이 특기할만 함.

o 또한 우리 정부는 금번 정부 최초보고서의 긍정 평가를 계기로 지난 4월

　유엔 인권위원회 위원국으로 피선된 한국의 위상이 실질적으로 공인받게

　됨에 따라 향후 국제무대에서 인권선진국으로서 세계적인 시각에서 다른

　나라의 인권문제도 거론할 수 있는 위상을 굳히는 성과도 거두었다고

　평가됨. 끝.

0013

長官報告事項

報 告 畢

1992. 7. 14.
國 際 機 構 局
國際聯合2課(39)

題 目 : 人權報告書 審議

第45次 人權理事會는 7.13. 午後 우리나라 最初報告書 審議를 開始,
駐제네바大使의 基調發言에 이어 各 委員들의 1次 質問이 있었는 바,
主要事項 아래 報告드립니다.

---

1. 槪 要

O 7.13. 會議에 18명 委員中 Pocar 議長포함 14명 參席
  - 委員 8명의 質問 終了(7.14.오전 의원 4명 추가질문)
  * 우리 代表團의 答辯은 7.15(수) 午後 豫定

O 主要 質問內容
  - 國家保安法 관련, 遡及效 不認定 問題, 反國家團體의 槪念, 死刑規定
    類型 等
  - 기타 法官의 地位 및 獨立性 保障, 規約의 留保條項 撤回 可能性,
    勞動法 改定意思 與否 等

2. 觀察 및 評價

O 모든 委員들이 우리 報告書가 人權關聯 法制 및 措置事項을 誠實하게
   說明하고 있음을 言及하고 그간의 民主化 進展과 人權伸張 狀況을 評價

O 대부분의 委員들은 國家保安法에 關心 表明, 具體的인 事例 提示나 理論的
   論理의 展開 보다는 用語의 定義 等 抽象的 質問

3. 參考 事項

O KNCC 人權委員長 및 事務局長, 辯協 人權委員長, 民辯 辯護士 3명 등
   傍聽하였으나, 特異事項은 없었음.

4. 言論對策

O 심의종료 후 조치. 끝.

0014

U.N. rights panel to review S. Korea

The Human Rights Committee will question South Korea July 13-15 on a human rights report submitted a year ago, the Foreign Ministry said yesterday.

The 18-member committee, in a study and comment session in Geneva, will also ask the Korean delegation whether Korean laws guarantee the implementation of rights protection. "The panel will not probe cases of human rights violations," said the ministry.

Ambassador to Geneva Park Soo-gil will receive the questions July 13 and present the answers July 15.

Seoul joined the International Covenant on Civil and Political Rights in April 1990 and submitted its first report on human rights conditions in July last year.

The committee's report is divided into two parts-economic, social and cultural rights, and personal and political rights, and will be presented to the U.N. General Assembly and other U.N. agencies.

Korea agreed to all articles except three-right to court appeal, double jeopardy and right to assemble.

Korea Herald page 1 92. 7. 11.

0015

문화일보 1면 92.7.14.

한국일보 2면 92.7.14.

0016

＊ 국민일보 '92.7.15 2면

한국人權 好轉 평가

유엔 '보안법은 개선여지많아'

[뉴욕=로이터] 유엔인권위원회는 14일 한국의 인권상황이 지난 수년간 부분적으로 신장돼 왔다고 평가하고 있다고 밝혔다.

그러나 국가보안법의 운용 일부 문제는 여전히 개선의 여지가 많다고 지적했다.

지난 13일부터 시작된 제45차 유엔인권위 회의에서는 한국정부가 제출한 제1차 인권규약에 관한 최초의 보고서에 대한 검토에서 한국정부가 6개 항목이 지난 적으로 추진해온 인권신장 노력을 개괄 평가하면서 한국사회의 인권개선 상황이 개발도상국의 모범이 되고 있다고 밝혔다.

인권위원회는 그러나 이날 한국의 진보된 일련의 특별에서 국가보안법의 운용, 국제인권규약 일부 부분에의 실천문제 일부 부분에 아직도 개선의 여지가 있다고 지적, 이에 대한 근본적인 개선이 감무돼야 할 것이라고 밝혔다.

한국人權 꾸준히 신장
保安法운용등엔 문제

유엔 人權委 지적

【브뤼셀=】유엔인권위원회는 14일 한국의 인권상황이 지난 수년간 꾸준히 신장돼 왔다고 평가하고 그러나 국가보안법의 운용등 일부 문제는 여전히 개선의 여지가 많다고 지적했다.

지난 13일부터 시작된 제45차 유엔인권위원회의는 한국정부가 제출한 국제인권규약에 관한 최초의 보고서에 대한 검토에서 한국정부가 6공화국 출범이후 지속적으로 추진해온 인권신장 노력을 높이 평가하면서 한국사회의 인권개선 상황은 개발도상 국의 모범이 되고 있다고 말했다.

인권위원회는 그러나 이날 한달동안 진행될 회의와 토론에서 국가보안법의 운용 ·국제인권관련 규약규정의 실천문제등 일부 분야에 있어서도 지적, 이에대한 근본적인 개선이 강구돼야할 것이라고 말했다.

적으로 추진해 온 인권신장 상황을 높이 평가하면서 한 국사회의 인권개선 상황은 개발도상국의 모범이 되고 있다고 말했다.

인권위원회는 그러나 이날 하루동안 진행될 회의와 토론에서 국가보안법의 운용, 국제인권관련 규약규정의 실천문제등 일부 분야에 대한 최종평가서도 같은날 발표될 예정이다.

안법과 관련, 한국의 분단 상황에 따른 특수성을 인정 하면서도 북한체제의 붕괴 및 남북관계의 개선상황에 비추어 보안법의 남용 가능성이 있다면서 특히 국가안보에 대한 정치적 소신의 강요가 가능한 문제점을 지적했다.

한국대표단의 인권위원회의 질의에 대해 15일 하오 담변하게 되며 한국인권에 대한 최종평가서도 같은날 발표될 예정이다.

韓國人權 꾸준히 신장

유엔인권委 평가

【브뤼셀】유엔인권위원회는 14일 한국의 인권상황이 지난 수년간 꾸준히 신장돼 왔다고 평가하고 그러나 국가보안법의 운용등 일부 문제는 여전히 개선의 여지가 많다고 지적했다.

지난 13일부터 시작된 제45차 유엔인권위원회의는 한국정부가 제출한 국제인권규약에 관한 최초의 보고서에 대한 검토에서 한국정부가 6공화국 출범이후 지속적으로 추진해온 인권신장 노력을 높이 평가하면서 한국사회의 인권개선 상황은 개발도상국의 모범이 되고 있다고 말했다.

인권위원회는 그러나 이날 하루동안 진행될 회의와 토론에서 국가보안법의 운용·국제인권관련 규약규정의 실천문제등 일부 분야에서 아직도 개선의 여지가 많다고 지적, 이에대한 근본적인 개선이 강구돼야할 것이라고 말했다.

한국 인권상황 나아졌으나
보안법 등 개선여지 많아

유엔인권위

【브뤼셀=연합】 유엔 인권위원회는 14일 한국의 인권상황이 지난 몇년간 꾸준히 신장돼 왔다고 평가하고 그러나 국가보안법의 운용 등 일부 문제는 여전히 개선의 여지가 많다고 지적했다.

지난 13일부터 시작된 제45차 유엔 인권위원회 회의는 한국 정부가 제출한 국제인권규약에 관한 최초의 보고서 검토에서 한국 정부가 6공 출범 이후 지속적으로 추진해온 인권신장 노력을 높이 평가하면서 한국 사회의 인권개선 상황은 개발도상국의 모범이 되고 있다고 말했다.

그러나 인권위원회는 이날 하룻동안 진행된 질의와 토론에서 국가보안법의 운용, 국제인권 관련 규약규정의 실천문제 등 일부 분야에서 아직도 개선의 여지가 많다고 지적하고 이에 대한 근본적 개선책이 강구돼야 할 것이라고 강조했다.

인권위 위원들은 6공 출범 이후 헌법을 비롯한 각종 인권관련 법령 개정과 헌법재판소 신설 등 제도 개혁, 사회안전법의 폐지, 집회 및 시위에 관한 법률과 국가보안법의 개정, 지방자치제에 따른 국민참정권 확대 등에 긍정적 의견을 보였다.

그러나 위원들은 국가보안법과 관련해 한국의 분단상황에 따른 특수성을 인정하면서도 냉전체제의 몰락, 남북관계의 개선 등에 비추어 보안법의 남용 가능성이 있다면서 특히 국가 안보의 개념에 대한 모호성, 국민에 대한 정치적 소신의 강요 가능성 등 문제점을 지적했다.

한겨레 92. 7. 16.

0019

한국保安法 수정 촉구

유엔人權委 "일부조항 공권력 공포 우려"

【제네바 21일=聯合】유엔인권위원회는 16일 한국의 인권상황에 진전이 있었다고 인정하면서도 한국의 국가보안법을 국제적인 기준에 맞도록 개정할 것을 촉구했다.

위원회는 14·15일 이틀간 진행된 청문회에서 한국의 보안법은 너무나 애매한 부분이 많아 한국인의 인권을 보장하기 어렵다고 말했다.

朴鈺洙 駐제네바대사에게 유고슬라비아의 인권전문가인 보진더 미트리여비치는 「보안법의 용어들은 일반 시민들에게 법으로 금지된 것과 그렇지 않은 것에 대한 구분을 어렵게하고있다」며 일부 조항은 공권력에 대한 공포와 강박관념을 야기하고 있다고 주장했다.

朴대사는 이에대해 한국정부는 국가보안법을 형법으로 편입시키기위한 작업을 추진중이나 對北관계및 문화적인 이유등으로 아직 완결하지 못했다고 밝혔다.

유엔人權委, 韓國 인권개선 평가
국가보안법운용등 일부문제 상존

(브뤼셀=聯合) 李鍾浩특파원 = 유엔인권위원회는 14일 한국의 인권상황이 지난 수년간 꾸준히 신장돼 왔다고 평가하고 그러나 국가보안법의 운용등 일부 문제는 여전히 개선의 여지가 많다고 지적했다.

지난 13일부터 시작된 제45차 유엔인권위원회 회의는 한국정부가 제출한 국제인권규약에 관한 최초의 보고서에 대한 검토에서 한국정부가 6共 출범이후 지속적으로 추진해 온 인권신장 노력을 높이 평가하면서 한국사회의 인권개선 상황은 개발도상국의 모범이 되고 있다고 말했다.

인권위원회는 그러나 이날 하루동안 진행될 질의와 토론에서 국가보안법의 운용, 국제인권관련 규약규정의 실천문제 등 일부 분야에서 아직도 개선의 여지가 많다고 지적, 이에대한 근본적인 개선책이 강구돼야 할 것이라고 말했다.

인권위 위원들은 한반도 분단상황에 따른 인권보장의 장애요인, 형사법상의 절차문제, 사형제도, 국가보안법의 적용문제, 여성과 어린이의 권리보장, 외국인 권리보호, 인권침해 예방을 위한 사전조처 등 인권분야를 폭넓고 상세하게 취급했다.

위원들은 6공 출범이후 헌법을 비롯한 각종 인권관련 법령개정과 헌법재판소 신설등 제도개혁, 사회안전법의 폐지, 집회및 시위에 관한 법률과 국가보안법의 개정, 지방자치제에 따른 국민참정권 확대, 언론의 비판감시 기능 활성화에 힘입은 인권침해 예방 등에 긍정적인 의견을 보였다.

그러나 위원들은 국가보안법과 관련, 한국의 분단상황에 따른 특수성을 인정하면서도 冷戰체제의 몰락, 남북관계의 개선 등에 비추어 보안법의 남용 가능성이 있다면서 특히 국가안보의 개념에 대한 모호성, 국민에 대한 정치적 소신의 강요가능성등 문제점을 지적했다.

한국대표단은 인권위원들의 질문에 대해 15일 오후 답변하게 되며 한국인권에 대한 최종평가서도 같은 날 발표될 예정이다.(끝)

(YONHAP) 920715 0811 KST

0021

```
GLGL
o0558 ASI/AFP-3121----
u i U.N.-rights-SKorea   07-14 0403
  South Korea's human rights record criticised
```

GENEVA, July 14 (AFP) - South Korea's application of the International
Agreement on Civil and Political Rights faced criticism here Tuesday by a
member of the United Nations human rights committee.

The Seoul government, which has ratified the 1966 agreement along with 110
other countries, defending its human rights record in a report submitted to
the committee late Monday.

According to the report: "The constitution ... has enormously contributed
to the political, economic and social development of the Republic of Korea and
to the protection of human rights.

"With regards to restrictions on fundamental human rights, the
constitution prescribed strict limitations on the government's power, in order
to prevent an abuse of power..."

French rights expert Christine Chanet said the 70-page academic report
"did not reflect reality" and added that South Korea was a "state without
rights."

She referred to studies by Korean non-governmental organisations, notably
Christian ones, which reported some 1,500 political prisoners in the country.

Chanet told AFP that as the country's penal system was to counter North
Korea, "everything can become a state secret."

In addition to the constitution, there was the National Security Law, of
which articles four and seven allowed "the detention of anyone" for a lengthy
period and could impose the death penalty.

The South Korean report set out the means by which individuals could
obtain reparations for any abuse of their rights. These would apply to any
torture cases, which is legally forbidden.

In a reference to the National Security Law, the report said that in
certain cases "freedom of expression, regarded as a cornerstone of democracy,"
would be restricted.

"The National Security Law is a special law to cope with the special
situation facing the Korean peninsula.

"The Korean people suffered a horrifying war for three years, started by
the North Korean attack on the South.

"Therefore most South Koreans are fearful of the North's agression and are
prepared to cope with the special situation of a divded nation," it said.

The South Korean representatives, ambassador Soo Gil Park and Kouk-Jin
Yoo, head of the justice ministry's human rights section, must reply Wednesday
to questions by the U.N. committee.
```
  jms/pc/cl
  AFP 141950 GMT JUL 92
AFP 142001 GMT JUL 92
```

0022

국제 심판대 오른 6공화국 '인권'

앰네스티 · ILO 들에서 '유엔 제소' 등 구체 대응

지난 3월 16일 법무부와 대전교도소는 발칵 뒤집혔다. 6.29선언 직후인 87년 7월4일 '재야침투 간첩' 혐의로 체포돼 징역 8년을 선고받고 대전교도소에서 복역중이던 장의균씨에게 미국의 대표적 국제 인권단체인 아시아 워치에서 인권상을 수여했기 때문이다. 아시아 워치는 정치적으로 박해를 받고 있다고 판정한 세계 각국의 문인들을 해마다 10명씩 뽑아 '표현의 자유를 위한 기금'으로 상을 수여한다. 그런데 올해 한국인으로서는 최초로 장의균씨가 선정돼 상금 1만달러를 받았던 것이다. 그동안 "국내에 정치범은 한명도 없다"고 늘상 주장해오던 정부로서는 이만저만한 낭패가 아닐 수 없는 일이었다.

비슷한 시기에 정부의 입장을 곤혹스럽게 하는 또 한가지 일이 벌어졌다. 영국 런던에 본부를 둔 세계적 인권단체인 국제사면위원회(Amnesty International)가 창립 30주년 기념 사업의 하나로 고난받는 세계 각국의 정치범 30명을 뽑아 그들의 삶을 비디오에 담아서 각국에 돌렸다. 그런데 30명 중에는 지난 84년 안기부에 의해 '재독일 유학생간첩'으로 지목돼 사형을 선고받았다가 무기로 감형돼 현재 서울구치소에 수감중인 김성만씨가 포함되어 있었던 것이다.

5공화국까지 국제사회에서 대표적인 인권침해 국가로 낙인찍혔던 한국은 경제성장과 올림픽 개최, 대통령 직선제에 의한 6공화국 등장으로 그같은 국제적 이미지를 개선하는 데 어느 정도 성공했다. 또 북방정책과 남북한 유엔가입 등 6공 들어 거둔 일련의 외교적 성과를 통해 국제사회에서 정치적 위상을 상당히 드높인 것도 사실이다.

그러나 이 과정은 한국의 인권문제를 국제무대에 공식적으로 끌어들인 결과를 가져오기도 했다. 유엔 가입으로 대표되는 외교적 성과는 회원국으로서 국제사회에서 져야 할 짐이 종전보다 무거워졌음을 뜻하기 때문이다.

국가보안법 · 장기수 · 대량 해직이 쟁점

6공의 인권상황 중에서 현재 국제여론의 주요한 관심 대상은 국가보안법과 장기수 문제, 그리고 교사 노동자 대량 해직과 관련된 문제들이다. 올해 들어서만도 이들 문제에 대한 국제 인권단체들의 구체적 대응이 꼬리를 물고 있다.

지난 6월 18일 미국의 로버트 케네디 인권재단은 '한국의 인권상황과 민주주의에 대한 보고서'를 통해 다음과 같은 내용을 발표했다.

"한국정부의 민주화 주장에도 불구하고 한국에는 국가보안법과 보호관찰법, 강제전향 등을 포함한 인권유린과 억압이 계속되고 있다. 법령 법집행관행 법집행당국 등이 일부 변화하고 있지만 한국정부는 헌법과 국제인권협약이 보장하는 기본인권 옹호에 충실하지 않으며 오히려 노대통령 집권 이전보다 더욱 정교하고 은밀한 방법으로 인권유린이 벌어지고 있다."

4월과 5월에는 세계교원단체연맹과 국제자유교원노조연맹이 결사의 자유를 위반했다는 이유로 한국정부를 유엔 산하 단체인 국제노동기구(ILO)에 공동으로 제소했다. 제소장에 따르면 "한국정부가 노조에 가입했다는 이유만으로 1천4백96명의 교사를 해고한 것은 ILO조약 제87조, 98조 위반이다. 해직교사들의 저항은 정부가 전교조를 탄압할 의도 때문에 나왔다. 한국정부는 조속하게 모든 해직교사를 복직시키고 전교조와 정상적인 관계를 정립해야 한다"고 촉구했다.

4월중에는 국제사면위원회가 유서대필 혐의로 실형을 선고받은 강기훈씨에 대해 공정한 재판을 받지 않았다는 사실을 우려하면서 한국정부에 이 사건을 재조사할 것을 촉구하고 나섰다. 사면위는 "이 사건의 주요한 증거는 국립과학수사연구소가 실시한 필적감정이었으며 재판부는 판결에서 국과수 문서분석실장의 감정 결과를 칭찬한 바 있다. 그런데 두달 후 바로 그 실장은 뇌물을 받고 허위감정을 해준 혐의로 체포되었다. 우리 국제사면위는 이 사건으로 인해 국과수의 김기설씨 유서 필적 감정에 대한 신빙성에 의혹을 품고 있다"고 밝혔다.

6공의 인권상황에 관심을 기울이는 국제여론 가운데 특히 눈에 띄는 것은 유럽 쪽이다. 한국의 올림픽 개최 및 노대통령의 대유럽외교 강화, 그리고 유럽통합 기운이 무르익어 가면서 유럽 지역에서 한국의 인권문제에 대한 관심이 부쩍 늘어난 것이다. 지난 2월13일 프랑스 스트라스부르그시에 있는 유럽의회 의사당 회의실에서는 '한국인권과 국가보안법'이라는 주제의 청문회가 열렸다. 유럽의회 녹색당이 주최하고 유럽의회 내 아시아대표단(Delegation 22)이 협력했던 이 청문회는 현재 한국의 인권상황이 호전됐다는 일반적 인식에 회의를 표시했다. 그 증거로는 6공 들어 구속된 정치범의 수가 계속 증가해 5천명 선을 넘고 있다는 점과, 인권침해의 핵심이 국가보안법이라는 점이 제시됐다. 3시간 반에 걸친 이 청문회는 "한국 민주화에 걸림돌이 되고 있는 국가보안법의 즉각 폐지와 한반도에 냉전 완화가 이뤄져야 한다"는 결의

미국과 유럽의 인권단체들은 6공화국의 '인권 신장' 주장에도 불구하고 전교조 1천5백여 교사의 대량 해직(관련 사진 위)이나 경찰의 과잉 폭력 진압(왼쪽) 등으로 국제적으로 공인된 기본권이 한국에서 충분히 향유되고 있지 않다고 주장한다. 특히 전교조 사태는 국제 노동단체들의 항의 속에 국제노동기구에 한국정부가 제소당하는 결과를 빚었다.

채택으로 끝맺음했다.

이밖에도 독일 함부르크시에서 운영하는 인권단체 '세계 정치범을 위한 재단'은 수감 중인 재야 인사 김근태씨와 민중 미술가 홍성담씨를 고문받은 정치범으로 규정하여 석방되면 함부르크시로 초청해 1년간 치료하고 모든 생활편의를 제공하기로 결정했다. 유엔 산하기구인 유네스코에서도 방북사건 관련자인 임수경씨와 문규현 신부를 양심수로 규정해 한국정부에 사면을 요청하고 나섰다.

이같은 국제 인권단체들의 움직임에 대해 우리 정부는 일관되게 "국내의 일부 재야세

강기훈씨의 유서대필 사건도 국제사면위가 재조사를 촉구하는 사안이다.

력 주장을 근거로 한 편견적인 자세"라며 유감을 표명해왔다. 노대통령 역시 외국의 국가원수들로부터 인권문제에 대한 지적을 받을 때면 "한국에 정치범은 없다"고 말하곤 한다. 구속된 사람들은 급속한 민주화 추세에 편승해 자유민주주의체제를 공공연히 부정하는 실정법 위반자들이기 때문에 양심수 혹은 정치범이라고 볼 수 없다는 논리이다.

국제인권이사회에 '한국 인권' 의제 상정

그런데도 국내외 인권단체들이 끊임없이 문제를 제기하자 정부도 과거처럼 수동적이고 소극적인 자세로 있을 수만은 없다고 판단하기 시작했다. 이미 유엔 회원국이 된 만큼 산하 인권단체 등을 통해 외교적 노력으로 국제 여론을 돌려보겠다는 것이다. 정부가 오는 7월13일과 15일 이틀에 걸쳐 스위스 제네바에서 열리는 국제인권이사회 회의에 정부대표를 참석시켜 질의 응답 시간을 갖는 것도 그같은 방침에서 나온 조처이다.

정부는 지난 90년 7월 인권보장을 위한 다자간 국제조약인 '경제적·사회적 및 문화적 권리에 관한 국제규약'(A규약)과 '시민적 및 정치적 권리에 관한 국제규약'(B규약)에 가입했다. 이어서 B규약 제40조의 규정에 따라 국내 인권상황에 관한 '최초 보고서'를 이미 제출했다. 주로 "6공 들어 민주화 조치로 인권상황이 급신장했다"는 내용을 담은 보고서이다.

정부대표로는 법무부 인권과장을 중심으로

로 한 법무부측 관계자 3명과 스위스 대사를 중심으로 한 외무부 관계자들이 참석할 예정이다.

그러나 이번 인권이사회 회의에는 그동안 국내 인권신장을 위해 활동해온 '민주사회를 위한 변호사 모임'(이하 민변)과 한국기독교교회협의회(KNCC·이하 기협) 인권위원회가 공동으로 반박보고서를 제출해 이에 대한 이사회의 판단과 평가도 주목된다. 반박보고서는 정부보고서의 문제점 및 한국 인권상황 전반에 걸친 평가에서 "6공 출범 직후 겉으로나마 다소 개선되었던 인권상황이 89년 이후 공안정국과 3당합당을 거치면서 크게 악화되어 왔다"고 전제하고 우리 사회 각 분야의 인권침해 사례와 법 제도의 인권침해 조항을 조목조목 담았다.

민변과 기협측은 천정배 조용환 변호사, 김경남 목사 등 5명의 대표를 7월초 제네바에 파견해 한국인권 개선을 위한 국제적 협조와 이해를 구하는 활동에 들어갔다. 국제사면위원회에서도 이번 회의에 한국의 인권문제가 단일 의제로 오른다는 점을 중시해 이사회에 별도로 6공화국의 인권보고서를 제출한 것으로 알려졌다.

이로써 제네바 인권이사회 회의장은 사실상 '6공의 인권 청문회'장이 될 전망이다. 국제사회에서 끊임없이 시비가 되어온 6공의 인권이 이번 공개회의 석상에서 어떤 점수를 받을지 관심을 끈다. ■

丁喜相 기자

0024

관리
번호 92
-655

외 무 부

종 별 : 지 급

번 호 : GVW-1394   일 시 : 92 0714 2200

수 신 : 장 관(연이,기정) 사본:법무부장관

발 신 : 주 제네바 대사

제 목 : 인권규약 보고서 심의(2)

연: GVW-1386

1. 금 7.14 10:00 회의가 속개되어 나머지 4 인의 위원이 질의를 한뒤 11:00 종료되었는바, 전일 제기된 질문외에 추가된 주요 내용은 아래와 같음.

   0 규약의 국내적 효력을 헌법과 동일하게 격상시킬수 있는지 여부

   0 공안관계 특별검사가 국가 보안법등 특별법 위반 사건을 다룰경우 무죄 추정 원칙이 침해될 가능성

   0 선택의정서에 의거 제출된 진정에 대해 인권이사회가 정부 조치에 반하는VIEW 를 채택할 경우 이를 국내적으로 반영할수 있는 구제조치

   0 남. 북간 이산가족들의 재결합을 위한 정부가 취한 조치

   0 공공복리에 근거한 기본권 제한의 구체적 설명

   0 고문행위로 기소된 경찰관의 재판결과

   0 재소자의 접견권 제한(장의균 사례 예시)

   0 대전 교도소에 미전향수 40 여명이 수용중이라는 보도에 대한 설명

   0 시위진압 경찰에 대한 정부의 업무 지침 내용

   0 한국내 소수민 현황

2. 명 7.15 오후에 실시될 아측 답변은 위원들의 질의를 규약조문별 및 주요 쟁점별로 묶어 정부입장에 따라 답변할 예정이며, 특히 편향적 시각의 질의에대하여는 그 편향성을 지적함과 동시에 인권 보장에 관한 분명한 정부의 입장을 밝히고자 함.

3. KNCC 및 민변측은 위원들을 개별접촉하여 질의요망 사항을 전달하였으며, 일부 질문은 이들의 부탁에 따라 개진된 것으로 보임. 한편 KNCC 와 민변측은명 7.15 당지에서 WCC 주선으로 기자회견을 가질 예정인 것으로 파악됨.

4. 이와 관련, 우선 7.15 (한국시간)중으로 법무부측에서 1 차 홍보를 실시함이

국기국	차관	1차보	분석관	청와대	총리실	안기부	법무부

적절한 것으로 판단되며, 향후 KNCC 측 회견내용이 국내에 보도될 경우 활용함이 좋을 것으로 사료됨. (보도자료 별첨)

5. 본직은 금 7.14 아국 보고서 심의를 참관하고 있는 김찬국 KNCC 인권위원장등 KNCC 및 민변측 인사를 오찬에 초대, 인권 보장과 관련한 정부의 기본입장 설명등 의견을 교환 하였음.

첨부: 보도자료(FAX) (GVW(F)-439)

(대사 박수길-장관)

예고 92.12.31. 까지

주 제 네 바 대 표 부

번호 : GVW(F) - 43ρ   년월일 : 20714   시간: 1800

수신 : 장   관(연이)

발신 : 주제네바대사

제목 :   회부 GVW 1394

총 4 매(표지포함)

보안통제	2
외신관통제	

43ρ-4-1

0027

보 도 자 료

재목 : 유엔인권이사회 우리의 국제인권규약 보고서 긍정평가

제 45차 유엔인권이사회는 지난 7. 13(월)부터 스위스 제네바의 유엔회의장에서
정부의 국제인권규약 최초보고서에 관하여 심도있는 검토를 한 결과, 한국 정부가
6공화국 출범이후 지속적으로 추진해온 민주화 및 인권신장 노력을 높이 평가
하고 이에 따른 성과를 매우 고무적인 일로 환영 하면서 한국사회가 인권보장에
있어 바람직한 방향으로 가고 있다고 평가를 하였음.   다른 한편 위원들은
위와 같이 괄목할만한 성과에도 불구하고 아국이 국가보안법의 운용, 규약규정의
구체적 실천문제, 일부 유보의 철회등 일부분야에서 아직도 개선해야 할 것이
있음을 지적하고 차기 보고서에서는 개선 노력이 반영되기를 희망하였음.

1. 인권이사회의 보고서 검토 과정

가. 수석대표 기조발언

0 동 인권이사회의 정부보고서 검토는18명의 인권이사회 위원중 14명이
   참석한 가운데 7. 13 오후 정부수석대표인 박수길 주 제네바대사의
   기조발언으로 시작되었음. 박수길 수석대표는 기조 발언을 통해
   우리의 보고서를 소개하면서 제 6공화국 헌법하에서 이루어진 인권
   신장과 민주화 진전. 특히 헌법소원제도의 활발한 운영과 민간차원의
   인권신장 노력등에 관하여 설명하고 보고서 제출이후 UN 가입,
   ILO 가입, 주요인권협약 가입. 남.북 교류협력 합의서 채결등 일련의
   진전 사항과 아울러 향후 인권신장을 위해 정부가 취할 제반 계획과
   조치들을 제시 하였음. 그중 특기할 사항으로는 고문방지 협약 가입

47가-4-2

0028

방침표명, 형법 및 형사소송법 개정 방향, 노동관계법 개정 검보등임.
이와 함께 박수길 수석대표논 정부가 앞으로도 헌법과 국제규약을
반영하여 국민의 인권신장을 위한 노력을 계속해 나갈 것임을
밝혔음. (첨부 - 수석대표 기조 발언)

나. 인권위원의 논평 및 질의

  o 7. 13-14 이틀간 참석위원 14명중 12명만이 우리 보고서에 대한 논평과
     질의 하였으며, 질의는 한반도 분단상황과 인권보장의 장애요인,
     형사사법상의 적법절차, 사형제도, 국가보안법 적용상의 제반문제,
     여성에 대한 평등보장, 아동의 권리보장, 외국인의 권리보호, 인권침해
     예방을 위한 조치등 인권관련 전 분야를 망라하여 폭넓고 상세하게
     개진되었음.

  o 위원들은 정부보고서를 평가함에 있어 특히 한국이 제 6공화국 출범이후
     이룩한 성과중에서 헌법 및 각종 인권관련 법령의 개정과 헌법재판소
     신설등 제도개혁, 사회안전법의 폐지와 집회및시위에 관한법률. 국가
     보안법 개정, 지방자치제도의 실시도 인한 국민 참정권 확대, 언론의
     비판과 감시기능의 활성화에 따른 인권침해 예방등에 긍정적인 평가를
     하면서 한국이 개방적이고 적극적인 인권보장 노력을 기울이고 있다고
     언급하였음.

  o 국가보안법에 관하여는 아국의 안보상황에 비추어 국가보안법의
     당위성을 인정하면서도 냉전체제의 붕괴, 남북관계의 개선등에 비추어
     동법 남용 가능성 특히 개념정의의 모호성, 정치적 소신의 강요 가능성등
     문제점을 지적하고 그에 대한 설명과 함께 개선 노력을 요청하였음.

  o 한편 여성차별, 신체의 자유, 집회결사의 자유, 재소자 처우등 기타
     인권 제약 요소에 관하여는 국제적 인권보장 기준에 비추어 이러한
     관계 법령의 운용이 어떻게 정당화 될 수 있는지에 관한 질의가 많았음.

0029

(C)A-4-3

다. 상기 위원들의 질의에 대해, 우리대표는 7. 15 오후 답변하게 되며, 정부의
    인권보장과 관련한 기본 입장을 심도있게 설명할 예정임.

2. 의의 및 평가

   O 금번 유엔인권이사회의 정부 최초보고서 평가는 국제무대에서 최초로 우리의
      인권 보장제도 및 운용 실태에 대하여 원칙적인면에서 긍정적인 평가를
      받았다는 점에 그 의의가 있으며, 다른 한편 특히 국가보안법의 남용
      가능성이 지적되는등 인권이사회가 아국의 인권 상황을 보는 시각을 확인
      하는 계기가 되었음.

   O 유엔 인권이사회는 우리정부의 최초보고서를 검토함에 있어 우리나라가
      국제사회에서 차지하고 있는 위치에 비추어 인권보장에 있어서도 선진국의
      수준과 기준으로 모든 질의와 평가를 개진 하였다는 점이 특기할만함.

   O 또한 우리정부는 금번 정부 최초보고서의 긍정 평가를 계기로 지난 4월
      유엔 인권위원회 위원국으로 피선된 한국의 위상이 실질적으로 공인받게됨에
      따라 향후 국제무대에서 인권선진국으로서 세계적인 시각에서 다른나라의
      인권 문제도 거론 할 수 있는 위상을 굳히는 성과도 거두었다고 평가됨.   끝.

0030

관리번호 92 -665

외 무 부

종 별 : 지 급

번 호 : GVW-1405   일 시 : 92 0715 2320

수 신 : 장관(연이 이기천 서기관)

발 신 : 주 제네바(정 달호)

제 목 :

1. 특별보고안을 정리, 아래 타전하니 공전내용 참조 조치 바람.

2. 보도자료는(FAX), 법무부측 작성한 것임을 참고, 적의 조치바람.

아래

92.7.13-15, 제네바에서 개최된 아국 인권규약 보고서 심의 결과를 아래 보고드립니다.

인권이사회의평가

0 88 년 현 정부 출범이후 민주화와 인권신장을 위한 법적, 정치적 조치를 포함한 가분야에서의 한국정부의 노력을 높이 평가

- 우리 대표단의 진지하고 성실한 답변 내용 치하

- 한국의 특별한 안보상황은 이해되나, 국가보안법등 안보관련 법령의 적용에 있어 기본적 인권이 제약될 수 있다는 점에 우려 표명

아국대표 설명 및 답변

0 기조발언 및 답변

- 민주화 진전 및 헌법재판소와 법원의 활발한 인권보장 활동, 인권관련 국내법령 개정등 소개

- 남북관계의 특수성에 따른 국가보안법의 당위성과 인권침해 소지 불식을 위한 조치 설명

- 고문방지협약 가입의사 및 형법, 노동법등 개정 방향 소개

0 최종발언

- 이사회 위원들의 평가를 진지하게 받아들이고 향후 인권신장 노력에 반영노력

향후 대책건의

0 인권신장 노력의 확실한 표명으로서 신속한 시일내 고문방지 협약 가입

국기국

o 인권규약 3 개 유보조항 일부 철회 검토.끝
독후파기

외 무 부

종 별 : 지 급

번 호 : GVW-1407 　　　　　　　　　　　　　 일 시 : 92 0706 0100

수 신 : 장 관(연이) 사본: 법무부장관(법무실장)

발 신 : 주 제네바대사

제 목 : 인권보고서 심의

　　회의결과에 대한 보도자료(필요시 홍보)를 별첨송부함.

　　첨부: 보도자료(GVW(F)-0445).끝

　　(대사 박수길-국장)

국기국　　　법무부

주 제 네 바 대 표 부

번호 : GVW(F) - 0445   년월일 : 20716   시간 : 0100

수신 : 장 관(영 애)

발신 : 주제네바대사

제목 : GVW-1409 첨부

총 3 매(표시도함)

보 관 통 제	

외 신 관 통 제	

445 - 3 -1

0034

보 도 자 료 (필요시 홍보)

제목 : 정부 인권보고서 유엔 인권이사회 검토결과

(한국인권상황이 획기적으로 개선되었다고 종합평가)

> 0 제45차 유엔인권이사회는 지난 7.13~15간 스위스 제네바 유엔회의장에서 정부보고서에 대한 심의를 마쳤음.
>
> 0 심의 결과 인권이사회는 아국의 인권상황이 "획기적으로 개선(tremendously improved)" 되었다고 종합 평가하였음.

1. 심의 경과

   0 7.13(월) - 박수길 주제네바대사 기조발언 및 위원질의

   0 7.14(화) - 위원질의

   0 7.15(수) - 정부답변 및 이사회 종합평가

2. 심의회 결과

   가. 정부보고서에 대한 위원들의 개별평가(individual comments)

   0 1988년 이후 제6공화국의 지속적인 민주화노력 및 인권신장 성과를 높이 평가하고, 아국의 인권보장 제도 및 운영의 획기적 향상등 성과를 매우 고무적인 일로 환영하며, 한국 사회가 인권 보장에 있어 바람직한 방향으로 나아가고 있음.

645-3-2   0035

    o   정부 보고서는 성실하고 체계적으로 작성된 우수한 보고서
        로써, 이번 심의와 관련 한국 대표단이 이사회 위원들의
        약 150여 질의사항 전부에 대해 자세하고도 설득력있는
        답변을 하였음을 공통적으로 지적하였음.

나. Pocar 의장의 종합평가(concluding observation)

    o   인권 이사회 전원의 공통된 의견을 종합하여, 결론적으로
        한국의 인권상황이 획기적으로 개선된 것에 감명을 받았다고
        전제하고, 한국이 인권선진국을 지향하여 개방적이고
        적극적인 정책을 구사하고 있는점을 높이 평가하면서 이제는
        한국이 국제무대에서 세계각국의 인권보장을 위하여 주도적
        역할을 수행해야 할 것임을 촉구하였음.

    o   그러나 국가보안법상 개정법규의 소급효 불인정, 국가기밀,
        간첩, 반국가 단체의 개념등 일부 분야에서 아직도 문제가
        있으므로 개선 노력이 필요함을 지적하였음.

3.   참고사항

  o   대표단은 심의회 종료직후 AFP 통신기자와 회견을 통하여 전일의
      AFP 외신 보도내용(프랑스 위원 Christine Chanet이 "한국은
      권리가 없는 국가 - Korea was a state without right" 라고
      언급하였다는 기사 부분)에 대하여 그 편향성과 외곡된 시각을
      반박하였고, 회견내용이 AFP에 보도 예상됨.

  o   위원들의 질의에 대한 아국정부의 답변은 150여개의 질의를 쟁점별로
      정확하게 분류하여 적극적으로 답변하였으며, 박수길 대사는 의장의
      종합평가에 대하여 종료발언(closing remarks)을 통해 위원들의
      평가가 비교적 적절한 것이었음을 언급하였음.

외 무 부

종 별 : 지 급

번 호 : GVW-1406

일 시 : 92 0715 2400

수 신 : 장관(연이,기정동문) 사본: 법무부장관

발 신 : 주 제네바 대사

제 목 : 인권규약 보고서 심의(3)

　　1. 금 7.15. 오후 개최된 인권이사회에서는 아국 대표단의 답변, 인권위원들의 종합평가(CONCULDING COMMENTS) 가 있었으며 본직의 최종 발언을 끝으로아국 보고서 심의를 마쳤는바, 금일 회의 내용을 아래 보고함.

　　가. 아국대표단 답변

　　0 답변은 전일 제기된 인권위원들의 질문에 대하여 본직이 아국입장을 아래와 같은 요지로 종합적으로 밝혔음(발언문 별첨송부).

　　0 88 년이후 아국의 민주화 및 인권신장에 대한 위원들의 평가에 사의 표명

　　- 아국인권 상황과 관련 일부 왜곡된 인식에 대한 우려 표명 및 반박

　　- 정치범 관련 주장에 대한 정부 입장 설명

　　- 일부 NGO 의 아국인권상황에 관한 자료의 허구성 지적

　　- 남북관계 설명

　　0 이어 유국현 법무부 인권과장이 위원들의 질문에 대해 아래와 같은 내용으로 세부적인 답변을 하였음

　　- 규약의 국내적 효력

　　- 국가보안법 관련 질문에 대한 종합적 설명

　　- 아국인권 관련 기구 현황

　　- 사형제도, 비상사태, 제소자 인권, 양심의 자유, 공정한 재판권리, 여성지위등에 대해 규약 조문별 정리 설명

　　나. 위원들의 평가(CONCLUDING COMMENTS)

　　0 금일 회의에 참석한 12 명 위원들은 아국 보고서의 체재내용 및 대표단의 충실한 답변을 높이 평가하고, 아국 인권상황과 관련, 6 공 출범이후 민주화 진전 및 인권향상을 위한 정부의 노력을 평가하였음

국기국	장관	차관	차관	1차보	분석관	청와대	안기부	법무부

92.07.16　　08:31
외신 2과 통제관 BX

0037

0 또한 위원들은 분단상황에 따른 아측의 어려움에 이해를 표명하면서도 정치적 상황의 특수성에 기인한 문제는 일상적인 법률로서 대응하는 것이 바람직하다는 입장을 밝히고 아국이 규약 가입을 계기로 기존 법률이 규약에 합치되는 여부 검토해 줄것을 요망함.

0 위원들은 평가의 많은 부분을 국가보안법등과 관련한 입장 표명에 할애하였는바, 국가보안법 일부 규정 내용 및 동법 적용상의 문제점을 지적하고 특히 아래 사항에 대한 시정을 요청함.

- 규정내용이 모호하거나 개념이 불분명한 일부 조항 개선 검토
- 동법이 반정부 인사에 대해 남용될 가능성 우려
- 피의자 장기 구속 인권침해 우려

0 이밖에 위원들은 아래 문제에 대해 정부의 정책적 검토를 요망함.

- 형법 및 국가 보안법등에 있어 사형대상 범죄 범위 축소
- 사상, 양심의 자유 보장과 관련 전향 및 교정교화 제도의 문제점
- 다른 나라에 비해 장기간 허용되는 구속기간 단축 필요
- 안기부의 수사활동에 따른 인권 침해가능성 우려 - 집회, 결사의 자유의 실질적 보장 강화

0 POCAR 의장은 상기위원들의 평가를 종합, 아국이 인권 이사회 활동에 적극 참여해준데 사의를 표명하고, 88 년 이후 아국내의 괄목할 만한 인권 신장을 높이 평가하면서 특히 인권보장을 위한 헌법재판소의 역할을 언급함.

0 동 의장은 금번회의에서 위원들의 질문 및 평가가 향후 아국내에서의 인권보장을 위한 입법활동 및 기존법률 검토에 활용되고 아울러, 국가보안법, 사형제도등에 관한 위원들의 의견이 반영되기를 희망함.

다. 종료 발언

0 본직은 종료발언을 통해 아국의 안본상황에 대한 인식부족에 따른 일부 위원들의 오류를 지적하는 한편, 금번 심의가 아국인권신장에 크게 기여할 것으로확신한다고 말하고 위원들의 의견과 우려를 본국 정부에 전달하겠다고 하였음

라. 차기 보고서 제출

0 의장은 회의 종료전 아국 2 차 보고서 제출시한이 96.4.9 로 결정 되었다고 발표함.

2. 기타

가. 본직은 이사회 종료후 AFP 기자와 회견, 7.14. 자 AFP 보도가 한국 인권상황을 근거없이 편향적으로 취급한데 대해 부당함을 지적하고, 이번 이사회 심의 과정에서 나타난 긍적적인 평가도 균형있게 다루도록 요청하면서 우리 인권보장의 진전 내용에 대해 자세히 설명하였음.

나. 한편 북한측에서 한창언 주제네바 공사 포함, 3 명의 직원이 회의를참관하였으며, 회의 종료후 대표단을 만나, 본직 기존연설 내용이 좋았고 금번한국보고서 심의가향후 북한의 보고서 작성 및 심의에 많은 참고가 될것이라고언급하였음. 동인들은 특히 남북관계 언급에 대해 관심을 가지고 참관한것으로보임.

3. 평가

가. 금번 보고서 심의는 88 년 이래 민주화 진전에 따라 우리의 인권상황이크게 신장하였음을 국제적, 객관적으로 인정받고 인권관련 법제도 및 운영상황이 유엔뿐만 아니라 일반에도 알려지게되는 계기가 되었음.

나. 대부분의 위원들은 인군상황 전반에 대하여 긍정적인 평가를 하였으며 특히 우리 보고서의 광범위한 내용 및 대표단의 체계적, 포괄적 답변을 높이 평가하였음.

다. 모든 위원들은 국가 보안법에 대해 많은 관심과 우려를 표명하면서 어려운 안보상황하에서도 정상적인 방법으로 법과제도를 운영하는 것이 바람직하다는 입장을 표명함.

4. 건의

가. 고문방지 협약 가입 추진

나. 인권 규약상 아국 유보의 철회 검토

다. 형법등 인권관련 법령 개정시 인권규약내용 반영

라. 인권규약 규정, 절차 및 금번보고서 심의 내용을 검토, 정책에 반영

첨부: 수석대표 모두 발언문(GVW(F)-0444)

(대사 박수길-장관)

예고:92.12.31. 까지

주 제 네 바 대 표 부

번 호 : GVW(F) - 0444   년월일 : 2.7/5   시간 : 2-4.00
수 신 : 장 관 (연이, 법무부, 기정)
발 신 : 주 제 네 바 대 사
제 목 : 첨부

총 7 매(표지포함)

보 안 통 제	

외신과 통 제	

0040

444-7-1

Republic of Korea
15 July 1992

Second Intervention

I would first like to express my thanks to the Chairman and Committee members for the serious interest that you have shown in the protection of human rights in Korea. I have reviewed and considered each of your points with utmost attention. They have made me ever more cognizant of the serious responsibility Korea shares with every democratic nation of the world for the universal protection of human rights.

I would like to express my appreciation to the Committee members who were kind enough to remark on the accomplishments that my government has made in improving human rights in the Republic of Korea. While I realize that there is still room for progress, I know that Korea's human rights policies are headed irreversibly in the right direction.

I only have a short time to address many serious concerns. Nevertheless, I will make my best effort to address each of these concerns. In order to respond to your questions to the fullest extent possible in the limited time before us, I have, first of all, tried to group responses to certain issues that attracted your particular attention into several broad categories. Other questions are answered by reference, where appropriate, to the Covenant.

Before turning to specific questions I wish to make a few comments with regard to some important misconceptions generated by our discussions yesterday about the real human rights situation in Korea.

0041

444-7-2

The misconceptions, in my view, are attributable to a few factors such as insufficient information provided by the government concerning its consistent efforts to improve the human rights situation, deliberate attempts in some quarters to magnify sporadic human rights violations, to create a wrong impression of Korea, and the impression drawn from the western media concerning the violent labour and student demonstrations particularly before 1988 in which club-swinging police were pitted against firebomb-throwing students.

In understanding the improved situation in Korea, one has to grasp the historical importance the Korean people attach to the June 29 Declaration for Democracy which I described in my Introductory Statement as a "turning point in our people's struggle for democracy". It is this democratic platform which has shaped the democratic agenda of the current administration.

When I stated in my opening remarks that the Korean people now live under the rule of law in a democracy free from the authoritarian tinges of the past, it was not intended as an idle rhetoric. It is through these democratic reforms, reflected in the new Constitution, that former dissident leaders are able to run for the presidency of the Republic this year, that the press is able to criticize the government without any restraints, and that every citizen is able to enjoy the human rights and have the violation redressed as provided for under the Constitution. Furthermore, you may recall that the recent General Assembly election results have almost deprived the ruling party of its majority. The influential National Assembly never stands idle in its role as a watchdog branch of the government particularly when important human rights violations occur. It is very often the case that the National Assembly undertakes an investigation into violations, the result of which could redress the situation and bring the government to account in one form or another.

2

0042

444-7-3

It is in this context that I could not conceal a sense of puzzlement about some comments which in my view did not take into account the enormous changes that have occurred since the inauguration of the new administration in 1988.

It may be recalled that there are more than 17 cases of laws that were declared unconstitutional by the Constitutional Court. The court also rendered an important decision supporting the restrictive application of the NSL. This has resulted in the revision of the NSL and its very restrictive application.

Some comments were also made about alleged "political prisoners". Let me make it clear that I sharply disagree with the concept of so-called political prisoner as often used in some quarters. Means never justify the end regardless of how noble an objective may be. Those who serve prison sentences for injuring policemen or destroying state property with firebombs can never be considered political prisoners in our legal system. Some comments were made to the effect that NSL is the "actual constitution",and Korea was depicted as if it had some insurgent movements in progress that necessitated extraordinary measures. Of course, this is not an accurate description of the situation. According to AFP dated the 14 of July, a member of the committee is quoted to have said "Korea is a state without rights". My reaction to this Report, if it is true, is that it is extremely unfair and unreasonable to characterize a democratic nation as a state without rights before even hearing this official response of the government to the many interesting questions raised during the past two days.

A brief word about the source materials which might have come to the attention of the members. Among the various sources, I found one source particularly disturbing for its lack of objectivity, balance and accuracy. For instance, the source writes that on March 20 this year the two Koreas jointly registered the South-North Agreement to the Secretariat of the UN under Article 102, perhaps in an attempt to make the NSL appear legally untenable

3

0043

444-7-4

in light of both Koreas' UN membership. However, both Koreas made
it clear that they do not consider the South-North Agreement as
an inter-state agreement, namely an international agreement. This
view is unambiguously reflected in a specific provision of the
agreement itself. It is also the height of absurdity when this
source writes that the works of E.H Carr and Bruce Cummings are
prohibited in Korea, let alone Marx or Lenin. I myself read these
books when I was a student and have seen them in both libraries
and book stores. The mere possession or reading of any book does
not constitute a crime under the law.

Before the legal issues are addressed, I would like to respond
to one question that was asked on the South-North dialogue.

4

0044

444-7-5

Concluding Remarks of Ambassador Park Soo Gil

1. I am pleased that we have reached a fruitful conclusion to two days of serious and productive dialogue between the distinguished members of the committee and my delegation. I take great pride in the fact that the Republic of Korea, for the first time in its history, has submitted its human rights record before the Committee for a collective evaluation through open and constructive dialogue. This was indeed an important step for my government and the Korean people, in terms of our commitment to promote universal human rights.

2. The results of your deliberation of the Initial Report of the Republic of Korea has made my government more fully aware of its serious responsibilities as an important member of the democratic community, while raising the consciousness of every Korean citizen of the human rights and fundamental freedom guaranteed under the Covenant and the Constitution. Indeed, the Committee has helped us raise the issue of human rights to an even higher level on Korea's domestic agenda.

3. We are pleased to note that your observations have been constructive, there were some points although on which I sharply disagree. However, we are happy with the positive assessment that you have made on the overall achievements of our democratic government since 1988.

0045

444-7-6

4. We will consider your positive comments as encouragement to increase our efforts to enhance human rights, and we will use your criticism as a catalyst to speed up our efforts to progress in the areas where improvement is needed. My country is irreversibly committed to democratic values and the fundamental freedom of its citizens. Our appearance before this Committee is testimony to this commitment, and you can count on the fact that our resolve to fulfill our human rights goals will increase.

5. Mr. Chairman, the road to the fulfillment of the world's human rights goals is long, but every step down that road is more satisfying than the last. The citizens of the Republic of Korea are now enjoying the satisfaction that human rights and democracy brings, but they will not rest now, because each and every Korean now knows that the further we travel down the road toward universal protection of human rights for all human kind, the better our world will become. No country can boast that it is blameless in its human rights record, and Korea is no exception. But the important thing in this regard is the resolute determination of the government to fulfil its commitment under the Covenant.

6. Mr. Chairman, I am sincerely grateful to all the members of the Committee for the open and fruitful dialogue which we have enjoyed during the last two days. I would like to take this occasion to promise that all of your comments and observations made during the last two days will be duly conveyed to my government. In addition, I would like to assure you that the questions that were not addressed in sufficient detail due to the time constraints, will be addressed at the time of our Second Human Rights Report. Lastly, Mr. Chairman, may I express my heartfelt thanks to you for your direction of the proceedings in a fair, judicious and able manner.

0046

444-7-7

우리나라 人權規約 報告書 審議

1992. 7. 16.

外 務 部

---

92. 7. 13-15間 제네바에서 開催된 第45次 人權
理事會의 우리나라 人權規約 報告書 審議結果를 아래
報告드립니다.

---

1. 人權理事會의 우리 報告書 審議

   ○ 우리나라는 90. 4. 加入, 90. 7. 發效한 ˝市民的,
   政治的 權利에 관한 國際規約˝에 따라 91. 7. 우리의
   同 規約履行에 관한 最初 報告書를 提出

   ○ 今番 理事會는 우리의 上記 報告書를 審議

   * 同 規約 當事國은 規約發效 1年後 및 그 후 每 5年
   마다 報告書를 提出하며, 同 報告書에 대한 理事會
   審議 開催

2. 우리代表(박수길 駐제네바 大使) 說明內容

   ○ 民主化 進展, 憲法裁判所와 法院의 활발한 人權保障
   活動, 人權關聯 國內法令 改正 等 第6共和國下
   에서의 人權伸張 措置 紹介

0047

o 南北關係의 特殊性에 따른 國家保安法의 當爲性과
  人權侵害 素地 拂拭을 위한 措置 說明
  - 특히, 우리의 安保狀況에 대한 認識不足에 따른
    一部 理事會 委員들의 誤謬 指摘
o 拷問防止協約 加入推進 意思 및 刑法, 勞動法
  改正 等 앞으로의 人權伸張 措置 方向 紹介

3. 人權理事會의 評價

  o 第6共和國 出帆以後 民主化 進展과 人權伸張을 위한
    法的, 政治的 措置를 포함한 우리 政府의 諸般
    努力을 높이 評價
  o 國家保安法 等 安保關聯 法令의 適用에 있어 基本的
    人權이 制約될 수 있다는 點에 關心과 憂慮 表明
    - 우리나라의 分斷에 따른 特別한 安保狀況에는
      理解 表示

4. 觀察 및 評價

  o 우리의 人權狀況이 크게 伸張하였음을 國際的으로
    認定받고 人權關聯 法制度 및 運營狀況을 널리
    알리는 契機
  o 委員들은 人權狀況 全般에 대해 肯定的 評價를
    하였으나, 어려운 安保狀況下에서도 正常的인 方法
    으로 法과 制度 運營이 바람직하다는 立場表明

0048

o 民主社會를 위한 辯護士 모임(民辯), 韓國基督教
協議會(KNCC) 等 在野團體의 反駁報告書 提出과
現地에서의 活動에도 불구, 우리 政府의 人權伸張
努力이 評價됨.

5. 弘報措置
   o 7.15. 人權理事會의 우리 報告書 審議 結果에
   대한 對言論 弘報措置

6. 向後 措置事項(關係部處間 協議, 措置 豫定)
   o 今番 報告書 審議內容을 檢討, 人權 關聯法令
   改正 및 政策立案時 反映
   o 人權伸張 努力의 일환으로서 早速한 時日內 拷問
   防止協約 加入 推進   - 끝 -

0049

우리나라 人權規約 報告書 審議

1992. 7. 16.

外 務 部

---

92. 7. 13-15間 제네바에서 開催된 第45次 人權
理事會의 우리나라 人權規約 報告書 審議結果를 아래
報告드립니다.

---

1. 人權理事會의 우리 報告書 審議

   ○ 우리나라는 90. 4. 加入, 90. 7. 發效한 '市民的,
     政治的 權利에 관한 國際規約'에 따라 91. 7. 最初
     報告書를 提出

     우리의 동규약이행에 관한

   ○ 今番 理事會는 우리의 上記 報告書를 審議

   * 同 規約 當事國은 規約發效 1年後 및 그후 每 5年
     마다 報告書를 提出하며, 同 報告書에 대한 理事會
     審議 開催

2. 우리代表 (박수길 駐제네바 大使) 說明內容

   ○ 民主化 進展, 憲法裁判所와 法院의 활발한 人權保障
     活動, 人權關聯 國內法令 改正 等 第6共和國下
     에서의 人權伸張 措置 紹介

0050

o 南北關係의 特殊性에 따른 國家保安法의 當爲性과
  人權侵害 素地 拂拭을 위한 措置 說明
  - 특히, 우리의 安保狀況에 대한 認識不足에 따른
    의사회
    一部 委員들의 誤謬 指摘
o 拷問防止協約 加入推進 意思 및 刑法, 勞動法 等
  改正 方向 紹介
  능 앞으로의 인권신장 2리

3. 人權理事會의 評價
  o 第6共和國 出帆以後 民主化 進展과 人權伸張을 위한
    法的, 政治的 措置를 포함한 우리 政府의 諸般
    努力을 높이 評價
  o 國家保安法 等 安保關聯 法令의 適用에 있어 基本的
    人權이 制約될 수 있다는 點에 關心과 憂慮 表明
    - 우리나라의 分斷에 따른 特別한 安保狀況에는
      理解 表示

4. 觀察 및 評價
  o 우리의 人權狀況이 크게 伸張하였음을 國際的으로
    認定받고 人權關聯 法制度 및 運營狀況을 널리
    알리는 契機
  o 委員들은 人權狀況 全般에 대해 肯定的 評價를
    하였으나, 어려운 安保狀況下에서도 正常的인 方法
    으로 法과 制度 運營이 바람직하다는 立場表明

0051

o 民主社會를 위한 辯護士 모임(民辯), 韓國基督教
  協議會(KNCC) 等 在野團體의 反駁報告書 提出과 現地
  에서의 活動에도 불구, 우리 政府의 人權伸張
  努力이 評價됨.

5. 弘報措置

  o 7.15. 人權理事會의 우리 報告書 審議 成果(결과)에
    대한 對言論 弘報措置

    ~~- 首席代表 基調發言, 人權委員의 論評 및 質疑
    意義 및 評價 等~~

6. 關聯 措置事項(關係部署와 協議, 措置 豫定)

  o 今番 報告書 審議內容을 檢討, 人權 關聯法令
    改正 및 政策立案時 反映

  o 人權伸張 努力의 일환으로서 早速한 時日內 拷問
    防止協約 加入 推進   - 끝 -

예): 92. 12. 31. 입안

0052

외 무 부

종 별 :

번 호 : GVW-1419   일 시 : 92 0716 2000

수 신 : 장 관(연이,법무부)

발 신 : 주 제네바대사

제 목 : 인권보고서 심의

연: GVW-1406

연호 표제회의시 본직의 최종발언 문안을 별첨송부함.

첨부: 발언문: GVW(F)-0447).끝

(대사 박수길-국장)

국기국   법무부

주 제 네 바 대 표 부

번호 : GVW(F) - 0447   년월일 : 20716   시간 : 2000

수신 : 장   관(6전이)

발신 : 주제네바대사

제목 : GVW-141P 첨부

총   5 매(표지포함)

보 안 통 제	𝑛
외신관 통 제	

Concluding Remarks of Ambassador Park Soo Gil

Mr. Chairman, as this is going to be the last occasion on which I am permitted to take the floor, I wish to make brief comments in light of what was just stated by the members of the Committee and then proceed to make a brief concluding statement. Mr. Chairman, the last two and half days of deliberations were indeed a valuable opportunity for us to exchange views with the members of the Committee on human rights issues which attract ever greater attention from the international community these days.

I am indeed very happy to note a clear trend, that a greater number of countries now take it for granted that human rights issues no longer fall under the exclusive domestic jurisdiction in the Article 2 (7) sense of the UN charter. It is for these reasons that we willingly subjected our human rights record to international scrutiny in the spotlight of public opinion.

Mr. Chairman, it is often said that realism without idealism is immorality and idealism without realism is impotent. By this, I mean to say resolutely that human rights issues of individual states must be examined and understood in the historical, cultural and even the politico-strategic context in which a country finds itself.

As regards some comments made on the definition of the terms "national spirit", "espionage" and other concepts, I am reminiscent, as a student of international law, of an interesting story about the difficulty of defining and interpreting any plain term used in our daily life. The Law

0055

447-5-2

of Treaties authored by Professor Mc Nair, one found a man, having a wife and children, made a will of conspicuous brevity consisting merely of the words "All for mother". No term could be clearer than "mother" but, fortunately or unfortunately, the deceased had his mother still alive. Claiming the authority of the administration of the will, the living mother argued that the estate left behind by her son belonged to her, while the wife of the deceased claimed the real estate on the grounds that the deceased's wife was always referred to as "mother" before their children in the family circle in the UK. The court decided in favor of the deceased's wife. The important lesson drawn from this story is that such plainest term as "mother" is susceptible to various interpretations, depending upon the context in which the term is used. It is understandable that some members expressed their concern about the term "national spirit" in the context of inculcating the prisoners to help them return to normal life when they are released. Furthermore, the term "national spirit" when translated into German reminds us of the leading ideology of Nazism, "Volksgeist". However, I would like to assure the Committee that what I meant by the term "national spirit" was the inculcation into the minds of prisoners the traditional and historical values unique to Korea, so that the prisoners can more easily adjust themselves to social life, as civic-minded citizens of the country.

With these brief comments in mind, I would like to say that we are indeed very happy to reach a fruitful conclusion to two and half days of serious and productive dialogue between the distinguished members of the committee and my delegation. I take great pride in the fact that the Republic of Korea, for the first time in its history, has submitted its human rights record before the Committee for a collective evaluation through open and constructive dialogue. This was indeed an important step for my government and the Korean people, in terms of our commitment to promote universal human rights.

0056

447-5-3

The results of your deliberation of the Initial Report of
the Republic of Korea has made my government more fully
aware of its serious responsibilities as an important
member of the democratic community, while raising the
consciousness of every Korean citizen of the human rights
and fundamental freedom guaranteed under the Covenant and
the Constitution. Indeed, the Committee has helped us
raise the issue of human rights to an even higher level on
Korea's domestic agenda.

We are pleased to note that your observations have been
constructive, although there were some points on which I
sharply disagree. However, we are happy with the positive
assessment that you have made on the overall achievements
of our democratic government since 1988.

We will consider your positive comments as encouragement to
increase our efforts to enhance human rights, and we will
use your criticism as a catalyst to speed up our efforts to
progress in the areas where improvement is needed. My
country is irreversibly committed to democratic values and
the fundamental freedom of its citizens. Our appearance
before this Committee is testimony to this commitment, and
you can count on the fact that our resolve to fulfill our
human rights goals will increase.

Mr. Chairman, the road to the fulfilment of the world's
human rights goals is long, but every step down that road
is more satisfying than the last. The citizens of the
Republic of Korea are now enjoying the satisfaction that
human rights and democracy brings, but they will not rest
now, because each and every Korean now knows that the
further we travel down the road toward universal protection
of human rights for all mankind, the better our world will
become. No country can boast that it is blameless in its
human rights record, and Korea is no exception. But the
important thing in this regard is the resolute
determination of the government to fulfil its commitment
under the Covenant.

0057

447-5-4

Mr. Chairman, I am sincerely grateful to all the members of the Committee for the open and fruitful dialogue which we have enjoyed during the last two days. I would like to take this occasion to promise that all of your comments and observations made during the last two days will be duly conveyed to my government. In addition, I would like to assure you that the questions that were not addressed in sufficient detail due to the time constraints, will be addressed at the time of our Second Human Rights Report. Lastly, Mr. Chairman, may I express my heartfelt thanks to you for your direction of the proceedings in a fair, judicious and able manner.

447-5-5

0058

외 무 부

원 본

종 별 :

번 호 : GVW-1424   일 시 : 92 0720 1600

수 신 : 장관(연이)

발 신 : 주 제네바 대사

제 목 : 민변등 재야 인사 기자회견 요지

　　인권이사회에서의 아국 보고서 심의관련, 당지를 방문중인 민변 및 KNCC 관계자들이 지난 7.14 오전 당지 WCC 회관에서 WCC 공보관계자들과 가진 기자회견 요지를 아래 보고함.

　　0 정부와 인권위원간의 대화는 한국인권이 국제적으로 인정 받고 개선될수 있는 좋은 기회

　　0 우리는 많은 심사위원들이 한국에서 사상의 자유, 표현의 자유, 평화집회의 자유등 기본권이 침해되고 있다고 올바르게 강조하고 있음을 목격

　　0 심사위원들은 정보기관(NSP)의 권력남용과 권력남용을 넓게 허용하고 있는 제반 절차법에 대해 깊은 관심 표명했음.

　　0 또한 심사위원들은 인권 개선을 위한 법적 자문과 제의를 한바, 이는 향후 사형범위 축소, 구금기간 단축, 안기부를 통제할 채제설치등을 하는데 있어 중요한 조치가 될 것으로 믿음.

　　0 우리는 정부 대표단에 대해 실망, 대표들은 국제인권 규약을 무시한채 남.북 긴장의 특수정치 상황을 들어 기본권 제한을 정당화 하는 주장을 되풀이 했으며, 현정부 출범이래 인권문제가 거의 없다고 말하면서 심사위원들의 귀중한 논평과 충고에 대한 진지한 자세가 결여되어 있었음.

　　0 우리는 정부가 인권 개선을 위한 심사위원들의 제의와 논평을 검토하여 필요한 조치를 취해줄 것을 촉구하며, 한국인의 인권을 향유할수 있도록 심사위원들과 한국인권에 관심있는 사람들이 계속적인 노력과 관심이 있기를 기대함.

　　0 위원들의 한국 인권 상황 관심과 권고에 감사함. 국제적 연대와 지원없이는 한국인권의 개선이 어려울 것임. 끝

　　(대사 박수길-국장)

국기국　　　장관　　　차관　　　1차보　　　분석관　　　청와대　　　안기부

예고 92.12.31. 까지

주 제 네 바 대 표 부

20, Route de Pre-Bois, POB 566 / (022) 791-0111 / (022) 791-0525(FAX)

▫▫▫▫▫▫▫▫▫▫▫▫▫▫▫▫▫▫▫▫▫▫▫▫▫▫▫▫▫▫▫▫▫▫▫▫

문서번호 제네(정) 2031-672

시행일자 : 1992. 7. 22

수신 : 외무부장관

참조 : 국제기구국장

선결			지시		
접수	일자시간		결재	대 사	
	번호	43213		차석대사	
처리자			공람	참사관	
담당자				서기관	

제목 : 아국인권보고서 심의 관련 UN Press Release

　　　　표제 UN Press Release를 별첨 송부합니다.

92. 7. 2 4

첨부 : '92.7.13, 14, 15일자 Press Release 각 4부. 끝.

　　　주 제 네 바 대

0061

주 제 네 바 대 표 부

년 호 : GVW(F) - 451   년월일 : 20121   시간 : 1802

수 신 : 장 관 (연이)

발 신 : 주 제네바대사

제 목 : 인권법어 관련 Press Release

총 4 매(표지포함)

보 안 통 제	

외신과 통 제	

재 부 처	청 와 실	차 관 실	일 차 보	이 차 보	외 정 실	문 화 원	아 주 국	미 주 국	구 주 국	중 아 국	국 기 구	경 제 국	통 상 국	문 업 국	의 연 인	청 와 대	안 기 부	공 보 처	경 기 원	상 공 부	재 무 부	농 수 부	동 자 부	환 경 처	과 기 처		
										O																	

451-9-1

0062

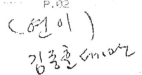

NATIONS UNIES · UNITED NATIONS ·

SERVICE DE L'INFORMATION · OFFICE DES NATIONS UNIES A GENÈVE
INFORMATION SERVICE · UNITED NATIONS OFFICE AT GENEVA

Press Release HR/3106
15 July 1992 (Afternoon)

HUMAN RIGHTS COMMITTEE CONCLUDES EXAMINATION OF REPUBLIC OF KOREA REPORT

Expresses Concern over National Security Law

The definition of political prisoners, the different approach of North Korea to unification, the working of the National Security Law and the rights of those detained under it were some of the issues explained by the delegation of the Republic of Korea in response to questions posed by the Human Rights Committee this afternoon.

Park Soo Gil, head of the delegation, told the 18-member Committee that in order to understand the improved situation in Korea, one had to grasp the historical importance the Korean people attached to the June 29 Declaration for Democracy. The Republic of Korea had to retain temporarily the National Security Law, said another member of the delegation, because terrorism was the instrument of the North's external policy. The National Security Law would remain in place until this policy of the North changed.

Following this intervention, members of the Committee offered their final comments on the initial report of the Republic of Korea on what it was doing to give effect to the International Covenant on Civil and Political Rights. While acknowledging the positive changes which had occurred in Korea since 1988, the members of the Committee in their final comments strongly criticized the persistence of the National Security Law, which some termed as unacceptable and others as totally incompatible with the International Covenant. Lengthy periods of pre-trial detention, the excessive use of force by the police and the long list of crimes punishable by the death penalty were also deemed as excessive and requiring reform measures.

The Korean delegation was composed of Park Soo Gil, Ambassador and Permanent Representative, Moon Bong Joo, Counsellor in the Permanent Mission, Chung Dal Ho, Director, United Nations Division II, Ministry of Foreign Affairs, and Yoo Kook Hyun, Director, Human Rights Division, Ministry of Justice.

(more)

0063

- 2 -   Press Release HR/3106
15 July 1992

The Committee will meet again Thursday morning, 16 July, at 10.00 a.m. to take up the third periodic report of Mongolia.

Intervention by Korean Delegation

Responding to questions posed by members of the Committee, PARK SOO GIL (Republic of Korea) said that some important misconceptions had been generated by the discussion in the Committee about the real human rights situation in the country. In order to understand the improved situation in Korea, one had to grasp the historical importance which the Korean people attached to the June 29 Declaration for democracy.

Mr. Park said he sharply disagreed with the concept of "so-called" political prisoners as was often used in some quarters. Those who served prison sentences for injuring policemen or destroying State property with firebombs could never be considered political prisoners in the Korean legal system, he declared.

YOO KOOK HYUN, replying to a question from the Committee about the South-North dialogue and unification, explained the unification formula. He stated that North Korea had a different approach to unification and it was difficult to predict the future of the current dialogue. The Republic of Korea had to retain temporarily the National Security Law because terrorism was the instrument of the North's external policy. Until such time as this policy changed the National Security Law would remain in force.

Under this Law, a person would not be punished simply because he harboured or expressed Communist ideas, as long as the ideas were not translated into illegal acts, such as violent attempts to overthrow the Government. In general, National Security Law convictions resulted from an act by the accused to overthrow the Government. In every case, the accused received full Constitutional safeguards, including the right to counsel, presumption of innocence, the right to present evidence in defence, a public trial and the right to appeal.

With regard to other questions, "reasonable cultural discrimination" was explained as differentiation based on a person's educational accomplishment. Fifteen crimes were subject to the death penalty, apart from crimes committed under the National Security Law. Violation of that Law was punishable by hanging. The maximum period of pre-trial detention could not, he said, exceed six months and when detention occurred, the family had to be notified. All inmates were free to meet relatives and friends, receive and send correspondence and read papers.

Turning to freedom of movement, he said that some restrictions were placed on travel to North Korea, for reasons of national security. Concerning freedom of expression, Mr. Yoo stressed that the Republic of Korea did not practise censorship; there simply was no list of banned books.

(more)

ㅆ51-4-3

0064

Concluding Comments by Committee Members

Members of the Committee, in their final comments, expressed the view that noticeable progress and positive changes had occurred in the Republic of Korea since 1988. They felt, however, that the persistence of the National Security Law was unnecessary and that the crimes punishable under it could be sufficiently dealt with by the Penal Code. One expert said the law was not only unacceptable, it was totally incompatible with the Covenant.

Most members also expressed concern about the unacceptable and excessive use of force by the police, the potentially abusable concept of State secret, over-lengthy periods of detention for purposes of interrogation, and the powers of the National Security Agency, which did not come under democratic controls. In the view of the members, the number of crimes punishable by the death penalty was too high and the spectrum of police activities which ran contrary to human rights provisions were too broad. They appealed to the delegation to consider curbing both.

As to the incorporation of civil and political rights in Korea's legislation, some members expressed concern about the absence of explicit reference to the freedoms of opinion and expression. One expert suggested that existing and pending laws be systematically checked against both constitutionality and the International Covenant on Civil and Political Rights.

One expert said he could understand why a State would be afraid of the use of force by a totalitarian State but could not understand the reasons for fearing the ideas coming from a totalitarian State. He expressed concern about the fact that visits to North Korea could take place only upon obtaining permission. Another expert said that the continuing political tension between North and South Korea created an atmosphere which hindered the full implementation of the Covenant's civil and political rights.

The feeling of danger by the Korean Government seemed to be translated into a type of logic which was incompatible with the Covenant, according to one expert. He felt that the ideas surrounding the National Security Law failed to orient Korean society or to convey correctly which type of behaviour was acceptable and which type was sanctioned and why. He suggested that Korea put behind its past and, from now on, rely on democracy and the rule of law to set standards of behaviour for its citizens.

* *** *

꾸준한 신장을 계속할 우리나라의 인권상황

― 인권이사회의 인권규약 최초보고서 검토를 계기로 ―

　　제45차 인권이사회(Human Rights Committee)는 92년 7월 13일부터 15일간
스위스 제네바의 유엔 회의장에서 우리 정부가 91년 7월 제출한 바 있는 "시민적.
정치적 권리에 관한 국제규약" 최초보고서에 관하여 우리나라 정부대표단이 참석한
가운데 심도있는 검토를 하였습니다.

　　인권이사회는 규약 산하조직으로서 규약 당사국 회의에서 선출되는 임기 4년의
18명의 인권법 분야 전문가로 구성되어 있습니다.

　　이번 인권이사회에 참석한 14명의 위원들은 우리 보고서에 대한 전반적인
평가와 함께 우리나라의 인권보장 법체제 및 운용현황에 대하여 상세하고 폭넓은
질의를 하였습니다.　위원들이 중점적으로 질의한 내용은 한반도 분단상황에 따른
인권보장의 장애요인, 인권규약의 국내적 이행보장, 형사사법상의 적법절차,
국가보안법 일부 규정 및 적용상의 문제, 사형제도, 법원의 독립, 규약 유보의
철회, 여성의 평등권 보장 등이었습니다.

　　위원들은 보고서에 대한 평가를 통하여 한국 정부가 제6공화국 출범이후
개방적이고 적극적인 인권보장 정책을 추진하고 있다고 긍정적인 평가를 내리면서,
특히 헌법 및 각종 인권보장 법령의 개정과 헌법재판소 신설 등의 제도개혁,
2개의 국제인권규약 및 선택의정서 가입 등을 통한 인권보장 강화 등을 구체적
성과로 들었습니다.　또한 우리 보고서의 체제와 내용이 모범적이었으며, 회의에
참가한 정부대표의 답변이 체계적이며 상세하였다고 평가하였습니다.

　　위원들은 우리의 분단상황에 따른 어려움에 이해를 표명하면서도 국가보안법
등 안보관련 법령상의 일부 규정내용과 동 법령들의 운용에 있어 기본적 인권이
제약될 가능성이 있다는 점을 지적하였으며, 사형범위의 축소, 구속기간의 단축,
정치적 의견에 따른 차별금지를 위하여 정부가 노력을 기울여 줄 것을 요청하였
습니다.

1

인권이사회에서의 인권보고서 검토는 보고서 제출국의 인권상황 자체를 논의하는 것이 아니며, 해당국이 규약의 이행과 관련하여 국내적으로 취한 입법적, 행정적, 사법적 조치가 규약의 이행을 보장하기 위하여 적합한지 여부를 보고서 내용 및 기타 참고자료를 기초로하여 검토하는 것입니다. 이러한 성격에 따라 통상적으로 보고서 검토는 인권보장을 향상하기 위한 인권이사회와 정부 대표단간의 "건설적인 대화"(constructive dialogue)라고 불리우고 있습니다.

정부는 금번 우리나라 보고서에 대한 인권이사회의 검토를 통하여 우리나라의 인권보장제도 및 운용실태에 대하여 권위있는 유엔 관련기관이 최초로 객관적인 평가를 함으로써, 이번 기회가 우리 국민의 인권신장을 위한 또 하나의 전기가 될 것이란 점에 큰 의의를 두고 있습니다. 금번회의에서 위원들이 내린 평가와 제기된 문제점은 향후에 우리 정부가 인권보장을 강화해 나가는데 있어 중요한 토대가 될 것입니다.

인권이사회 토의과정 및 결과

수석대표 기조발언

우리나라 대표단의 수석대표인 박수길 주제네바 대사는 7월 13일 기조발언을 통하여 보고서의 주요내용을 소개하면서 제6공화국 출범이후 이룩한 인권신장과 민주화 진전을 설명하였습니다. 특히 대통령 직접선거, 사법부 독립 강화와 헌법 재판소 설치, 헌법 및 법령에서의 기본권 보장 강화, 인권관련 법령의 광범위한 개정, 사형대상 범죄의 축소, 지방자치제 확대실시 등에 관하여 상세히 언급하였습니다.

또한 박수길 대사는 1991년 보고서 제출 이후 인권관련 주요 진전사항으로서 국제노동기구(ILO)에의 가입, 아동권리협약의 비준, 난민협약 및 의정서 가입 추진 등을 설명하고, 인권신장을 위하여 향후 정부가 취할 조치에 대하여는

2

0067

시민적.정치적 권리에 관한 국제규약(B규약) 한국 최초 인권보고서 제출 및 심의, 1991-92. 전5권 (V.5 1992.7.10-10월)   73

고문방지협약에의 가입방침, 형법 및 형사소송법의 개정방향, 노동관계법 개정 검토 현황 등을 언급하면서, 정부가 앞으로도 헌법과 국제인권규약에 입각하여 국민의 인권신장을 위한 노력을 계속 경주해 나갈 것임을 밝혔습니다.

한편 박수길 대사는 한반도 분단에 따른 긴장상태가 규약의 이행에 영향을 주는 요인중의 하나라고 전제하고, 평화와 통일을 위한 대화를 적극 추진하면서, 자유민주주의 체제를 위해하고 전복하려는 세력을 견제하여야 하는 우리 정부의 입장을 밝히고, 현단계에서 안보관계 법률의 존치 당위성을 설명하였습니다.

인권위원들의 논평 및 질의

7월 13일 오후와 14일 오전에 걸쳐 계속된 인권위원들의 논평 및 질의에는 14명의 참석 위원중 12명이 참가하였습니다. 위원들은 우리 보고서와 수석대표의 기조발언을 통하여 설명된 그간의 민주화 진전과 인권신장의 성과를 긍정적으로 평가하면서 아래와 같이 논평과 함께 규약이행과 관련한 문제점에 대하여 질의를 하였습니다.

전반적 논평

O 1988년 제6공화국 출범이후 민주화 진전과 인권상황의 개선은 괄목할만 하며, 이를 위한 정부의 노력을 평가함.

O 한국보고서는 규약이 정하는 기준과 지침에 따라 충실하고 상세히 작성되어 있어 그 내용과 체계면에서 뛰어나며, 특히 규약의 각 조문에 맞추어 인권관련 법제 및 정부의 조치사항을 망라하고 있음.

O 한반도 안보상황의 특수성은 인정되나, 냉전체제의 몰락 및 이에 따른 남북한 관계의 개선 움직임에 비추어 국가보안법 등 안보관계 법령의 신중한 적용 및 개선이 요망됨.

3

0068

- 규약의 국내적 효력 및 국내법으로서 직접적용 가능 문제
- 반국가단체 및 비밀의 개념 등 국가보안법상의 제문제
- 남북대화 현황 및 이산가족 재결합을 위한 정부조치
- 영장주의의 예외조치가 광범위하게 인정되는 근거
- 장기간의 구속기간 인정에 따른 인권침해 방지책
- 고문 등에 의한 자백의 효력
- 재소자의 면접권 보장
- 법관의 독립성 보장 제도
- 군사법원의 지위 및 상소권 보장
- 선택의정서에 의거한 국내적 구제 절차
- ILO 가입을 계기로 한 노동법 개정 문제
- 한국내 소수민족 현황
- 규약유보의 철회 가능성
- 사형대상 범죄의 유형 및 범위
- 여성에 대한 실질적 평등 보장

우리 대표단의 답변내용

7월 15일 회의에서 박수길 대사는 인권위원들의 논평과 질의에 대하여 우리 정부입장을 아래와 같이 종합적으로 밝혔습니다.

- 88년 이후 우리나라의 민주화와 인권신장에 대한 위원들의 평가에 주목함.

- 우리 인권상황과 관련한 일부 왜곡된 인식에 대한 우려 표명과 함께 정치법 문제를 언급한 일부 위원의 편향된 시각에 대한 반박

4

0069

- 우리나라는 여하한 동기에서든 폭력, 방화 등으로 실정법을 위반한
  사람을 정치범으로 보는 견해를 수용할 수 없음.

O 위원들의 논평에 참조된 일부 자료의 오류 및 왜곡 지적

O 위원들의 논평 내용이 인권증진을 위한 정부시책에 반영되도록 노력

O 인권규약상의 의무이행을 위한 정부의 확고한 의지 표명

인권위원들의 질의에 대하여는 대표단의 일원인 법무부 인권과장이 인권규약의
조문별로 상세히 답변을 하였습니다.

인권위원들의 최종 평가(Concluding Comments)

우리 대표단의 답변에 이어 인권이사회의 Fausto Pocar 의장(이태리)을 포함한
12명의 위원들이 이번 우리 보고서에 대한 검토를 마치면서 동인들의 최종 평가를
아래와 같이 밝혔습니다.

O 1988년 이래 민주화 진전과 인권상황 개선을 위한 정부의 노력을 평가함.
   특히 Pocar 의장은 한국의 인권신장이 인상적이라고 언급함. 또한
   위원들은 보고서의 체제 및 내용, 정부대표단의 답변이 성실하고 모범적
   이었다는데 의견을 같이함.

O 분단상황에 따른 어려움을 이해하나, 정치적 상황의 특수성에 기인하는
   문제는 일반 법률에 의하여 대처하는 것이 바람직함. 또한 규약가입을
   계기로 기존의 법령이 규약에 합치되는지 여부를 검토할 것을 요망함.

O 죄형법정주의에 따라 국가보안법상 일부 조항에 있어 내용이 모호하거나
   개념이 불분명한데 따른 문제점의 개선이 요망됨.

O 사형대상이 되는 범죄의 범위를 축소하고 다른 나라에 비하여 장기간
   허용되는 구속기간의 단축을 위한 정부의 정책적 검토를 희망함.

인권이사회에서의 보고서 검토제도 개요

보고서의 성격

O 시민적.정치적 권리에 관한 국제규약 제40조에 의하여 각 당사국은 규약 발효후 1년 이내에 규약의 이행을 위하여 취한 조치에 관하여 인권이사회에 보고서를 제출하도록 되어 있음. (그 이후에는 매 5년마다 정기 보고서를 제출)

인권이사회(Human Rights Committee) 구성

O 인권이사회는 시민적.정치적 권리에 관한 국제규약에 의해 설치된 협약 기구로서 규약 당사국 회의에서 선출되는 임기 4년의 18명의 위원으로 구성되며, 위원들은 통상적으로 국제법과 인권법 분야의 전문가임.

O 인권이사회는 매년 3차례의 회의를 제네바 또는 뉴욕에서 개최함.

인권이사회에서의 보고서 검토

O 인권이사회는 매 회기마다 5-6개 국가의 보고서를 검토하며, 회의결과를 유엔 경제사회이사회와 총회에 제출함.

O 92.7.13-7.31간 개최되는 제45차 회의에서는 우리나를 비롯하여 몽골, 벨라루스 및 페루 등 4개국의 보고서가 검토됨.

우리나라 보고서 제출 경위

O 1990년 4월 10일   시민적.정치적 권리에 관한 국제규약 가입서 기탁
O 1990년 7월 10일   상기 규약이 우리나라에 대하여 발효
O 1991년 7월 31일   우리나라 최초 보고서 제출
O 1991년 11월   우리나라 최초 보고서 유엔문서로 발간, 배포

6

0071

시민적.정치적 권리에 관한 국제규약 요지

O 전문, 6부 53개조로 구성

O 실체 규정(제1조-제27조)

제1조   자결권 및 자원처분권

제2조   모든 종류의 차별금지 및 기본권의 침해에 대한 효과적 구제보장

제3조   남녀평등권 확보

제4조   비상사태하에서의 기본권 보장

제5조   규약에 인정되지 아니한 이유로 인한 기본권의 경시 금지

제6조   생명권

제7조   고문 금지

제8조   노예제도 및 강제노동 금지

제9조   신체의 자유와 안전에 대한 권리

제10조   피구속자에 대한 인도적 대우

제11조   계약상 의무의 이행불능을 이유로 한 구금 금지

제12조   거주이전 및 퇴거의 자유

제13조   합법적 거류외국인의 추방요건 및 구제

제14조   공정한 재판을 받을 권리

제15조   형법불소급의 원칙

제16조   법률상 인격인정

제17조   사생활, 가정, 통신의 침해 금지

제18조   사상, 양심 및 종교의 자유

제19조   표현의 자유 및 그 제한의 한계

제20조   전쟁선전 금지

제21조   평화적 집회의 권리

제22조   노동조합의 결성을 포함한 결사의 자유

제23조   가정의 보호, 혼인의 자유와 혼인 관련 남녀평등 보장

제24조   아동의 보호

제25조   참정권

제26조   법앞의 평등 및 법의 평등한 보호를 받을 권리

제27조   소수민족의 보호

O 실시규정(제28조-45조)

- 규약준수 보장을 위한 조치로써 인권이사회 설치 및 보고서 제출의무를 규정

O 최종 규정(제48조-53조)

- 규약의 발효 및 개정 관련 규정

인권관련 주요기구

경제사회이사회 산하 기구

O 유엔 인권위원회(Commission on Human Rights)

- 1946년 설립된 경제사회이사회 산하의 기능위원회

- 경제사회이사회에서 선출되는 임기 3년의 53개 위원국으로 구성

  * 우리나라는 93-95년 임기의 위원국으로 피선

- 매년초 1차례씩 6주간 일정으로 제네바에서 회의를 개최, 유엔에서 다뤄지는 인권문제 전반에 대하여 토의하고, 회의결과를 경제사회 이사회에 보고

O 유엔 인권소위원회(Sub-Commission on Prevention of Discrimination and Protection of Minorities)

- 1947년 설립된 인권위원회 산하기구

8

0073

- 인권위원회에서 선출되는 임기 4년의 26명의 위원으로 구성
- 매년 4주간 일정으로 제네바에서 회의를 개최, 인권전반에 대한
  연구활동, 경제사회이사회 및 인권위원회에서 위임하는 인권문제를
  토의하고 동 결과를 인권위원회에 보고

인권협약 산하 주요조직

O 인권이사회(Human Rights Committee)
- 시민적.정치적 권리에 관한 국제규약 산하 조직
- 임기 4년의 18명의 위원
- 매년 3차례 회의 개최

O 경제적.사회적.문화적 권리 위원회(Committee on Economic, Social
and Cultural Rights)
- 경제적, 사회적, 문화적 권리에 관한 국제규약 산하조직
- 임기 4년의 18명의 위원
- 매년 1차례 회의 개최

O 기타 협약 산하조직
- 인종차별철폐 위원회
- 여성차별철폐 위원회
- 아동권리 위원회
- 고문방지 위원회   - 끝 -

9   0074

외 무 부

110-760 서울 종로구 세종로 77번지 / 전화 (02) 723-8934 / 전송 (02) 723-3505

문서번호 연이 2031-/26

시행일자 1992.7.23.

수신 문화협력국장

참조

취급		장 관	
보존			
국 장	전결		
심의관			
과 장			
기안	김 종 훈		협조

제목 외교문제 해설 자료송부

　　　92.7.13-7.15간 제네바에서 개최된 제45차 인권이사회(Human Rights
Committee)의 우리나라 인권규약 최초보고서 심의 결과를 "외교문제 해설"로
발간, 배포하여 주실 것을 요청하오니 협조하여 주시기 바랍니다.

첨부 : 상기 자료 1부. 끝.

0075

2 외교문제해설

우리의 人權伸張 努力에 대한 國際的 評價

——人權理事會의 人權規約 最初報告書 檢討를 계기로 본다

제45차 人權理事會(Human Rights Committee)는 92년 7월 7일부터 15일까지 스위스 제네바의 유엔 회의장에서 우리 정부가 91년 7월 제출한 바 있는 「市民的·政治的 權利에 관한 國際規約」 最初報告書에 관하여 우리나라 정부대표단이 참석한 가운데 심도있는 검토를 하였습니다.

이번 인권이사회에 참석한 14명의 위원들은 全般的인 評價와 함께 우리나라의 人權保障과 運用現況에 대하여 상세하고 폭넓은 질의를 하였습니다. 위원들이 중점적으로 질의한 내용은 한반도 분단상황에 따른 여러 유의 인권보장의 제약요인, 인권구제의 국내적 이행보장, 형사사범상의 적법절차, 국가보안법 등 법령 운구조와 등 법집행상의 문제, 사형제도, 법원의 독립, 구속 유보의 문제, 여성의 평등권 보장 등이 있습니다.

위원들은 우리가 제6공화국 수립이후 통하여 온 한국 정부가 제6공화국 수립이후 취하여 온 積極的이고 긍정적인 인권보장 정책을 추진하고 있다고 긍정적인 인권보장 정책을 주진하고 있다고 긍정적인

평가를 내리면서 특히 憲法의 改正과 憲法裁判所 設置 등의 制度改革, 2개의 國際人權規約 및 選擇議定書 加入 등을 통한 人權保障 强化 등을 구체적 성과로 들었습니다. 또한 우리 보고서의 내용이 상세하고 충실하여, 회의에 참가한 정부대표의 답변의 성실성도 높이 평가하였다고 평가하였습니다.

위원들은 우리의 분단상황에 따른 여러 음에 이해를 표명하면서도 國家保安法 등 일부 規範내용과 등 법령들의 운용에 있어 基本的인 人權이 削約될 가능성이 있다는 점을 지적하였으며, 사형범위의 축소, 구속기간의 단축, 정치적 이견에 따른 차별금지를 위하여 정부가 노력을 기울여 줄 것을 요청하였습니다.

인권이사회에서의 인권보고서 검토는 보고서 제출국의 인권상황 자체를 논의하는 것이 아니라, 해당국의 「規約」의 이행과 관련하여 국내적으로 취한 立法的, 行政的 및 司法的인 조치가 이행을 보장하기 위하여 적합한지 여부를 보고서 내용 및 기타 참고자료를 기초로 하여 검토하는 것입니다. 이러한 성격으로 보고서 검토는 人權保障을 同고조하기 위한 정부 대표단과 해당 委員會간의 "建

人權理事會(Human Rights Committee) 構成

△ 인권이사회는 「시민적·정치적 권리에 관한 「규약」에 의해 설립된 협약기구로서 「규약」 당사국 회의에서 선출되는 임기 4년의 18명의 위원으로 구성되며, 위원들은 통상적으로 국제법과 인권법 분야의 전문가임.

△ 인권이사회는 매년 3차례의 회의를 제네바 또는 뉴욕에서 개최함.

人權理事會에서의 報告書 檢討

△ 인권이사회는 매 회기마다 5-6개 국가의 보고서를 검토하며, 회의결과를 유엔 경제사회이사회에 제출함.

△ '92.7.13-7.31간 개최되는 제45차 회의에서는 우리나라를 비롯하여 몽골, 벨리루스 및 페루 등 4개국의 보고서가 검토됨.

우리나라 報告書 提出 經緯

△ 1990년 4월10일 시민적·정치적 권리에 관한 국제규약 가입서 기탁

△ 1990년 7월10일 상기 규약이 우리나라에 대하여 발효

△ 1991년 7월31일 우리나라의 최초 보고서 제출

△ 1991년 11월 우리나라의 최초 보고서를 유엔 문서로 발간, 배포

人權關聯 主要機關

유엔 經濟社會理事會 傘下 機構

△ 유엔 인권위원회(Commission on Human Rights)

- 1946년 설립된 경제사회이사회 산하의 기능위원회
- 경제사회이사회에서 선출되는 임기 3년의 53개 위원국으로 구성
* 우리나라는 93-95년 임기의 위원국으로 피선

- 매년조 1차례씩 6주간 일정으로 제네바에서 회의를 개최, 유엔에서 다루어지는 인권문제 전반에 대하여 토의하고, 회의결과를 경제사회이사회에 보고

△ 유엔 인권소위원회(Sub-Commission on Prevention of Discrimination and Protection of Minorities)

- 1947년 설립된 인권위원회 산하기구
- 인권위원회에서 선출되는 임기 4년의 26명의 위원으로 구성
- 매년 4주간 일정으로 제네바에서 회의를 개최, 인권전반에 대한 연구활동, 경제사회이사회 및 인권위원회에 위임하는 인권문제를 토의하고 동 결과를 인권위원회에 보고

人權協約 傘下 主要組織

△ 人權理事會(Human Rights Committee)

- 시민적·정치적 권리에 관한 국제규약에 관한 산하조직
- 임기 4년의 18명의 위원
- 매년 3차례 회의 개최

△ 경제사회문화적 권리 위원회(Committee on Economic, Social and Cultural Rights)

- 임기 4년의 18명의 위원
- 매년 1차례 회의 개최

△ 기타 협약 산하조직

- 인종차별철폐 위원회
- 여성차별철폐 위원회
- 아동권리 위원회
- 고문방지 위원회

◆편집·제작: 문화협력국 홍보과(720-2339)

設的인 對話"(constructive dialogue)로 불려지고 있습니다.

정부는 금번 우리나라 보고서에 대한 인권이사회의 검토를 통하여 우리나라의 人權保障制度 및 運用實態에 대하여 권위있는 유엔 관련기관이 최초로 客觀的인 評價를 함으로써, 이번 기회가 우리 國民의 人權伸張을 위한 또 하나의 轉機가 될 것이란 점에 큰 의의를 두고 있습니다. 우리정부는 금번 회의에서 위원들이 내린 평가와 제기된 문제점을 향후 우리국민의 人權保障을 強化해 나가는데 있어 중요한 토대로서 활용해 나가고자 합니다.

人權伸張 및 民主化 크게 進展

우리나라 대표단의 수석대표인 박수길 주제네바 대사는 7월 13일 기조발언을 통하여 보고서의 주요내용을 소개하면서 제6공화국 출범이후 이룩한 人權伸張과 民主化 進展을 설명하였습니다. 특히 대통령 직접선거, 사법부 독립 강화와 헌법재판소 설치, 헌법 및 법령에서의 기본권 보장 강화, 인권관련 법령의 광범위한 개정, 사형대상 범죄의 축소, 지방자치제 확대실시 등에 관하여 상세히 언급하였습니다.

또한 박수길 대사는 1991년 보고서 제출 이후 인권관련 주요 진전사항으로서 국제노동기구(ILO)에의 가입, 아동권리협약의 비준, 난민협약 및 의정서 가입추진 등을 설명하고, 人權伸張을 위하여 향후 政府가 취할 措置에 대하여는 고문방지협약에의 가입방침, 형법 및 형사소송법의 개정방향, 노동관계법 개정 검토 현황 등을 언급하면서, 정부가 앞으로도 헌법과 국제인권규약에 입각하여 국민의 인권신장을 위한 노력을 계속 경주해 나갈 것임을 밝혔습니다.

한편 박수길 대사는 한반도 분단에 따른 긴장상태가 「규약」의 이행에 영향을 주는 요인중의 하나라고 전제하고, 평화와 통일을 위한 대화를 적극 추진하면서, 自由民主主義 體制를 危害하고 顚覆하려는 세력을 견제하여야 하는 우리 정부의 입장을 밝히고, 현단계에서 安保關係 法律의 存置 當爲性을 說明하였습니다.

人權委員들의 論評 및 質疑

7월 13일 오후와 14일 오전에 걸쳐 계속된 人權委員들의 論評 및 質疑에는 14명의 참석위원중 12명이 참가하였습니다. 위원들은 우리 보고서와 수석대표의 기조발언을 통하여 설명된 그간의 민주화 진전과 인권신장의 성과를 긍정적으로 평가하면서 아래와 같이 論評과 함께 規約 履行과 關聯한 問題點에 대하여 질의를 하였습니다.

全般的 論評

o 1988년 제6공화국 출범이후 민주화 진전과 人權狀況의 改善은 괄목할만하며, 이를 위한 政府의 努力을 평가함.

o 한국보고서는 규약이 정하는 기준과 지침에 따라 충실하고 상세히 작성되어 있어 그 내용과 체제면에서 우수하며, 특히 규약의 각 조문에 맞추어 人權關聯 法制 및 政府의 措置事項을 망라하고 있음.

o 한반도 안보상황의 특수성은 인정되나, 냉전체제의 몰락 및 이에 따른 남북한 관계의 개선 움직임에 비추어 국가보안법 등 안보관계 법령의 愼重한 適用 등 改善이 요망됨.

主要 質疑內容

o 「規約」의 國內的 效力 및 국내법으로서 직접적용 가능 문제

o 반국가단체 및 비밀의 개념 등 국가보안법상의 제문제

o 남북대화 현황 및 이산가족 재결합을 위한 정부조치

2

0077

○ 영장주의의 예외조치가 광범위하게 인정되는 근거
○ 장기간의 구속기간 인정에 따른 인권침해 방지책
○ 고문 등에 의한 자백의 효력
○ 재소자의 면접권 보장
○ 법관의 독립성 보장 제도
○ 군사법원의 지위 및 상소권 보장
○ 선택의정서에 의거한 국내적 구제 절차
○ ILO 가입을 계기로 한 노동법 개정 문제
○ 한국내 소수민족 현황
○ 「規約」유보의 철회 가능성
○ 사형대상 범죄의 유형 및 범위
○ 여성에 대한 실질적 평등 보장

우리 代表團의 答辯內容

7월 15일 회의에서 박수길 대사는 인권위원들의 논평과 질의에 대하여 우리 정부입장을 아래와 같이 종합적으로 밝혔습니다.

○ 1988년 이후 우리나라의 민주화와 인권신장에 대한 위원들의 평가에 주목함.
○ 우리 인권상황과 관련한 일부 왜곡된 인식에 대한 우려 표명과 함께 정치법 문제를 언급한 일부 위원의 偏向된 視角에 대한 反駁
 - 우리나라는 여하한 동기에서든 暴力, 放火 등으로 實定法을 違反한 사람을 정치범으로 보는 견해를 수용할 수 없음.
○ 위원들의 논평에 참조된 일부 자료의 오류 및 왜곡 지적
○ 위원들의 논평 내용이 인권증진을 위한 政府 施策에 反映되도록 노력
○ 인권규약상의 의무이행을 위한 정부의 確固한 意志 表明

인권위원들의 질의에 대하여는 대표단의 일원

인 법무부 인권과장이 인권규약의 條文別로 상세히 답변을 하였습니다.

人權委員들의 最終 評價

우리 대표단의 답변에 이어 인권이사회의 Fausto Pocar 의장(이태리)을 포함한 12명의 위원들이 이번 우리 보고서에 대한 검토를 마치면서 最終 評價를 아래와 같이 밝혔습니다.

○ 1988년 이래 민주화 진전과 인권상황 개선을 위한 정부의 노력을 평가함. 특히 Pocar 의장은 한국의 인권신장이 인상적이라고 언급함. 또한 위원들은 보고서의 체제 및 내용, 정부대표단의 답변이 성실하고 진지하였다는 데 의견을 같이함.
○ 분단상황에 따른 어려움을 이해하나, 정치적 상황의 특수성에 기인하는 문제는 一般 法律에 의하여 對處하는 것이 바람직함. 또한 「規約」가입을 계기로 기존의 법령이 「규약」에 합치되는지 여부를 검토할 것을 요망함.
○ 죄형법정주의에 따라 국가보안법상 일부 조항에 있어 내용이 모호하거나 개념이 불분명한 데 따른 문제점의 개선이 요망됨.
○ 사형대상이 되는 범죄의 범위를 축소하고 다른 나라에 비하여 장기간 허용되는 구속기간의 단축을 위한 정부의 정책적 검토를 희망함.

人權理事會에서의 報告書 檢討制度 槪要

報告書의 性格

「시민적·정치적 권리에 관한 국제규약」 제40조에 의하여 각 당사국은 규약 발효후 1년 이내에 「규약」의 이행을 위하여 취한 조치에 관하여 인권이사회에 보고서를 제출하도록 되어 있음. (그 이후에는 매 5년마다 정기 보고서를 제출)

3

0078

주 제 네 바 대 표 부

20, Route de Pre-Bois, POB 566 / (022) 791-0111 / (022) 791-0525(FAX)
▨▨▨▨▨▨▨▨▨▨▨▨▨▨▨▨▨▨▨▨▨▨▨▨▨▨▨▨▨▨▨▨▨▨▨▨▨▨

문서번호 제네(정) 2031- 696

시행일자 1992. 7. 23

수신 장 관

참조 국제기구국장

선결			지 시	
접	일자 시간		결	
수	번호	**43211**	재	
처 리 과			공	
담 당 자			람	

제목 인권보고서 심의 기록 송부

연 : GVW - 1450

연호 표제 아국보고서 심의 회의록(Summary Record) 별첨 송부합니다.

첨부 : 상기 보고서 5셑. 끝.

92. 7. 2 4

주 제 네 바 대 사

0079

CCPR

**International covenant
on civil and
political rights**

Distr.
GENERAL

CCPR/C/SR.1150
17 July 1992

Original: ENGLISH

HUMAN RIGHTS COMMITTEE

Forty-fifth session

SUMMARY RECORD OF THE 1150th MEETING

Held at the Palais des Nations, Geneva,
on Monday, 13 July 1992, at 3 p.m.

Chairman: Mr. POCAR

CONTENTS

Consideration of reports submitted by States parties under article 40 of the
Çovenant

Initial report of the Republic of Korea

This record is subject to correction.

Corrections should be submitted in one of the working languages. They
should be set forth in a memorandum and also incorporated in a copy of the
record. They should be sent <u>within one week of the date of this document</u> to
the Official Records Editing Section, room E.4108, Palais des Nations, Geneva.

Any corrections to the records of the public meetings of the Committee at
this session will be consolidated in a single corrigendum, to be issued
shortly after the end of the session.

GE.92-16357/4668B

0080

<u>The meeting was called to order at 3.15 p.m.</u>

CONSIDERATION OF REPORTS SUBMITTED BY STATES PARTIES UNDER ARTICLE 40 OF
THE COVENANT

<u>Initial report of the Republic of Korea</u> (CCPR/C/68/Add.1)

1.   <u>At the invitation of the Chairman, Mr. Soo Gil Park, Mr. Bong Joo Moon,
Mr. Dal Ho Chung and Mr. Kook Hyun Yoo (Republic of Korea) took places at the
Committee table.</u>

2.   <u>Mr. Soo Gil PARK</u> (Republic of Korea), introducing the initial report of
the Republic of Korea (CCPR/C/68/Add.1), said that his country had acceded to
the two International Covenants on Human Rights in 1990 in order to
consolidate the protection of human rights in Korea and to join the
international effort to promote them throughout the world. The consideration
of its initial report was an important event, and he hoped it would lead to a
constructive dialogue on how the Republic could better fulfil its commitments
under the International Covenant on Civil and Political Rights. The event had
already attracted the attention of the media and various human rights groups
in his country and would encourage his Government in its firm undertaking to
enhance the human rights of the Korean people.

3.   Every effort had been made to ensure that the structure and content of
the report complied with the Committee's guidelines, and all possible
information had been included to provide as full a picture as possible of
human rights protection in the Republic of Korea. Since the laws of the
Republic were based on the written law system, the emphasis of the report was
on legal and institutional aspects, but decisions of the Constitutional Court
and other courts, as well as relevant administrative measures, were also
mentioned. In view of the fact that major advances in human rights protection
had been made since the inauguration of the present Government in early 1988,
the report focused on developments since that time.

4.   Under the Constitution, as revised on 29 October 1987, institutional
measures had been strengthened to embody genuinely democratic principles, and
to enhance the protection of human rights and fundamental freedoms. The
Korean people regarded the Constitution, based on the 29 June 1987 Declaration
for Democracy, as a turning-point in the struggle for democracy. It provided
for the election of the President of the Republic by direct popular vote,
instead of by indirect vote as previously, thus widening the scope of popular
participation. It also strengthened the power of the National Assembly
<u>vis-à-vis</u> the administration by, for example, reinstating its power to review
the actions of the latter. In the area of justice, it had reinforced the
independence of the judiciary by improving the procedure for appointing
judges. It had also established the Constitutional Court, which, in addition
to reviewing the constitutionality of laws at the request of courts, ruled on
petitions by individuals seeking redress of human rights infringements caused
by acts of the State. More than 30 cases of infringements had been redressed
since the introduction of the system in September 1988 - which represented a
significant improvement in the human rights situation. The constitutional
provisions dealing with human rights and fundamental freedoms had also been

amended to enhance protection. For example, strict procedures to be followed
in the event of arrest or detention had been written into the Constitution,
and the rights of criminal suspects and defendants strengthened.

5.   To give effect to these constitutional provisions, the relevant laws and
regulations had been amended, and the related procedures improved. The
Government had also made improvements in the penal administration and had
instituted legal aid programmes. In accordance with the spirit of article 10
of the Constitution, assuring the human worth and dignity of citizens, and
implying a right to life as affirmed in article 6 of the Covenant, the
Government had amended the Special Criminal Act to abolish the death penalty
for 15 types of crime. The Government was also undertaking a review aimed at
further reducing the applicability of the penalty by amendments expected to be
enacted by the end of the current year. The application of the controversial
National Security Law and the Act concerning Assembly and Demonstration had
also been restricted in order to eliminate misinterpretation or abuse.

6.   Local autonomy, which, although written into the Constitution since the
birth of the Republic, had not been implemented except for a brief period in
the 1960s, had become a reality, and legislative council elections had been
held nationwide in March and June 1991.

7.   The people of the Republic were now living under the rule of law in a
democracy, completely free from the authoritarian tinges of the past. Human
rights and fundamental freedoms, including freedom of the press, were
guaranteed and safeguarded. Accession to the Covenant had been an important
part of those democratic processes. Only a true democracy could open its
doors to public scrutiny, and it was to be noted that the Republic of Korea
had made a declaration recognizing the competence of the Committee under
article 41 of the Covenant and had also acceded to the Optional Protocol.
Thus, the human rights of the population were henceforth under international
protection, reinforcing the extensive domestic protection provided by the
Constitution. Every effort had been made to publicize those international
instruments, and the texts had been translated and published in the Korean
language, along with a compilation of the Committee's proceedings and
important decisions. Measures had also been taken to educate law enforcement
officials in the provisions and procedures set forth in the Covenant and in
the Constitution. Citizens of the Republic could take special pride in having
a whole week set aside for commemoration of the Universal Declaration of Human
Rights, and 10 December was celebrated as Human Rights Day in order to remind
the people of the spirit of the Universal Declaration and of the rights they
enjoyed in a democracy. All the rights provided for in the Covenant were
guaranteed by the Constitution, which stipulated that all treaties duly
concluded and promulgated should have the same effect as domestic laws.
Together, the two instruments formed the centrepiece of human rights law of
the Republic, and it was noteworthy that the Constitutional Court had invoked
article 18, paragraph 2 of the Covenant in its landmark decision of
1 April 1991 on the constitutionality of a provision of the Civil Code. The
Republic did maintain three reservations to the Covenant with regard to
specific provisions that conflicted with domestic law, namely article 14,
paragraphs 5 and 7 and article 22, but they were only partial in nature and
were not intended to disavow the specific rights provided for in the Covenant;
they sought only to maintain limitations prescribed in the relevant domestic

0082

laws as explained in the report. His Government firmly believed that the reservations did not represent a derogation from the basic principles embodied in the Covenant, but it was reviewing its position to see whether their scope could be further limited.

8. The admission of the Republic of Korea to membership of the United Nations in September 1991 had given additional momentum to its Government's efforts to promote universal human rights in accordance with the Charter, and by subsequently becoming a full-fledged member of the International Labour Organisation in December 1991, the Republic had strongly endorsed international endeavours to ensure the protection of fundamental trade union rights. The Republic had also ratified the Convention on the Rights of the Child in December 1991 and was shortly to become a party to the Convention relating to the Status of Refugees and its Protocol, pending the consent of the National Assembly. No less importance should be attached to the actions of individuals and groups, and he believed that the increase in the number of human rights cases being brought to the courts was evidence of popular confidence in the fair application of the law. In addition, private human rights groups were increasing their monitoring activity.

9. One of the most important factors affecting the implementation of the Covenant was the tense situation resulting from the division of the Korean peninsula. Following its liberation from Japanese colonial rule in 1945, Korea had been caught between two opposing ideologies, and the Northern aggression in 1950 had brought untold misery upon the Korean people and consolidated the division of the country. Since that war, the two parts of Korea had confronted one another militarily, as well as ideologically, across the 38th parallel. Consequently, it was not until 1991, following the end of the cold war, that the two sides had succeeded in engaging in serious dialogue and begun to seek a way to reunify the nation peacefully. The Agreement on Reconciliation, Non-Aggression and Exchanges and Cooperation had been concluded in February 1992 and had led to a series of regular consultations that were expected to narrow the gap between the two Koreas in every field. That was, however, only a cautious first step, and it was natural that a country which had been nearly overthrown by invasion should feel unable to relax its guard against further aggression. Armed forces totalling 1.5 million were in a military stand-off along the 38th parallel, and, despite the end of the cold war, the Armistice Agreement had still not been replaced by a peace settlement. The Republic of Korea was accordingly obliged to guard against subversion of its liberal democratic system. It was very unfortunate that North Korea should still maintain a clause in the preamble of the platform of the Korean Workers' Party, which took precedence over its Constitution, declaring as its basic policy the "realization of the people's revolution for national liberation in South Korea" - in other words, the communization of the whole peninsula. Accordingly, the National Security Law adopted by the Republic to protect its security and the integrity of the system still had its _raison d'être_. In spite, therefore, of the call in some quarters for abolition of the Law, it was the national consensus that it should be maintained: no democracy could be so tolerant as to allow the forces of revolution to overthrow its free system. It was, however, his firm belief that, when a peace agreement was signed and South-North relations normalized, the National Security Law would become irrelevant. In the meantime, the Government remained determined to eliminate any infringement of

0083

human rights resulting from application of the Law, beyond the restrictions permitted by the Constitution and the Covenant, as was instanced by its incorporation into the Law in May 1991 of the substance of a 1990 Constitutional Court decision limiting its scope. The decision provided clearer and narrower definitions of such concepts as "endangering national security and survival" and "endangering the basic liberal democratic order".

10. As part of its future programme to promote universal human rights, his Government planned to accede to the Convention against Torture and Other Cruel, Inhuman or Degrading Treatment or Punishment. It was also finalizing amendments to the Penal Code and the Code of Penal Procedure to reinforce the principle of nullum crimen sine lege, and to introduce measures for more effective review of warrants. As a new member of the ILO, it was also preparing to accede to various ILO conventions, and it had set up a working group consisting of an equal number of representatives of workers, employers and legal experts to streamline labour-related domestic laws. The group was also considering an amendment to the Labour Union Act to allow multiple unions in a single workplace, which was at present prohibited. The Republic would thus continue its endeavours to improve its institutions and practices relevant to human rights and to incorporate the spirit and principles of the Constitution and the Covenant into the daily life of the people.

11. His Government would also take an active part in promoting human rights at the international and regional levels. It had high expectations of the World Conference on Human Rights to be held in June 1993, in which it was particularly anxious to participate actively as the Republic had been elected to the Commission on Human Rights for a term starting in 1993.

12. He hoped that the explanations and statements given would assist the Committee in understanding the status of the protection of human rights in the Republic of Korea, and he would be pleased to answer to the best of his knowledge any questions which members of the Committee might wish to put.

13. Mr. ANDO congratulated the delegation of the Republic of Korea on the timely submission of its report, which generally followed the Committee's guidelines and, in addition to an account of legislative provisions, gave some useful statistical and factual information. He commended the Republic's decision to accede not only to the Covenant but also to the Optional Protocol and to make the declaration provided for in article 41.

14. Throughout Korea's long history Japan had learnt much from it in the cultural, religious and philosophical spheres. It was, therefore, particularly unfortunate that, as it had become modernized, Japan had adopted aggressive policies which had led to the invasion of Korea in 1905 and colonial domination by Japan from 1910. The division of the peninsula after liberation at the end of the Second World War had been followed in 1950 by the outbreak of the Korean war. He wished to express his deep sympathy with the Korean people over that recent tragic history, and to express his personal sorrow and apology for the role that Japan had played in it.

15. He appreciated the willingness expressed by the delegation to enter into constructive dialogue with the Committee as a contribution to solving any human rights problems that might exist. It was in that spirit that he would

request clarification on a number of matters in the report. The first
concerned the statement in paragraph 5 that the Covenant had the same legal
effect as domestic laws. If that was so, what occurred when new domestic
legislation was enacted? Did such enactment leave room for conflict between
the new legislation and the Covenant?

16. Paragraph 29 of the report, referring to article 2 of the Covenant,
quoted article 11 (1) of the Republic's Constitution, which prohibited
discrimination on grounds of sex, religion or social status. There were,
however, other possible grounds for discrimination, such as those enumerated
in article 2, paragraph 1 and article 26 of the Covenant, including political
opinion. He wished, therefore, to ask whether there were any differences
between the grounds for discrimination in the Constitution and the Covenant.

17. Turning to the section of the report relating to article 3 of the
Covenant, he welcomed the fact that, by acceding to the Covenant, the Republic
of Korea had committed itself to eliminating all discrimination against
women. It was, however, a well-known fact that, irrespective of legislative
measures, many kinds of de facto discrimination could exist in a society, as
was indeed the case in his own country, Japan. He would, therefore,
appreciate a brief account of any such de facto discrimination that might
exist in the Republic and any affirmative action being taken to eliminate it.
In that connection, he noted the statement in paragraph 87 (d) of the report
concerning the right of both husband and wife to seek a division of the joint
property on the basis of their contribution to its formation, which seemed to
imply separation of matrimonial property. But in practice, when two people
lived together in marriage, there was bound to be some property held in common
between them, and in certain social situations the husband's share was likely
to be greater than the wife's. He would therefore like more information about
the matrimonial property situation in the Republic of Korea and about any
measures to ensure a more equitable balance between husband and wife.

18. In relation to article 4 of the Covenant, the report indicated (para. 89)
that article 37 (2) of the Constitution provided for restrictions of freedom
and rights in cases of emergency. However, article 4, paragraph 2 of the
Covenant laid down that, even in time of public emergency, no derogation was
permissible from a number of articles of the Covenant relating to basic
rights, and he would welcome information on specific categories of rights from
which no derogation was possible under the law of the Republic of Korea.

19. Different aspects of the application of the National Security Law would
no doubt be addressed by other members of the Committee. He himself would
merely ask, in connection with that part of the report which dealt with the
prohibition of torture and cruelty committed in the performance of official
duties (art. 7), for additional information on the facts which had led to the
Supreme Court decision referred to in paragraph 138.

20. Paragraph 150 of the report, relating to article 9 of the Covenant, noted
"a discrepancy between the norms of the Code of Criminal Procedure and the
actual practices of investigatory agencies" in the matter of detention. How
soon, in fact, after a person had been taken into custody, was his or her
family informed?

0085

21.   In connection with article 10 on the humane treatment of detained persons, he asked at what age criminal law was applicable in the Republic of Korea. The report (paras. 167 and 206) left some doubt as to the exact definition of "juveniles".

22.   The announced liberalization with regard to liberty of movement (art. 12) was to be welcomed. What, however, were the de facto and de jure situations as far as visits to North Korea were concerned?

23.   The Republic of Korea, like Japan, had been affected by the arrival of the so-called "boat people". He asked, against the background of article 13 of the Covenant, what legal provisions in the former country affected the admission or expulsion of such persons.

24.   Referring to paragraph 204 (b) (iii) of the report, he requested clarification concerning the possible restriction of the right to communicate with counsel, as provided under article 14 of the Covenant.

25.   Also in connection with article 14, and more specifically the right to appeal, he noted the reservation made by the Government (para. 211 of the report) on the grounds that "military trials under extraordinary law may not be appealed except in case of death sentences". Why was that right denied in the case of lesser sentences?

26.   Freedom of expression in the Republic of Korea obviously remained adversely affected by the very real trauma of the country's recent history, but the amendments to the National Security Law announced in paragraph 247 of the report were a promising sign. Nevertheless, the amended Law, notably its article 7 (5), still seemed too broad in scope and too vague in some of its provisions. Perhaps further review of the situation was called for. He also understood that, together with the application of legal sanctions, attempts were sometimes made to impose the recantation of beliefs: that was certainly in conflict with article 18 of the Covenant, and he invited the delegation of the Republic of Korea to comment on the matter.

27.   Welcoming the entry of the Republic of Korea into the International Labour Organisation (ILO), he added that, according to information received, certain private university or school teachers' unions had been dissolved. Freedom of association was thus, perhaps, another matter which merited further review.

28.   In relation to article 24 of the Covenant, and paragraph 294 of the report, concerning the protection of working children, he asked for additional information on measures to prevent the employment of children at an age when they should be enrolled in compulsory education.

29.   Finally, with regard to article 25, and more particularly the question of restrictions on political rights (para. 308 of the report), he inquired why, inter alia, journalists were prohibited from becoming founders or members of a political party.

30.   Mr. DIMITRIJEVIC, welcoming the delegation of the Republic of Korea, commented on the topicality of a report that reflected the conscious efforts

0086

being made in many parts of the world to achieve gradual and peaceful social
development in a direction that led away from all forms of authoritarianism,
repression and constraint deriving from international circumstances. His
chief regret concerning the document before the Committee was that - perhaps
understandably in view of their recent promulgation and because of their
importance as a foundation for the defence of human rights - it dwelt rather
too much on the letter of the new constitutional and legislative provisions
and was insufficiently detailed with regard to the factual situation and
specific actions to guarantee those rights and eliminate inadmissible
practices. The state of affairs with regard to prostitution (para. 67) was a
case in point.

31. The statement in article 37 (1) of the Constitution of the Republic of
Korea, cited in paragraph 3 of the report, that "Freedoms and rights of
citizens shall not be neglected on the grounds that they are not enumerated in
the Constitution", taken in conjunction with paragraph 5 of the report, was of
considerable legal interest. He asked whether such non-enumerated provisions
had actually been applied or invoked with the force of domestic laws since the
adoption of the present Constitution, and whether the highest judicial bodies
of the land had actually read into the Constitution some rights that formed
part of the spirit of the times or of natural law.

32. Concerning article 6 of the report and the right to life, he noted from
paragraph 101 of the report the provisions according to which criminal
punishment, including the death penalty, was enforced in the Republic of
Korea. Welcoming the recent limitation of the categories of crimes subject to
the death penalty, he added that a cursory reading of the National Security
Law led to the conclusion that an inordinate number of offences still carried
that penalty, and requested details on the subject. Similarly, and in
connection with paragraph 110 of the report, dealing with the subject of
abortion, he asked in what circumstances abortion was not considered a crime.

33. With regard to article 7, he requested further information as to whether
the non-admission of confessions derived from torture and other harsh
treatment was fully effective.

34. It was not altogether clear from the report what restrictions were placed
on pre-trial detention, but it seemed that such detention must not exceed
30 days in the case of ordinary offences and an additional 20 days, apparently
to permit further investigations, where alleged offences under the National
Security Law were involved. He commented that the lengthier period seemed
hardly justifiable, given the experience, common to many countries, of the
generally expeditious functioning of special investigatory agencies acting
under national security laws.

35. As far as the Republic of Korea was concerned, it seemed to him that the
central issue in the matter of guaranteeing the rights covered by the Covenant
related to the actual status of the National Security Law, albeit in its
amended, "milder" form. The principal concerns which it addressed, especially
in relation to articles 15 and 19 of the Covenant, were defined in somewhat
vague terms which, in his view, could lend themselves to interpretations
inconsistent with the letter and spirit of the Covenant and result in
sanctions for acts that might not be truly dangerous for the State, criminal

0087

or even reprehensible, as well as undue restrictions on the freedom of expression, association and assembly. Further, as Mr. Ando had observed, certain pressures seemed on occasion to be applied to obtain the recantation of beliefs and other unseemly actions taken to inquire into people's thoughts. "Preventive" censorship in the form of banning certain forms of expression also appeard to be practised.

36. In conclusion, and notwithstanding the anxiety which he had expressed with regard to the overall impact of the National Security Law, he acknowledged that the comprehensive report before the Committee reflected a sincere endeavour to provide information about positive developments following a period during which the country's very existence had indeed been threatened. He commended its systematic presentation and expressed the view that it would be of great assistance to the Committee and the delegation of the Republic of Korea alike in what he hoped would be a constructive dialogue.

37. Mr. AGUILAR URBINA joined in commending what he found to be a well-prepared report, likely to stimulate useful dialogue. Like the earlier speakers, however, it left him with a number of questions and doubts, more specificially because of its relative failure to describe the actual situation obtaining in the country.

38. Noting with interest, like the previous speaker, the statement that the Covenant had the same effect as domestic laws without the enactment of separate domestic legislation (para. 5), he asked whether its provisions had in fact been applied or invoked before the courts. Notwithstanding the statement he had alluded to, could a national law in any way derogate from a provision of the Covenant?

39. Those concerns, which centred on the general status of the Covenant in relation to the legislation of the Republic of Korea, also prompted him to seek further clarifications with regard to the National Security Law as well as other enactments which affected a number of the Covenant's provisions. He noted that a number of non-governmental organizations claimed that the National Security Law was, in effect, the country's Constitution.

40. Article 11 (1) of the Constitution prohibited discrimination on various grounds which, however, seemed to be more limited than those laid down in the Covenant (para. 29 of the report). He would welcome more information on that point. Paragraph 44 of the report said that foreigners were not allowed to hold public office; did that apply to all public posts, without exception?

41. Paragraph 48 of the report stated that any law relating to criminal penalties which was found to be unconstitutional would be declared null and void. What consequences had that provision had? Did it, for example, apply to the National Security Law, whose scope had now been restricted? He would also like to know whether prosecutors were subject to executive or to judicial authority.

42. Turning to article 3 on equality of rights between men and women, he noted from paragraph 67 of the report that prostitution was a criminal offence in the Republic of Korea. He would like to know whether the procurement of women for prostitution was also a criminal offence. Paragraph 69, dealing

with the participation of women in society, stated that women and men had
enjoyed equal political rights since the establishment of the "Korean
Government". Why was the reference to the "Korean Government", rather than
the "Korean State"? Paragraphs 73 and 74 dealt with the position of women in
the legal profession and political life: he inquired whether there were any
laws to protect women against discrimination in those fields.

43. With reference to article 4 of the Covenant, he noted that, under the
Constitution of the Republic of Korea, the President was empowered to enforce
emergency measures only during the period when the survival of the State was
at stake (para. 92 of the report). That was surely a very vague concept; it
might even be interpreted to mean that emergency measures could be prolonged
until the two halves of the Korean nation had been reunited. Under
article 76 (1) of the Constitution, the President could assume emergency
powers in circumstances rather more wide-ranging than those laid down in the
Covenant (para. 90 of the report). Would the provisions of the Covenant take
precedence over the Constitution in such a case, and would the Covenant be
applicable directly or only through the courts? To what extent were
article 76 of the Constitution, and also article 37 (2), (which dealt with
admissible restrictions on the rights of citizens), compatible with the
Covenant?

44. In respect of article 6 of the Covenant, dealing with the right to life,
he noted that a large number of offences carried the death penalty in the
Republic of Korea. Paragraph 103 stated that the death penalty could be
imposed under the Criminal Code and "the other related regulations", and he
would welcome more details about the latter. In the same paragraph, it was
stated that the death penalty was limited to crimes which threatened "the very
existence of the State"; he would like to know exactly which crimes were
involved. In that connection, he understood that as many as 50 offences under
the National Security Law were subject to the death penalty. He was concerned
to read in paragraph 109 of the report that the death penalty could be imposed
for robbery. Moreover, there had been no successful appeals against death
sentences since 1986 (para. 108 of the report). He would welcome more
information about the statement in paragraph 113 that "the detention of
persons sentenced to death is to secure the execution of the death penalty".

45. Paragraph 125 of the report described possible limitations on the rights
of people suffering from three categories of communicable diseases. He would
like to know how the rights of those people were restricted in practice.

46. Turning to article 7 of the Covenant, he asked for more information about
the decision of 1981 in which the Supreme Court had rejected a confession made
under duress (para. 138 of the report). According to information he had
received, there had been other cases where defendants had been tortured or
otherwise ill-treated in order to extract a confession.

47. In respect of article 8 of the Covenant, he noted that it was a criminal
offence to kidnap a person in order to take him out of the country (para. 141
of the report). He would like to know whether kidnapping alone was also a
criminal offence. Paragraph 146 stated that the right of conscientious

0089

objection to military service was not included in the right to freedom of conscience under the Constitution, and he would welcome more information on that point.

48. With reference to article 9 of the Covenant, he asked how many political prisoners there were in the Republic of Korea; according to information in his possession, they numbered some 1,300. Article 12 (1) of the Constitution referred to "preventive restrictions" which might be imposed in certain circumstances; what were those restrictions? He was concerned to note that people suspected of an offence under the National Security Law could be detained without trial for up to 150 days. How was a prisoner's welfare guaranteed during that time?

49. In respect of article 10 of the Covenant, he would like to know whether there were different categories of prisoner, and whether a prisoner might be transferred from one category to another, depending perhaps on his degree of ideological rehabilitation. What were the regulations governing solitary confinement?

50. He noted that the section of the report dealing with article 12 of the Covenant (paras. 192 and 193) made no mention of the Resident Registration Law (para. 227). What were the provisions of that Law, and was it connected with the Security Surveillance Law, under which anyone suspected of offences under the National Security Law could be kept under surveillance for up to two years?

51. In respect of article 14 of the Covenant, he noted that, under the Constitution of the Republic of Korea, defendants had the right to a prompt trial (para. 200). However, undue haste might prevent the defendant from adequately preparing his defence. What were the practical effects of that provision? Paragraph 204 said that the State would appoint a defence counsel if the defendant was unable to do so but, in that case, was extra time allowed for the defence counsel to prepare the case? It appeared that the accused had no automatic right to question witnesses: indeed, the accused might be excluded from the court in some circumstances, which would preclude him from cross-examining the witness, even if permission was granted. He would welcome more information on that point and also on the imposition of the death penalty by military courts.

52. In regard to article 18 of the Covenant, dealing with freedom of thought, conscience and religion, he inquired whether anyone had been coerced into renouncing a belief in Communism in the Republic of Korea. He was concerned about the provisions of article 2 (1) of the National Security Law and wondered how far it was compatible with the provisions of the Covenant.

53. Finally, he would like more details about the restrictions on political activity by people who had been declared incompetent (para. 306). It was further stated that certain teachers and journalists were forbidden to found or join a political party and that new parties could not be established with the same political platform as a party which had been banned (para. 308). Which parties had already been banned, and why?

54. Mr. EL SHAFEI welcomed the Republic of Korea's accession to the International Covenants on Human Rights and the Optional Protocol. The report

0090

was a detailed one, which acknowledged the restriction of some fundamental
rights in the Republic of Korea, but it did not tell the whole story.
Admittedly, the country had been seriously affected by the cold war over a
long period and had suffered bouts of insurgency, but they had been met by
excessive and arbitrary use of force and by ill-treatment, torture and the
abuse of authority to an extent which was unacceptable in a democratic
country. It was to be hoped that the new attitude displayed by the Government
of the Republic of Korea, as shown by its accession to the international human
rights instruments and its presence at the current session of the Committee,
meant that the excesses of the past would never be repeated.

55. The Committee's main concern in considering the report was to establish
how the legislation of the Republic of Korea could be made more compatible
with the provisions of the Covenant. He would like to hear more about
developments since the submission of the report which would show the
Government's commitment to such changes.

56. He inquired whether there was a State body responsible for the protection
of human rights. Moreover, the delegation had stated that the Covenant had
the same force as domestic law in the Republic of Korea. What happened in
cases of infringement of rights guaranteed by the Covenant but not recognized
under domestic law? He asked whether there had been any court decisions based
directly on the provisions of the Covenant. He would also like more details
about measures to guarantee the independence of judges, particularly the
regulations governing their appointment, tenure and removal.

57. It seemed that the Constitutional Court could only rule on the
constitutionality of a law on the basis of a decision by a lower court: could
it also consider allegations of unconstitutionality submitted by individuals?
He hoped that the Government would soon take action to make several of its
laws, including the National Security Law, the Security Surveillance Law, the
Labour Dispute Adjustment Act and the Act concerning Assembly and
Demonstration, more compatible with the Covenant. He could see that such
provisions had been necessary in the past, but the time had surely come to
amend or repeal them.

58. Mr. MAVROMMATIS said that there had clearly been considerable progress in
the protection and promotion of human rights in the Republic of Korea since
the end of the cold war. Nevertheless, the Committee had received allegations
of a large number of violations, particularly in respect of relations between
the two Korean States, the rights of long-term political prisoners, the right
to a fair trial, the presumption of innocence and freedom of expression.
However, the Government's determination to tackle the problems had been
demonstrated by its accession to the Optional Protocol to the International
Covenant on Civil and Political Rights. The report before the Committee was a
good one but, like many others, it made general statements without backing
them up with specific facts and gave no details of the actual situation in the
country or of difficulties in implementing the provisions of the Covenant.
For example, the report stated that the Constitution did not conflict with the
Covenant (para. 6), but it made no mention of other legislation. The Covenant
had the same force as domestic law without any need for specific domestic
legislation to that effect (para. 5), but he wondered how that principle
applied to the non-self-executing provisions of the Covenant.

0091

59.   Article 11 (1) of the Constitution prohibited discrimination on a number of grounds (para. 29), but they did not include such fundamental criteria as race, colour, birth and, in particular, political belief, and he felt that the list should be enlarged.

60.   There were a number of other points on which additional information was needed.   In regard to the punishability of offences, for example, article 1 (1) of the Criminal Code seemed to contradict article 15 of the Covenant.   With regard to the imposition of the death penalty, an explanation was needed of the various degrees of murder, not all of which could be considered as heinous crimes justifying the imposition of the death penalty. More detailed information was required regarding means of securing the independence of the judiciary: did judges enjoy security of tenure, were their emoluments safeguarded, did they had the right to resign from office, were they immune from civil charges in respect of their duties, and so forth? The importance of elaborate provisions for ensuring the independence of the judiciary could not be overemphasized.   It would also be useful to have an explanation of the national legal structure, the jurisdiction and competence of the various courts, their hierarchical relationship and the right of appeal.

61.   In regard to article 25 of the Covenant, the unexplained provision in the Political Party Act prohibiting certain teachers and journalists from becoming founders or members of a political party seemed to contradict not only the Covenant but also article 13 (2) of the Constitution of the Republic of Korea.   It was important to know whether it was the Constitution or the Political Party Act that prevailed.

62.   Finally, the report seemed to make a rather restricted interpretation of religious and cultural minorities.   It would be interesting to have more information about the country's religious composition.

63.   Mr. MYULLERSON expressed appreciation of the efforts made in the Republic of Korea in recent years to promote human rights.   The Government's initial report, which had been drafted in accordance with the Committee's guidelines, contained a great deal of useful information.   There were, however, certain gaps that should be mentioned.

64.   The statement in the report on the right of peoples to self-determination was an instance in which further information was needed.   The right of peoples to self-determination covered not only their right to found independent States but also their entitlement to democracy and to choose their own economic, social, political and cultural system.   He wondered what the views of the Republic of Korea were in that respect.   In connection with the references in the report to Palestine and South Africa, he noted that Korea was itself a divided country and that problems of self-determination were very topical, given the movement towards reunification.   It had been reported in the media that the conditions put forward by North Korea for reunification were not acceptable to the Government of the Republic of Korea.   It would be interesting to hear the Government's own conditions.

0092

65. In regard to paragraph 29 of the report, he wondered why article 11 (1) of the Constitution mentioned only three grounds of discrimination. No mention was made, for example, of religion or political opinion, as referred to in the Covenant.

66. Paragraph 89 of the report, on emergency actions and orders and the possible proclamation of martial law, stated that article 37 (2) of the Constitution provided that restrictions on the freedom of citizens could not infringe on the essential aspects of fundamental rights. It did not, however, define those essential aspects. Paragraph 93 referred to control over the exercise of emergency powers but did not define the powers of the President or say what control was exercised over his powers.

67. Paragraph 149 of the report, on article 9 of the Covenant, described the rather wide grounds on which detention without a warrant was permitted, including violations of the National Security Law. The provision for extending the period of detention, referred to in paragraph 154, would appear to violate the presumption of innocence.

68. Regarding article 12 of the Covenant and the right of citizens to move freely, he asked whether there were any restrictions on visits by citizens of the Republic of Korea to North Korea. He also asked for further information on the term of office of judges. He believed that the Government had recently granted longer terms than the customary 10 years and noted that life tenure was one of the best guarantees of an independent judiciary. Regarding the reference to military courts in paragraph 211, he asked what categories of cases were tried by such courts and what was the meaning of the term "extraordinary law".

69. The application of the National Security Law gave him some concern. While he understood the raison d'être for the Law, he felt that the recent changes in the overall situation might have made it seem less necessary. Apparently, the Law was used not only against agents of North Korea but also against critics of the Government of the Republic of Korea, the simple possession of Marxist literature being regarded as grounds for imprisonment.

70. Mr. SADI said that the presentation of the report constituted a dramatic break with the past and the start of a new era in the Republic of Korea. He had been particularly impressed by the inclusion in the delegation of the Director of the Human Rights Division of the Ministry of Justice.

71. He understood that the preparation of the report had generated considerable publicity within the country. Such publicity would help to guarantee the implementation of the Convenant and he would welcome further information on the attention given to it. It was important for such publicity to be directed to the public at large as well as to professional legal circles. He wondered whether the situation had changed perceptibly since the Government had ratified the Covenant. Detailed information on the number of times it had been invoked would enable the Committee to establish a link with the general evolution of the human rights situation in the country.

0093

72. Broad concern had been expressed by several members of the Committee about the application of the National Security Law. He understood that its application was subject to judicial review but wondered how far the courts were able to control it. Apparently, the Supreme Court was not empowered to decide on the legality of martial law.

73. He hoped that the Government would shortly be able to withdraw its reservations to articles 14 and 22 of the Covenant. It had been said that the Confucian tradition prevailing in the Republic of Korea made it difficult for the Government to meet some of its treaty obligations, particularly in respect of discrimination against women. Other countries with strong religious traditions had encountered similar problems and further information on the evolution of the situation and the course of public opinion would be useful to those countries.

74. Miss CHANET commended the report for its full and detailed account of constitutional protection for civil and political rights and measures to ensure the implementation of the Covenant, but regretted the absence of information on the day-to-day difficulties encountered in promoting respect for human rights.

75. She associated herself with the questions asked by previous speakers about the hierarchy between the provisions of the Covenant and those of the Constitution. She welcomed the Government's withdrawal of its reservation to article 23 and hoped that those to articles 14 and 22 would also be withdrawn shortly. She noted that the reservations were drafted in very broad terms although, according to the report, they applied to very specific cases: certain procedures in military trials which could not be appealed against except in the case of death sentences, and restrictions on the trade union rights of public officials. It ought to be possible to cover those two exceptions without having to enter a reservation in respect of the articles as a whole.

76. She would welcome more information on the structure of the judiciary, including the training and recruitment of judges and arrangements for disciplinary action against them where necessary.

77. Paragraph 18 of the report referred to the Government's efforts to make the contents of the Covenant fully understood, particularly by public officials. She would welcome more information on the way the Government intended to inform the public in general of the provisions and spirit of the Covenant.

78. She noted from paragraph 48, on the remedies for the infringement of rights guaranteed by the Constitution, that in cases where the Constitutional Court ruled in favour of the petition, new action had to be taken in accordance with the decision. She asked how many such cases had occurred. She would also like an explanation of the term "reasonable discrimination" used in paragraph 35.

79. In connection with article 4 of the Covenant, paragraph 94 of the report said that the restrictions on fundamental rights in the case of an emergency did not refer explicitly to the absolute fundamental rights of article 4 of

0094

the Covenant but to the "essential" aspect of the freedoms or rights referred
to in the Constitution. She asked whether certain fundamental rights, such as
the right to life or freedom from torture, could in fact be suspended during
an emergency. She had a similar question in regard to article 6 and the death
penalty. She recalled that it was the Committee's view that the death penalty
should be exceptional and applied only in the case of very serious crimes.
Conceptions of what constituted a serious crime could differ. She would like
to know, therefore, what crimes were still subject to the death penalty since
the amendment of the Special Criminal Act.

80. Regarding article 9 of the Covenant, she would like more information on
the role of the National Security Planning Agency. She asked whether the
Agency was empowered to detain and interrogate suspects. According to
information from non-governmental organizations, there had been instances in
which persons had been held for a very long time without trial under the
National Security Law. She asked whether there was any limit in the Law to
the time of such detention. She noted that, according to paragraph 247 of the
report, amendments had been adopted to the National Security Law in 1991 in
order to reduce the scope of its application, and she wondered whether that
might pose any problems in regard to article 15 of the Covenant. Another
question in respect of the National Security Law arose under article 4 and the
definition of espionage. The crime of the betrayal of secrets, as included in
the Law, was extremely vague. In case law, the Supreme Court seemed to define
as secret any political, social or economic information available. The
revelation of such information could be regarded as a crime subject to the
death penalty, which could in turn pose problems in regard to articles 15, 18
and 19 of the Covenant. Concerning article 14, the report stated that a
confession under torture was not to be admitted as evidence of guilt.
According to Amnesty International, however, a person was currently serving a
sentence of life imprisonment by reason of such a confession. She asked
whether the delegation could confirm or deny the report. She noted that
paragraph 242 stated that one of the purposes of the Broadcasting Act was "to
help the formation of public opinion" and asked for an explanation of that
phrase. She wondered whether efforts to promote anti-communism were still
current in the Republic of Korea despite the changes that had taken place in
the world.

<u>The meeting rose at 6 p.m.</u>

UNITED
NATIONS

**International covenant
on civil and
political rights**

CCPR

Distr.
GENERAL

CCPR/C/SR.1151
24 July 1992

ENGLISH
Original: FRENCH

HUMAN RIGHTS COMMITTEE

Forty-fifth session

SUMMARY RECORD OF THE 1151st MEETING

Held at the Palais des Nations, Geneva,
on Tuesday, 14 July 1992, at 10 a.m.

Chairman: Mr. DIMITRIJEVIC

CONTENTS

Consideration of reports submitted by States parties under article 40 of the
Covenant (<u>continued</u>)

Initial report of the Republic of Korea (<u>continued</u>)

Third periodic report of Belarus

GE.92-16364/4706B

0096

<u>The meeting was called to order at 10.10 a.m.</u>

CONSIDERATION OF REPORTS SUBMITTED BY STATES PARTIES UNDER ARTICLE 40 OF THE COVENANT (agenda item 4) (<u>continued</u>)

<u>Initial report of the Republic of Korea</u> (CCPR/C/68/Add.1) (<u>continued</u>)

1.   The CHAIRMAN invited the members of the Committee to continue their consideration of the initial report of the Republic of Korea and requested the last speakers to put their questions to the Korean delegation.

2.   Mr. HERNDL welcomed the presence in the Committee of a high-level Korean delegation and thanked the Government of the Republic of Korea for the quality of its report, which had been submitted within the time limit and prepared in accordance with the Committee's guidelines. He warmly congratulated the Republic of Korea on its accession to the Covenant and the Optional Protocol, thus making it possible for persons within its jurisdiction, and not only citizens of the Republic, to apply to the Committee directly.

3.   Referring to the Covenant's relationship with the domestic laws of the Republic of Korea, he noted that, under article 6 (1) of the Constitution, the Covenant had the same effect as domestic laws, and that meant that it ranked as an ordinary law. In that connection, he was not sure whether it might not be better for it to rank as a constitutional law so that its precedence in the national legal system would be guaranteed. Laws enacted subsequently might, for example, be contrary to some of the provisions of the Covenant and, if the Covenant had the same rank as ordinary laws, the <u>lex posterior</u> rule would apply, so that some provisions of the Covenant would have no effect. He would also like to know whether the Covenant was regarded as a directly applicable instrument because, if it was, it could be directly invoked in the Republic of Korea by the law enforcement authorities, namely, the administrative authorities and the courts.

4.   With regard to remedies available to individuals, he asked what effect petitions filed by individuals would have, since the law provided only that the State had an obligation to consider such petitions, but did not say what specific action had to be taken on them. He also wished to know whether the remedies referred to in paragraph 14 of the report could be filed simultaneously, for example, whether an appeal against a decision handed down as a result of a petition could be lodged while the litigation procedure was under way in the same case. He would like some explanations about the role of the prosecutor, as referred to in paragraph 10 of the report, and about guarantees of his independence, as well as about the specific or general responsibilities entrusted to the human rights consultation centres established by the prosecutor.

5.   As to the implementation of article 2 of the Covenant, the provisions of article 11, paragraph 1, of the Constitution might require some amendments, for discrimination appeared to be prohibited only on certain grounds, whereas the provisions of article 2 of the Covenant were much broader in scope. In

0097

respect of the implementation of article 6 of the Covenant, the Committee had
always clearly stated that the death penalty could be imposed only for the
most odious and serious crimes. There was no doubt that the Government of the
Republic of Korea had carefully thought out the reasons for deciding to
maintain that penalty, but he would like some clarifications concerning the
circumstances in which it was actually applied, for, under national laws,
widely varying penalties, which could range from five years' imprisonment to
death, could be applied for practically the same offences. The provisions of
article 12 of the National Security Law stating that any person who had made
false accusations was liable to the penalty provided for in the corresponding
article, also called for some explanations: what was the corresponding
article?

6.   With regard to the implementation of article 9 of the Covenant, he would
like to have some clarifications about the logic of the reasoning reproduced
in paragraph 153 of the report because, in his view, the right of the accused
to a speedy trial, on the one hand, and, on the other, the fact that a
confession made under duress as a result of unduly prolonged detention was not
admitted as evidence of guilt were two entirely separate ideas. As to the
right of convicts to communicate, as dealt with, for example, in paragraph 168
of the report, which stated that an inmate was permitted to see other persons
"when deemed necessary" and "except in limited cases where the meeting is
deemed harmful for the rehabilitation of the inmate", he requested information
on the Chang Ui-gyun case, which had been recently brought to the Committee's
attention. Mr. Chang had apparently been prohibited from receiving visits in
Taejeon prison because he was regarded as an "ideological criminal". He asked
what the Korean authorities meant by "ideological criminal" and how such
status could influence the measures taken for the prisoner's rehabilitation in
society.

7.   Referring to the implementation of article 15 of the Covenant and, in
particular, to the retroactive effect of a decision of unconstitutionality, he
requested some explanations on why reference was made to the retroactive
effect of a decision of unconstitutionality, since it was clearly stated that
any law which was declared unconstitutional would lose its effect "from the
decision date". He also noted that very few details were given on the
implementation of article 27 of the Covenant and that it was indicated only in
paragraph 312 of the report that no minorities existed in the Republic of
Korea. He would like to know whether that was really true.

8.   Mrs. HIGGINS welcomed the Korean delegation and thanked the Government of
the Republic of Korea for having submitted a carefully ordered and detailed
report that had been prepared in accordance with the Committee's guidelines.

9.   She asked how the Korean authorities planned to ensure that the
population was informed of the implications of the commitments the Government
had undertaken as a result of its accession to the Covenant and the Optional
Protocol, how the population would be informed of the dialogue that had
started with the Committee - particularly the final observations which would
be formulated following the consideration of the periodic reports of the State
party - and how the Government would give effect to the decisions taken under

0098

the Optional Protocol concerning the authors of communications within its
jurisdiction. Like the other members of the Committee, she hoped that the
last reservations formulated by the Government of the Republic of Korea would
rapidly be withdrawn.

10.   With regard to the implementation of article 6 of the Covenant, she
welcomed the plans to amend criminal law in order to abolish the death
penalty. She would like to know what instructions were given to members of
the police in connection with the use of force during public demonstrations.
Referring to the implementation of article 7 and to paragraph 136 of the
report, she asked whether studying the Constitution was really enough to make
law enforcement officers refrain from the practice of torture and whether it
might not also be a good idea for instruction to be provided on the
international undertakings of the Republic of Korea with regard to the
prohibition of torture. She noted that paragraph 137 of the report indicated
that 29 public officials had been prosecuted for inflicting torture, but there
was no indication of what the outcome of those proceedings had been. She
therefore asked how many officials had been found guilty and what penalties
had been imposed on them. She would also like to know who conducted
interrogations and by virtue of which powers, whether the Government ensured
that accused persons were not tried by their own superiors and whether there
were any plans to set up an independent body to carry out inquiries into cases
of that kind.

11.   Referring to the implementation of article 9 of the Covenant, she
requested information on the draft amendments to the Criminal Code, which
had last been revised in 1975, and on the revision of the Code of Criminal
Procedure. As to arrest before investigation, she noted that the Constitution
Court had called for the amendment of some articles of the National Security
Law because it had considered that detention lasted too long. In her view,
however, a minimum reduction of the length of time that could be as long as
50 days was still not enough, bearing in mind the provisions of article 9,
paragraph 3, of the Covenant, as well as the general comments and decisions
of the Committee. She would also like to know whether there were any real
obstacles to the reopening of the cases of persons who had been detained for
many years and who claimed that they had been convicted in the past on the
basis of confessions obtained under torture. Could such persons not benefit
from the positive changes in the situation that had recently occurred in the
Republic of Korea?

12.   In the case of the implementation of article 14 of the Covenant, she
asked whether the fact that there were special prosecutors and special public
security legislation might not jeopardize the implementation of the principle
of the presumption of innocence and what instructions were given to the courts
in order to ensure that that principle was respected, particularly for persons
accused under the National Security Law. She also asked whether it was true
that some trials were held in prisons. If there were not enough lawyers,
as was the case in many other countries in the world, the accused had to be
defended by members of his family and by friends and such persons therefore
had to be given every facility for access to prisons, but that appeared to
give rise to some problems.

0099

13. With regard to the implementation of article 19 of the Covenant, she
believed that there were still some 40 political prisoners in the Republic of
Korea. In that connection, she was not sure that the condition under which
such prisoners could not be released unless they had given up their opinions
and their beliefs was compatible with the provisions of the Covenant. She
also wondered whether some provisions of the National Security Law did not
specifically apply to persons whose opinions were different from those of the
Government or to trade union members or political dissidents. Referring to
the implementation of article 21 of the Covenant, she noted that the Act
Concerning Assembly and Demonstration had recently been amended, in 1989.
She nevertheless wished to know why an authorization had to be obtained in
advance in order to organize meetings or demonstrations, in how many cases
such an authorization was refused and why. As to the Social Surveillance Act,
which had been promulgated in 1989 only and applied to persons released after
having served their sentence, her view was that, as a rule, persons who had
paid their debt to society should be free from any surveillance. She
therefore asked why such an act had been promulgated and, in particular,
whether its provisions were compatible with those of the Covenant.

14. Mr. PRADO VALLEJO welcomed the ratification of the Covenant and the
Optional Protocol by the Republic of Korea, which was thus demonstrating its
willingness to make progress towards full respect for human rights. He also
welcomed with satisfaction the report by the State party, which had been
prepared in accordance with the Committee's guidelines. Although the report
contained full information on domestic laws, which did not seem to have many
gaps, it provided little information on the problems and difficulties
encountered in the practical application of the laws.

15. Like the other members of the Committee, he hoped that the Republic of
Korea would withdraw the reservations it had made to some provisions of the
Covenant and, in particular, to article 14, paragraph 5, a natural and
essential provision which merely referred to the right to review by a higher
court in the event of an error committed by an ordinary court.

16. In addition to the considerable development efforts it had been making,
the Republic of Korea had also been working hard to ease tensions with
neighbouring North Korea and to reduce antagonism and violence that could
only lead to human rights violations. In that connection, he would like to
know what stage had been reached in the negotiations being held to solve the
serious problem of the separation of families and to bring about their reunion.

17. He was concerned about the fact that, under the National Security Law,
it was possible to arrest anyone who had spoken with North Koreans and that
particularly harsh measures were taken against persons imprisoned for that
reason. In his view, those were practices that should no longer be used.
He was also concerned about the fact that the National Security Law required
political prisoners who had left prison after serving their sentences to
report to the police every three months, that it made it possible to prohibit
demonstrations, even peaceful ones, and that it allowed detention by the
police for up to 50 days (para. 154), which was much longer than usual.

0100

18.   There had been many complaints of torture in respect of the Republic of Korea. It was pointed out, for example, that the authorities took a long time to institute an investigation in the case of a complaint of acts of torture. He would like to have some clarifications on the rules adopted to prevent such acts and on the complaints to which he had just referred because those were important elements for assessing the implementation of the Covenant. In the event of a complaint that detainees were being tortured, was it possible for independent bodies such as the Red Cross to enter prisons and visit prisoners to determine whether the complaint had any basis in fact?

19.   Paragraph 89 of the report relating to article 4 of the Covenant stated that, under the Constitution, the freedom and rights of citizens could be restricted by law only when absolutely necessary for national security, the maintenance of law and order or "public welfare". He would like to know what was meant by "public welfare". He also wished to know the maximum period authorized for pre-trial detention and how the remedy of habeas corpus worked, since periods of detention could be very long.

20.   He asked how many political prisoners there were in the Republic of Korea, since the figures quoted varied greatly. In that connection, attention had been drawn to the case of some prisoners of opinion who had been detained for 30 years. He wished to know whether any of them had been given reductions in sentence or other types of pardon provided for the benefit of some prisoners in many pieces of legislation. In the Republic of Korea, political prisoners could apparently not benefit from such measures if they were communist or regarded as such and if they did not give up their ideas, and that was not in conformity with recognized basic human rights standards.

21.   When the Republic of Korea had ratified the Covenant, he would like to know whether the text had been published and disseminated so that all persons would be informed of their rights and the remedies and guarantees available to them, even under international instruments. Such dissemination was important for the implementation of the Covenant.

22.   Mr. WENNERGREN, referring to article 107 of the Constitution and administrative remedies and, in particular, to paragraph 14 of the report, which stated that "The Supreme Court has the power to make a final review" of the constitutionality of decrees and administrative regulations, asked whether that meant that there were no administrative courts in the Republic of Korea and that the Supreme Court was, as it were, a supreme administrative court. He also wished to know the procedure for bringing a case before the Supreme Court.

23.   With regard to article 6 and the death penalty, he had been suprised to learn from paragraph 112 of the report that the minimum age for the death penalty was now 18 years and that there was also a possibility of "the death sentence of a juvenile who is less than 18 years of age". He would like some clarifications on that point and asked whether the death penalty was carried out by hanging or otherwise. As to abortion, paragraph 110 of the report

0101

stated that the voluntary interruption of pregnancy was authorized for "eugenic" reasons. He would like to know what that meant, whether a woman could be required to have an abortion for such reasons and whether a diagnosis of the foetus was carried out.

24. Referring to article 7 and torture, he requested statistics on the prosecution and punishment of officials who had committed acts of torture and on the penalties imposed on them. With regard to article 8 and forced labour during detention, paragraph 145 of the report stated that the Criminal Code provided for penal servitude "with a certain amount of labour", which should be defined. He would also like some statistics on solitary confinement, cases in which it was used and conditions under which prisoners were subjected to that regime.

25. Paragraph 246 of the report referred to the National Security Law under the heading of freedom of expression, but the commentary in the report suggested that the authors were actually dealing with freedom of conscience in the context of freedom of expression. Moreover, article 37 of the Constitution provided that fundamental rights could be subjected to restrictions when necessary for national security, the maintenance of law and order and public welfare, but, even in that case, the restrictions must not jeopardize any essential aspect of the right in question (para. 244 of the report). Freedom of conscience or opinion was, however, a fundamental right that must be respected. Under the heading "penitentiary system" (para. 165), reference was made to the purpose of the Penal Administration Act, which was to reform and rehabilitate convicted persons to return them to a normal life in society through moral training and the cultivation of a sound and stable personality. In his view that was a kind of indoctrination.

26. The CHAIRMAN said that the first phase of the consideration of the initial report of the Republic of Korea had now been completed, since the members of the Committee had asked their questions, which the delegation of the State party would answer later. The meeting would be suspended to enable the Committee to welcome the delegation of Belarus.

The meeting was suspended at 11.10 a.m. and resumed at 11.30 a.m.

Third periodic report of Belarus (CCPR/C/52/Add.8)

27. At the invitation of the Chairman, Mr. Dashuk, Mr. Ogurtsov and Mr. Galka (Republic of Belarus) took places at the Committee table.

28. Mr. DASHUK (Republic of Belarus), Minister of Justice, introducing his country's third periodic report, said that, since the consideration of the second periodic report and the submission of the third periodic report to the Committee in July 1990, enormous changes had taken place in the political, social and economic life of Belarus. He would therefore give a brief description of the many reforms that had been under way for the past two years, drawing attention to the most important. As far as details and the implementation of the Covenant were concerned, his delegation would then try to give exhaustive replies to the questions the members of the Committee would ask.

0102

29.   Under the new law on the election of deputies to the Supreme Soviet and local soviets which had been adopted in 1989, a new Parliament had been elected, as had the Supreme Soviet and the local soviets composed of deputies of the people.   Voters had been able to choose from among several candidates the one they considered most worthy of representing them, on the basis of the programme submitted to them.   Some 40 parliamentary seats had gone to the opposition, namely, the Belarusian Popular Front, which had been formed during the period preceding the elections.   The presence of a strong opposition had had repercussions on the work of the supreme legislative bodies and on the consideration of matters submitted to Parliament.   The laws and decrees adopted genuinely reflected the will and interests of the citizens of the Republic.

30.   On 27 July 1990, during its first session, the Supreme Soviet had adopted the Declaration of State Sovereignty, an extremely important document which had not had any equivalent in 70 years of Soviet power and which, for the first time, proclaimed the sovereignty of the Republic, the supreme and independent authority as a matter of right.   The Declaration provided for the supremacy of the rule of law and the independence of the Republic of Belarus in relations with other countries and expressed the desire of the Republic to establish itself as a State subject to the rule of law.

31.   According to article 1 of the Declaration on State Sovereignty, the Republic of Belarus was recognized as a sovereign State on the basis of the existence of the Belarusian nation and its inalienable right to self-determination; the Belarusian language was established as the State language; and the people took precedence in the choice of its destiny.   The inalienable rights of the Republic of Belarus as a sovereign State were in conformity with the generally recognized rules of international law; the Republic defended the nation State and had an insignia, a banner and a national anthem.   Any attempt to overthrow the Belarusian nation State by force, by the activities of political parties or collective organizations or by individual activity was punishable by law.

32.   Article 2 of the Declaration stated that citizens of all nationalities were part of the Belarusian people and regarded as full nationals of the Republic.   Their rights were exercised directly and through State bodies. Only the Supreme Soviet could take decisions on behalf of the entire people of the Republic.   Article 3 provided that State sovereignty was exercised in the name of a higher interest, which was development in well-being, freedom and respect for the dignity and life of every citizen on the basis of respect for individual rights, in accordance with the Constitution of the Republic and the international obligations it had undertaken.

33.   Under article 4 of the Declaration, the Republic of Belarus defended the honour, health, rights and interests of citizens and guaranteed them social protection.   Citizens were protected by the Republic even beyond its borders and the Republic regulated matters of citizenship, particularly in respect of persons who wanted to leave the territory.

0103

34. According to article 5 of the Declaration, the soil, subsoil and airspace were the exclusive heritage of the Belarusian people, which enjoyed an exclusive right of possession, use and allocation of its resources. The Republic had set up the National Bank, which was subordinate to the Supreme Soviet; it had established its own financial system and credit system, organized its tax and customs regime independently and was entitled to create its own monetary system. According to article 6, the territory of the Republic must be respected in its unity and integrity. It could not be changed or used without the agreement of the Republic and all boundary problems were settled by way of agreements concluded by the Republic with sovereign States in the form of treaties which had to be ratified by Parliament.

35. Article 7 of the Declaration provided that the Constitution and laws took precedence in the territory of the Republic. All citizens, as well as non-citizens, State bodies, enterprises, institutions and organizations established or operating in Belarusian territory had to abide by the laws in force in the Republic. The separation of the legislative, executive and judicial powers was an important principle on which the rule of law in the Republic of Belarus was based.

36. Under articles 8 and 9 of the Declaration, the Republic decided independently on the establishment in its territory of organizations for the protection of nature and natural resources and it guaranteed the people protection against ecological risks. Moral and cultural matters were settled independently, as were questions relating to information and education. The Republic guaranteed the use of the Belarusian language in all areas of social life, ensured respect for national traditions and protected national and historical treasures in its territory, which were the exclusive property of the Republic and citizens.

37. Article 10 of the Declaration of Sovereignty related to the right of the Republic to set up its own armed forces under the supervision of the Supreme Soviet. It governed all matters relating to the installation and deployment of armed forces throughout the territory, as well as conditions for military service. It provided, _inter alia_, that no foreign armed force, military base or weapon could be installed in the territory without the agreement of the Supreme Soviet. The Republic had declared its intention to proclaim the territory a nuclear-free-weapon zone and, eventually, to become a neutral State.

38. According to article 11 of the Declaration, the Republic of Belarus had the sovereign right to set up, of its own accord, a union with other States and to separate from that union.

39. The provisions of the Declaration were being implemented by the Supreme Soviet of the Republic and as a result of the adoption of a new constitution and other laws. Thus, a law of 25 August 1991 had given the Declaration the rank of a constitutional law. The Supreme Soviet, meeting on 25 August 1991 in special session, had undertaken to amend and supplement

the Constitution in force. For example, it had amended article 72, which now provided that the Constitution of the Republic took precedence over all other laws and that the legislation of the former Soviet Union continued to be in force as long as it was not incompatible with the national Constitution. It had also amended article 73 guaranteeing the indivisibility of the territory, which could not be changed or used in any way without the agreement of the Republic. In that connection, all boundary problems were settled by agreement between the Republic and the States concerned.

40. A Supreme Soviet decree dated 25 August 1991 also guaranteed the economic and political independence of the Republic. All enterprises, organizations and institutions established in the territory of the Republic were its property, except for those whose management had been transferred to the competent bodies of the former Soviet Union, in accordance with the law on the transfer of authority which had entered into force on 1 January 1992.

41. In 1991, Parliament had adopted a nationality act which determined the conditions for the acquisition, retention and loss of citizenship of the Republic. It had also adopted a law on the crest and flag of the Republic in 1991 and had organized a competition for the composition of the national anthem.

42. A new customs law had been enacted in April 1992 and a text governing banking activity, bankruptcy and the protection of tax payers' interests had been adopted on 14 December 1991.

43. Popular voting by referendum had been regulated in detail in a legislative text adopted on 13 June 1991 and, at its 1992 winter session, Parliament had drafted a set of texts on military service. On 20 September 1991, the Supreme Soviet had issued a decree on relations between local bodies and the military authorities, as well as between those authorities and the State Security Committees of the former Soviet Union.

44. A law on self-management and the local economy establishing the basic principles and general orientation of the economy had been adopted on 20 February 1991 and had already been amended several times because its implementation had revealed some negative aspects. On 27 February 1992, Parliament had adopted a very important law establishing that the people held power and was the only source of the authority of the State, such sovereignty being exercised directly or through the intermediary of bodies set up to represent it. The law stipulated that the most important task of State bodies was to provide all the services the people needed and to guarantee that its rights, freedoms and legitimate interests were safeguarded. It prohibited any interference in the activities of State associations and bodies and vice-versa, except as otherwise expressly provided, prohibited the State from financing political parties and other political associations and guaranteed every citizen access in full quality to public service, as well as the right to join social associations.

0105

45. The requirements for the publication and entry into force of all legislative texts of the Republic adopted by the Supreme Soviet were also provided for in a law which made their publication compulsory within 10 days of their adoption. International treaties concluded by the Republic also had to be published in the newspapers in Belarusian and in Russian so that each citizen might be informed of them.

46. One of the most important laws adopted since the submission of the third periodic report was the law putting an end to the monopoly of the Communist Party and establishing a multi-party system. The transition to a market economy had required other changes in the Constitution and a number of new laws had been drafted and adopted to govern matters such as land ownership, leases, activities of enterprises, foreign investments, bankruptcy, employment, culture, the possibility of concluding international treaties, education, the legal regime governing the territory contaminated as a result of the Chernobyl disaster and the protection of veterans, disabled persons, young persons and the family.

47. By decision of Parliament, the draft Constitution of the Republic of Belarus had been published in the media and the result had been tens of thousands of replies by citizens expressing their wishes. All the competent experts and State bodies had also studied the draft, on which a constitutional commission had been working for two years. The details of the text were not known, but, having taken part in its preparation, he could assure the Committee that one of its basic features was that it took account of all the international obligations assumed by the Republic of Belarus and that the protection of human rights occupied a very important place. A mechanism had been set up to guarantee the protection of human rights and there were plans to organize voting to elect deputies according to a multi-party system. The Republic would thus have a Parliament, a constitutional court and a court of appeal. The separation of the three powers would be fully guaranteed. In April 1992, Parliament had undertaken a legal reform and, although there was still a great deal to be done, many new texts already existed, such as the Criminal Code, the Civil Code, the Code of Criminal Procedure, the Code of Civil Procedure, a law containing the judiciary regulations, the Labour Code, the Family Code and the Administrative Code.

48. On 14 January 1992, the Supreme Soviet had ratified the Optional Protocol to the International Covenant on Civil and Political Rights and had made the declaration provided for in article 41 of the Covenant. He also drew attention to the ratification of ILO Convention No. 160 (on labour statistics), the Convention on the Rights of the Child and the Convention on Psychotropic Substances. As a State party to the Convention against Torture and Other Cruel, Inhuman or Degrading Treatment or Punishment, the Byelorussian Soviet Socialist Republic had submitted a report to the Committee against Torture in 1989.

49. His delegation was at the disposal of the Committee for any clarifications and explanations it might like to have.

0106

50.   The CHAIRMAN invited the delegation of Belarus to reply to the questions contained in section I of the list of issues (M/CCPR/92/32), which read:

"I.   Constitutional and legal framework within which the Covenant is implemented; right to self-determination; non-discrimination and equality of the sexes; and rights of persons belonging to minorities (articles 1, 2, 3 and 27)

(a)   Please clarify the legal and practical consequences of the dissolution of the Soviet Union and the establishment of the Commonwealth of Independent States on the implementation of the rights set forth in the Covenant and their enjoyment by individuals in Belarus.   What is the actual status of legislation in the field of human rights in Belarus?

(b)   What has been the impact on the actual implementation of the Covenant of the adoption of the Act on the Status of Judges of 4 August 1989, the Contempt of Court Act of 2 November 1989, and the Foundations of Legislation on the Judicial System of 17 November 1989 (paras. 50 to 58 of the report)?

(c)   What is the position of Belarus regarding the first Optional Protocol to the Covenant?

(d)   Please elaborate on the new systems of power being established both nationally and locally, in provinces, cities and rural areas (para. 84 of the report).

(e)   What measures have been taken or contemplated to ensure consistency between any new constitutional provisions or other legal instruments and the Covenant?

(f)   Please comment on what improvements, if any, have occurred in the situation of minorities since the consideration of the second periodic report.   Please provide statistical data on minorities described in the Covenant.

(g)   Please elaborate on the activities undertaken to enhance the role and status of women during the reporting period, particularly by the women's councils mentioned in paragraph 29 of the report."

51.   Mr. DASHUK (Republic of Belarus) said that the Declaration of Sovereignty confirmed the exercise of the right to self-determination, which, until the adoption of the Declaration, had been only a principle that had had no effect.   The Declaration guaranteed the rights of citizens and minorities and strengthened them even more.   The dissolution of the USSR had, of course, given rise to economic disruptions, but, as far as the rights of citizens were concerned, there had been an enormous step forward, although that did not necessarily mean that there had been serious violations of human rights in Belarus before 1990.   After the ratification of the Covenant, many texts had

0107

been adopted to guarantee the exercise of human rights. At present, those guarantees were being expanded and increased. It should be pointed out that nearly all the laws enacted since 1990 included a provision stating that, if a particular question was not covered by a law, the international rule applied.

52. With regard to question (b), he pointed out that, since the third periodic report had been submitted to the Committee, the Republic of Belarus had equipped itself with new laws, particularly on conditions of admission to the profession of judge. Since 3 July 1990, when a law had been adopted along those lines, judges and assessors of the Republic were qualified and had to be sworn in. As part of the reform of the judicial system, there were plans to establish a court of appeal and eliminate the institution of people's assessors. It was also being proposed that some minor criminal offences should come within the jurisdiction of a single judge, whereas more complex cases would be tried by three judges. Various measures had been taken to guarantee the independence of judges and strengthen their authority. For example, the Criminal Code penalized any interference in the powers of judges and established criminal responsibility in the event of threats against judges, contempt of court, refusal to testify, withholding evidence, obstruction of the operation of the court and refusal to enforce a court decision. According to another recommendation, judges had to be appointed without delay. Judges were elected at the regional level for 10 years, and that was an improvement compared to the past situation, although it was not a complete guarantee. In any event, the Government and Parliament were fully aware of the importance of the independence of the judiciary and would do everything possible to strengthen it even more.

53. With regard to the question asked in paragraph (c), he said that the Republic of Belarus had ratified the first Optional Protocol to the Covenant on 14 January 1992.

54. As to paragraph (d), the question of regional and local autonomy was important and complex. In February 1991, Parliament had adopted various texts on that question and there were many legislative provisions relating to it. In general, an end had been put to the representation of what had been known as the "nomenklatura" of the Communist Party within the organs of power. At present, those bodies were composed of persons who had a spirit of initiative and cared about respect for democracy. The legislation in force prohibited being both a deputy and a member of a party. At all levels of power, efforts were being made to improve the economic situation of citizens and guarantee respect for their rights. The Soviets now were very different from those of the past. Deputies no longer systematically adopted the texts submitted to them, as they had done before. In appointing judges, they carefully considered each file, taking account primarily of the qualifications of candidates, and they made very specific recommendations in every case.

55. There were differences and oppositions within each Soviet and they were to be welcomed.

0108

56. Although he had partially answered the question asked in paragraph (e), he added that, on the whole, the provisions of the Covenant had been respected in his country since the submission of the second periodic report. However, the legislation in force still had some important gaps. For example, in the event of unlawful arrest or detention, it did not provide for adequate remedies and, in that sense, its provisions were not up to international standards. Moreover, the rights and interests of citizens were not always sufficiently protected by the law. The new legislation being prepared would fill all those gaps and be designed particularly to protect rights and freedoms. He assured the Committee that each provision of the Covenant was being carefully studied as part of the legislative reform and that his country's next periodic report would provide further information on all those questions. A set of draft laws would be submitted to Parliament at its autumn session and their adoption should make it possible to bring national legislation more fully into line with the provisions of the Covenant. Other problems included the under-representation of lawyers in court, the fact that the Supreme Court sometimes heard cases which were within the jurisdiction of a court of first instance and the fact that the Ministry of the Interior exercised functions that were not within its terms of reference, such as issuing passports and permits or registering citizens. The role of the police would also have to be reappraised, for its task was basically to prevent delinquency and guarantee the security of citizens. It was also necessary to redefine the functions of the public prosecutor, who had to assist judges in their work, not impose his views on them. There could be no independence of the judiciary if the public prosecutor could be made responsible for investigations. There were also not enough lawyers. They numbered about 1,000, but they did not meet needs, far from it. Moreover, the profession of lawyer should be exercised more and more in the private sector. The reform that was under way was moving in that direction. He also noted that the State Security Committee (KGB) was now undergoing a complete restructuring, which had been badly needed.

57. Referring to paragraph (f), he said that 77 nationalities now lived together in Belarus. The four main minorities were Ukrainians, Russians, Poles and Jews. As a general rule, the rights of national minorities were fully respected in the Republic, which had a long tradition of political stability. The Belarusian people had suffered greatly during the Second World War, one out of four - some said one out of three - having been killed, and it knew the price of friendship among peoples. The authorities therefore set great store by ensuring harmonious coexistence with the different national minorities. A draft law on the question of minorities would, moreover, probably be adopted on second reading at the autumn session of Parliament. He also noted that the members of national minorities in Belarus enjoyed the same rights as all other citizens of the Republic. In addition, Belarusians who left the new Baltic Republics because of the harsh requirements they had to meet, particularly as far as knowing the language of the country was concerned, could freely return to Belarus, where they were welcomed. He had no knowledge of any case of the denial of Belarusian citizenship. Many Ukrainian, Polish and Jewish social and trade union organizations, inter alia,

0109

had been officially registered by the authorities of the new Republic. The aim of those organizations was to defend the rights and interests of the minorities they represented. Under the legislation in force, moreover, national minorities could request Parliament to include the consideration of important questions of concern to them in its agenda.

58. Replying to the question contained in paragraph (g), he said that the legislative provisions on the status of women, pregnancy, children and adolescents had been amended considerably. The law of 28 June 1992 relating to the family, pregnancy and women's work contained a number of provisions which usefully supplemented the existing legislation. Pregnant women were thus better protected and their working conditions had been made more flexible, without any reduction in wages. For example, women were entitled to one year of maternity leave. Mothers below age 18 were entitled to 18 months' paid leave to raise a child and, throughout that period, received allowances from the State for themselves and for their children. After that, a woman could take unpaid leave to raise her child until it had reached the age of three. She then received allowances for the child only. It was also prohibited to dismiss a pregnant woman or a woman whose children were below the age of three. If the enterprise where she had been working before her pregnancy was closed down, the management of the enterprise or the State then had to find her another job.

59. Under the Family Code, women and children enjoyed legal protection by the State. As a general rule, everything was done so that women could combine bringing up children and work, especially by giving them advantages in the workplace.

60. As an even more general rule, women took an active part in the political life of the country. Many of them held posts as ministers, deputies, physicians, etc. and the authorities paid a great deal of attention to the economic problems they encountered. The status of women had never given rise to any real problems in Belarus, where women's committees played an important role and women were generally particularly dynamic.

61. The CHAIRMAN thanked the Belarusian delegation for its detailed replies to the questions contained in section I of the list. He invited the members of the Committee to continue their consideration of the third periodic report of Belarus (CCPR/C/52/Add.8) at a subsequent meeting.

The meeting was called to order at 1.05 p.m.

0110

International covenant
on civil and
political rights

Distr.
GENERAL

CCPR/C/SR.1154
20 July 1992

Original: ENGLISH

HUMAN RIGHTS COMMITTEE

Forty-fifth session

SUMMARY RECORD OF THE 1154th MEETING

Held at the Palais des Nations, Geneva,
on Wednesday, 15 July 1992, at 3 p.m.

Chairman: Mr. POCAR

CONTENTS

Consideration of reports submitted by States parties under article 40 of the
Covenant (underline continued)

Initial report of the Republic of Korea (underline continued)

This record is subject to correction.

Corrections should be submitted in one of the working languages. They
should be set forth in a memorandum and also incorporated in a copy of the
record. They should be sent within one week of the date of this document to
the Official Records Editing Section, room E.4108, Palais des Nations, Geneva.

Any corrections to the records of the public meetings of the Committee at
this session will be consolidated in a single corrigendum, to be issued
shortly after the end of the session.

GE.92-16411/4676B

0111

The meeting was called to order at 3.15 p.m.

CONSIDERATION OF REPORTS SUBMITTED BY STATES PARTIES UNDER ARTICLE 40 OF THE COVENANT (agenda item 4) (continued)

Initial report of the Republic of Korea (CCPR/C/68/Add.1) (continued)

1.   The CHAIRMAN invited the delegation of the Republic of Korea to answer the questions raised by Committee members.

2.   Mr. Soo Gil PARK (Republic of Korea) thanked Committee members for their appreciation of his country's achievements in the field of human rights. Nevertheless, the questions members had raised revealed a number of misconceptions, due perhaps to a lack of information from the Government or deliberate attempts by certain parties to exaggerate isolated human rights violations.

3.   The Declaration for Democracy of 29 June 1987 had truly been a turning-point in the history of the Korean people. The subsequent democratic reforms, embodied in the new Constitution, had made it possible for former dissident leaders to run for the presidency in 1992, for the press to criticize the Government without restrictions and for the human rights of all citizens to be guaranteed. In the recent National Assembly elections, the ruling party had almost lost its majority. The Assembly frequently investigated allegations of human rights violations and brought the Government to account where necessary.

4.   Some of the comments made by Committee members did not seem to recognize the enormous changes which had taken place in the Republic of Korea. Seventeen laws had been declared unconstitutional by the Constitutional Court, which had also restricted the application of the National Security Law. Members had talked about "political prisoners": however, the legal experts of the Republic of Korea did not consider that people convicted of injuring police officers or throwing firebombs at State property could be considered political prisoners. Members had further described the National Security Law as the "de facto Constitution" and had inferred that the unrest in the Republic of Korea was so great as to make extraordinary measures necessary. That was simply not true.

5.   Some of the material which Committee members had possibly used in preparing their questions - and one source in particular - was notable for its lack of objectivity, balance and accuracy. For instance, the source in question had stated that the two Koreas had registered the South-North Agreement with the Secretariat of the United Nations in March 1992 under Article 102 of the Charter of the United Nations. In fact, it was stated quite clearly in the Agreement itself that it was not to be considered an international accord. Moreover, the same source had alleged that the works of E.H. Carr and Bruce Cummings, let alone those of Marx and Lenin, were prohibited in the Republic of Korea. He had read those works himself as a student, and they were still widely available. The mere possession or reading of any book was not a crime in the Republic of Korea.

0112

6.   The relations between the two Koreas were among the most important factors affecting the human rights situation.   The signing of the agreement on reconciliation, non-aggression, exchanges and cooperation and the joint declaration on the denuclearization of the Korean peninsula within the past year had raised hopes of a dialogue between the two sides.   In May 1992, three bodies had been established to work on a basic agreement governing unification.   However, the two sides' differences on the nuclear issue had hindered progress in the negotiations, although he hoped that a spirit of mutual compromise would yet achieve results.   It was also to be hoped that an agreement would soon be reached on family reunion; at present, separated family members were not even allowed to telephone or write to one another.

7.   The reunification of the Korean peninsula must be based on the three principles of self-determination, peace and democracy.   His Government's plan was to establish a provisional Korean commonwealth, which would promote peaceful coexistence, national homogeneity and the economic, cultural and social integration of the two Koreas.   The commonwealth would be composed of a council of presidents, a council of ministers, a council of representatives and a joint secretariat, as well as a resident liaison office in each capital.   After that, the legislative body of the commonwealth – the council of representatives – would draft and promulgate a constitutional law for a unified Korea by means of democratic procedures.   Finally, a general election would be held under the new constitutional law to elect a unified parliament and government.   Unfortunately, however, the other side took a different approach to reunification, and it was thus difficult to predict the outcome of the current dialogue.

8.   Mr. Kook Hyun YOO (Republic of Korea) said that many members had asked about the relationship between the Constitution of the Republic of Korea and the Covenant.   Under article 6 (1) of the Constitution, the Covenant had the same effect as domestic law.   He could not accept the claim that the guarantees contained in the Covenant might be overturned by subsequent domestic legislation, since such a suspicion underestimated the Republic of Korea's commitment to human rights and the increasing public awareness of the rights enshrined in the Covenant, thanks to the Government's public awareness campaign.   Moreover, since the principal rights enshrined in the Covenant were also embodied in the Constitution, any conflicting domestic legislation would be deemed unconstitutional.   If an individual claimed that his rights under the Covenant had been infringed, the court would normally rule on the basis of domestic legislation; in the rare cases where that was not possible, the Covenant could be invoked directly by the courts.

9.   Article 37 (1) of the Constitution stated that the freedoms and rights of citizens could not be neglected on the pretext that they were not enumerated in the Covenant: it was his Government's official position that that article covered all the rights enshrined in the Covenant, except those in respect of which the Government had entered reservations.

10.   In reply to Mr. El Shafei's question about the remedies available to persons whose human rights had allegedly been violated, he said that individuals were free to activate the procedures outlined in the Optional Protocol to the Covenant.   In reply to Mrs. Higgins' question as to what measures the Government would take if the Committee expressed views on a case

0113

under the Optional Protocol, he could only say that the Government would make every effort to reflect the Committee's views in its future legislation. Mr. Herndl had asked about the remedy of petitions: a complaint lodged by a petitioner would be dealt with by the relevant administrative agency and, if the petitioner was not satisfied with the result, he was automatically entitled to lodge a complaint with the court.

11. The Government of the Republic of Korea was endeavouring to establish a dialogue with North Korea while coping with a very real threat of destabilization and military provocation. Until the other side stopped using terrorism as an instrument of its foreign policy, his country was bound to retain the National Security Law. His Government did not agree with the view that North Korea's participation in the current dialogue was a sign of a change of heart. The National Security Law was strictly applied and interpreted in accordance with the Constitution and the Covenant: it was only used to counter subversive acts which endangered national security and the democratic order.

12. It had been suggested that article 7 of the National Security Law infringed the freedom of speech and the freedom of the press, art, creativity and education; such restrictions were far beyond its scope. It had further been alleged that articles 3 and 7 infringed the freedom of association. However, the latter articles prohibited only the activities of anti-State organizations which endangered national security. Article 10, which had also been criticized, was designed not to infringe freedom of conscience, but to obtain necessary information about criminal acts which threatened national security.

13. In order to preclude any abuse of the National Security Law, the Government had incorporated into it the substance of a decision of the Constitutional Court of April 1990, which had defined "activities endangering national security and survival" to cover explicit communist activities, infiltration of the national territory or an attempt to destroy the constitutional system. "Activities endangering the basic liberal democratic order" had been defined as activities which made it difficult to maintain majority rule exclusive of violence and arbitrariness and a legal order based on liberty and equality, or activities which destroyed the existing order. The term "anti-State organization" had been defined as covering organizations which purported to assume authority over the State on behalf of the Korean people or to overthrow the State of the Republic of Korea. It was not possible to be convicted under the National Security Law simply for harbouring or expressing communist ideas or for having a positive opinion about North Korea, provided that those sentiments did not lead to the commission of illegal acts.

14. Miss Chanet had asked about the definition of espionage under the National Security Law. The concept was actually defined in the Criminal Code as the collection, divulging and transmission of national secrets (which comprised not only military secrets, but also political and economic information) on the instructions of anti-State organizations or their members. The provision covered only information which might jeopardize national security, and it was not invoked unless there had clearly been an attempt to pass information to North Korea with the knowledge that the

0114

information would endanger the Republic of Korea. People had been convicted
under the National Security Law if they had attempted or advocated the
overthrow of the Government by violent revolutionary means. In all cases,
defendants had enjoyed the full constitutional safeguards which ensured a fair
trial.

15. The amendment to the National Security Law was not retroactive: the old
law still applied to acts which had taken place before the amendment. The
country's legal experts considered that amendments should not be retroactive
unless they were designed to redress wrongs or eliminate contradictions in the
existing law.

16. Members of the Committee had asked about the role of the prosecutor's
office. Prosecutors were officials of the executive branch, coming under the
authority of the Ministry of Justice, and were guaranteed independence by the
Prosecution Organization Act. Prosecutors had to possess the same
qualifications as judges, pass a highly competitive examination and complete a
two-year training course. In order to preserve their political neutrality,
they could not be suspended except by impeachment or conviction for certain
crimes, and their salary levels were guaranteed. They were responsible for
investigating and prosecuting cases, supervising the police and submitting
requests to the courts for the application of the law. Prosecutors working on
public security cases did not possess any special qualifications. A body
called the National Security Planning Agency gathered domestic security
information about communist and subversive activities and conducted
investigations in a limited number of cases, including alleged violations of
the National Security Law.

17. There were three levels of court - district courts, high courts and the
Supreme Court, as well as the Constitutional Court and military courts. The
Constitutional Court ruled on the constitutionality of the law, impeachment
cases, the dissolution of political parties and conflicts of jurisdiction.
Judges served for 10 years, and could be reappointed for further terms. They
could not be dismissed except by impeachment or conviction for certain
offences, and their political activities were restricted.

18. Mr. Herndl and other members had remarked on the small number of grounds
for possible discrimination laid down in article 11 of the Constitution. He
wished to make it clear that the list was a purely indicative one, and other
grounds, such as differences in political opinion, were not excluded.

19. Mr. Aguilar Urbina had inquired about a foreigner's right to hold public
office. Foreigners were not guaranteed the right to hold public office, but
the Government did employ foreigners on a contract basis. Only citizens of
the Republic of Korea were entitled to vote or engage in political activity.

20. Miss Chanet had asked what constituted "reasonable cultural
discrimination": that term was intended to cover differentiation based upon a
person's educational accomplishments.

21. A question had also been asked about the de facto status of women.
Despite the advances in women's status, most female workers were still in
low-paid jobs, and there were few women in senior academic posts. There were

not enough State child-care facilities for low-income families, and the traditional discrimination against women still lingered on. The Government had endeavoured to eliminate the traditional stereotypes, promote women's participation in social and economic activities and increase welfare facilities.

22. Under the 1945 Nationality Act, women were obliged to take their husband's nationality on marriage and to be naturalized if the husband was naturalized. The Republic of Korea had lodged a corresponding reservation to the Convention on the Elimination of All Forms of Discrimination against Women. However, the Government was considering an amendment to the Nationality Act to bring it into line with international standards.

23. Concerning the protection of human rights under a state of emergency, article 37 (2) of the Constitution stipulated that, even if it were necessary to restrict certain rights, it was not permissible to restrict the "essential aspects" of a freedom or right. That term safeguarded all the rights referred to in article 4 (2) of the Covenant. Under article 76 of the Constitution, the President could issue an emergency order in times of insurgency, external threat, natural calamity or serious financial or economic crisis. If the National Assembly subsequently found that the emergency order was not justified, it would be revoked forthwith.

24. Mr. Prado Vallejo had asked about the definition and application of the terms "national security", "maintenance of order" and "public welfare" with reference to the imposition of restrictions in certain, very limited circumstances laid down in the Constitution, the Criminal Code and the National Security Law. "National security" meant the countering of foreign aggression and the safeguarding of the liberal democratic order. "Maintenance of order" meant the preservation of the public and social order necessary for a normal life. "Public welfare" referred to the interests and well-being of the public. The term was used in a positive sense which went beyond the maintenance of order, being used in laws concerning economic and social rights, the environment, land use, town planning and the protection of green spaces.

25. Mr. Dimitrijevic had asked about the law on abortion. Although abortion was penalized under the Criminal Code, the Maternal and Child Health Act permitted exceptions in cases of rape, incest and threats to the health of the mother. The Government was considering an amendment to the Criminal Code to take those exceptions into account. The reference in the report to abortions for eugenic reasons (CCPR/C/68/Add.1, para. 110) covered cases where the foetus was severely deformed.

26. Turning to the subject of the death penalty, he said that, besides the offences covered by the National Security Law, 15 crimes were subject to the death penalty under the Criminal Code. As Miss Chanet had noted, the death penalty could be imposed in cases of robbery, but that would not happen unless there were vile aggravating circumstances. The death penalty was a rare exception, not the rule, in the Republic of Korea. The Government had already considerably reduced the number of capital offences and intended to progress further in that direction.

0116

27.   Members of the Committee had referred to a claim that 50 offences under the National Security Law were subject to the death penalty. However, the National Security Law dealt with only one crime - anti-State activities which endangered national security - and many offences referred to in the law, such as murder for the purposes of insurrection, were also covered by the Criminal Code. Under the Penal Administration Act, the death penalty was carried out by hanging.

28.   Several members had raised the question of protection against torture and inhuman treatment. The courts would not accept a confession unless it could be proved beyond reasonable doubt that it had been made voluntarily. Following an investigation into the unnatural death of Jong Chul Park in January 1987, five police officers had been convicted and sentenced to prison terms of between 3 and 10 years. In response to Mr. Wennergren's question about the number of police officers who had been convicted of torturing prisoners, he could say that six officers had been sentenced to prison for 2-10 years, 14 had received suspended sentences and 9 more cases were awaiting trial. Places of detention were inspected regularly: prosecutors inspected the detention premises of the investigative authorities at least once a month, and the Ministry of Justice inspected all prisons at least 10 times a year. Any complaints of inhuman treatment were investigated immediately by the prosecutor's office.

29.   Miss Chanet had referred to the case of Ki Rae Park. His conviction had been based on objective evidence, and not on a confession extracted under torture, as had been alleged. Ki Rae Park's prison sentence had been reduced for good behaviour, and he had been released on probation on 25 May 1991.

30.   Mrs. Higgins had inquired about the situation of long-term prisoners. Such prisoners had been convicted of attempts to overthrow the Government by violence or to disrupt the liberal democratic political system. The Government could not afford to release prisoners unless it was sure that their release would not jeopardize national security. It therefore considered every application for early release on its merits.

31.   Several questions had been raised about the period of detention as referred to in paragraph 154 of the report. The term referred to the time that elapsed between the date of arrest and the date of the final court judgement. Such detention could not exceed six months and the court must render its judgement during that period or release the suspect. In response to the question on how the court reviewed the legality of a detention, he said that a suspect detained pursuant to a warrant, or his lawyer, legal representative, spouse or other family member, cohabitant or employer, could submit an application for an examination of legality to an appropriate court. The court must then examine the case promptly and either dismiss the application or order the release of the detainee. The prosecutor, the defence counsel and the applicant could appear before the court and present their views. Arrest or detention must be followed immediately by notification of the detainee's family.

32.   Several questions had been raised in connection with article 10 of the Covenant, concerning treatment of prisoners, and also in that context inquiries had been made about the correctional education of inmates, which

also had implications for articles 18 and 19. As well as punishment, the purpose of the correctional system was the prevention of further crimes and the rehabilitation of prisoners. To accomplish the latter, inmates received correctional education aimed at cultivating sound civic values with a view to preventing the recurrence of crimes. Such prison education programmes were a common feature of almost all modern prison systems. Inmates incarcerated under the National Security Law also participated in correctional education programmes, including exchanges of views about competing ideologies, the goal being that a prisoner's re-entry into society should not pose a problem for the country. Comparative discussion of ideologies in the hope that a prisoner would absorb democratic ideals did not constitute "forced conversion". Inmates whose beliefs, if translated into action, might pose a threat to the Republic were not eligible for parole. Apart from that exception, all inmates received equal treatment and had equal rights, including family visits. No special restrictions were imposed on those who had violated the National Security Law. Meetings with relatives and friends lasted for 30 minutes and the period could be extended on request if approved by the prison authorities.

33. Unconvicted detainees were entitled to meet relatives once a day. The Constitutional Court had decided, in January 1992, that article 62 of the Penal Administration Act was unconstitutional because it prohibited an unconvicted detainee from meeting his attorney without being accompanied by a prison officer. The Government planned to revise the relevant laws and regulations in order to reflect that decision. The term "sound national spirit", which had given rise to questions, was an attempt to render the original Korean and should be interpreted as the restoration of a prisoner's moral sense. The term "voice prevention tool" also used in the report meant a gag, as commonly used in many countries.

34. In connection with article 12, on freedom of movement, Mr. Ando had asked a question about visits to North Korea by South Koreans. Since the hope of peaceful reunification had yet to be fulfilled, some restrictions were placed on travel to North Korea, in accordance with paragraph 3 of article 12, which provided for restrictions on freedom of movement for reasons of national security. The Government hoped that it would soon be possible for the restrictions to be lifted. The Special Act Governing Intra-Korean Exchanges and Cooperation already authorized visits to North Korea for certain specified purposes with government approval. Regarding the registration of residence, a statute called the Residence Registration Act applied.

35. A question had been asked in connection with article 13 about the treatment of Vietnamese boat people. The Government was working with UNHCR to provide humanitarian assistance to boat people until they could be resettled in their country of ultimate destination or a third country willing to accept them. So far, about 1,220 boat people had been resettled in third countries after arriving in the Republic of Korea. One hundred and forty-five boat people were still residing in a temporary accommodation camp.

36. In response to several questions about article 14 of the Covenant, he said that the Republic's Code of Criminal Procedure was based in part on the Anglo-American adversary system. It provided for the right to assistance by defence counsel and the right to remain silent. The suspect could designate his own counsel and communicate with him, and counsel could participate in the

0118

execution of search warrants, evidentiary procedures and reviews of the
legality of arrests. There were no exceptions to a suspect's right to
communicate with counsel. He noted that the last sentence of paragraph 153 of
the report, on speedy trial, should be deleted.

37. In response to inquiries about the military courts, he said that the
Military Court Act specified the procedures to be applied by military justice
and guaranteed the fundamental rights of the defendant in the same way as the
civil courts' Code of Criminal Procedure. The only exception was the right to
appeal. For certain specified crimes, in particular espionage, the military
court was the court of final instance. However, if a defendant was sentenced
to death, a mandatory appeal to the Supreme Court was guaranteed regardless of
the charge. Civilians were rarely subject to military justice, but it could
apply to civilians who committed such crimes as military espionage, supply of
contaminated food to soldiers, and unlawful activities in respect of prisoners
of war and sentries under martial law. In that connection, the phrase
"extraordinary law" in paragraph 211 of the report should read "extraordinary
martial law", as declared in states of siege or on the outbreak of war.

38. A question had been asked in connection with article 19 about the
protection given to freedom of expression. He emphasized that the Republic of
Korea did not practise censorship. There was no list of prohibited books.
The writings of Marx and Lenin, together with other communist works, were
freely available in bookstores and university libraries. Nor was there any
censorship of academic conduct. The confusion on the issue could be traced to
a provision of the National Security Law imposing restrictions on propaganda
that could destabilize the Republic. The publication, copying, transportation
or dissemination of propaganda for the purpose of jeopardizing national
security was forbidden.

39. As far as preventive censorship in other media was concerned, three
laws - the Performance Act, the Movies Act and the Act Concerning Records and
Video Materials - imposed very limited restrictions on movies, records and
tapes for the purpose of maintaining public order and morality. They were
fully in accordance with both the Constitution of the Republic and article 19
of the Covenant. Film producers were required to register and films were
classified, as in many other countries, to protect children from
indiscriminate sex and violence. Under the Performance Act, scripts and
scenarios written by nationals of countries with which the Republic had no
diplomatic relations were reviewed by the Performance Ethics Committee, which
was composed of civilian specialists.

40. A question had been raised by Mrs. Higgins about the requirement for
advance notice of public assembly. On receiving notice of an assembly or
demonstration, the police examined it to see whether the gathering would occur
at a prohibited time and place and whether it would disrupt traffic. As long
as it conformed to the regulations, the assembly or demonstration could
proceed as scheduled. If it had the potential to create violence or posed a
clear threat to public order and safety, a prohibition order was issued,
nullification of which could be sought in the courts. In determining the
potential for violence, all the relevant circumstances were reviewed,
including the purpose of the assembly or demonstration, the organizers' past
record, their capacity to control the demonstrators and the plans for the

0119

demonstration, for example, whether attacks on public agencies appeared to be contemplated. On 1 June 1991, the Government had established an Assembly and Demonstration Consideration Committee and had issued objective standards for limiting prohibitions on assemblies with a view to the better protection of human rights.

41. In reply to the question by Mr. Mavrommatis concerning the provision prohibiting certain teachers and journalists from joining certain political parties, he said that the Government was of the view that strict impartiality in party politics was required of teachers and journalists. The Government also considered that the Political Parties Act was compatible with article 25 of the Covenant. However, when a specific case involving that article was brought before a court, the court would have the opportunity to examine the Government's opinion.

42. A question had been asked about the grounds for the dissolution of political parties. Article 8 of the Constitution stated that, if the purpose or activities of a political party were contrary to the fundamental democratic order, the Government could bring an action for its dissolution in the Constitutional Court and the political party would then be dissolved or not in accordance with the Court's decision. Under that provision, a communist party which intended to create a communist regime through a revolution of the proletariat was banned.

43. A question had been asked under article 24 of the Covenant about safeguards against child labour. The Government was making every effort to prevent the employment of children in bars or in the entertainment business. Those efforts included educational seminars for management and the inspection of premises.

44. In reply to Mr. Herndl's question about minorities, in connection with article 27, he said that Korea was a homogeneous nation with a distinct population sharing a common language and culture and more than 4,000 years of history. There were, however, approximately 51,000 resident foreign nationals, of whom 23,500 were Chinese. In 1991, about 80 people had become naturalized citizens, most of them being of Chinese origin. All of them enjoyed fundamental human rights in every field, pursuant to the Constitution and to the Covenant.

45. In conclusion, he thanked the members of the Committee for their thoughtful and thorough questions and comments on human rights in the Republic of Korea.

46. The CHAIRMAN invited the members of the Committee to comment on the replies to their questions.

47. Mr. WENNERGREN thanked the delegation of the Republic of Korea for its very helpful replies, which he believed had given the Committee a better understanding of the situation regarding human rights in Korea. Nevertheless, although on the face of it the country's Constitution seemed to contain all that was required for a democratic state under the rule of law, the situation was not entirely clear. For example, he had some difficulty understanding why the right to freedom of opinion was not specifically mentioned in the

0120

Constitution. There was a conceptual tradition in that field, and to claim that freedom of opinion was covered by the right to freedom of conscience did not altogether satisfy the requirements of the Covenant. The argument that the so-called umbrella clause, article 37 of the Constitution, whereby various rights and freedoms were not to be neglected on the grounds that they were not enumerated, covered the point was not adequate. To ensure real freedom of thought and freedom of opinion a solid structure of explicit rules was needed.

48. Article 37 went on to say that the freedoms and rights of citizens could be restricted by law when necessary, but that even when such restriction was imposed, no "essential aspect" of the particular freedom or right should be violated. He hoped that when the second periodic report was presented that term would be fully explained. The freedoms and rights referred to in article 37 were all enshrined in the Covenant and it should not be necessary to say in the Constitution that they should not be neglected.

49. He noted from the reply regarding judicial supervision of detention that complaints could be made to the court, which was then obliged to review the matter. According to article 9 (3) of the Covenant, however, anyone arrested must be brought promptly before a judge and the detainee or his relatives should not need to make a special request. The Government should take steps to bring the rules regarding detention into compliance with article 9 (3). He also noted that there was no mention of the security police in the Criminal Procedure Act, although it was important for detention under the National Security Law also to be subject to judicial supervision. That point too should be addressed in the second periodic report. He recognized that the area was a difficult one for most countries, all of which possessed a secret police but were loath to discuss the matter. Nevertheless, citizens were entitled to protection in that respect also and it was not clear from the report and the replies what the real situation was in the Republic of Korea.

50. The Committee had learned a great deal from the report and the highly informative replies to its questions and he looked forward to learning still more from the second periodic report. He hoped that the delegation of the Republic of Korea had also learned what was needed to bring all its procedures into full compliance with the Covenant.

51. Mrs. HIGGINS thanked the delegation for its painstaking and detailed replies to the Committee's questions. She believed she was typical of the Committee members as a whole in sensing a forward movement in the Republic of Korea and a significant shift of approach. She assured the delegation that the Committee's comments were intended only to help advance that process. She also assured the delegation that while the members of the Committee received information from a variety of sources, thus did their own research and made their own assessments. She was gratified that the Republic of Korea had become a party to the Covenant and that it had accepted the Optional Protocol, as well as joining ILO. She was also pleased to learn that consideration was being given to the possibility of withdrawing its reservations to the Covenant. She had been impressed to hear about the progress that had been made in regard to legal aid and towards narrowing the scope of operation of the National Security Law. She had learned that internal dissent was now possible and that the Constitutional Court was playing a vigorous and independent role. At the same time, it was evident that more needed to be

done. The next task should be to check existing and pending laws
systematically not just for constitutionality but for compliance with the
Covenant. As had been pointed out, the Constitution itself did not altogether
cover all the rights enshrined in the Covenant.

52. Notwithstanding the narrowing scope of the National Security Law, she was
still concerned that a continuing need was felt for such a law. It had been
explained in the reply that the underlying objective was to eliminate and
control the activities of anti-State organizations in order to prevent the
building up of a non-democratic, specifically a communist, State. Ultimately,
that could only be done by winning the hearts and minds of the people. The
ordinary law should be able to cope with activities of the kind referred to.
She noted that, for instance, the crime of homicide was already covered by the
Criminal Code and could be dealt with through the ordinary law. She felt
similar concern about the Security Surveillance Law. The broad definition of
State secrets in connection with the definition of espionage was potentially
open to abuse.

53. She hoped that the list of offences liable to the death penalty,
mentioned in connection with article 6 of the Covenant, could be further
reduced. The rehabilitation of prisoners was also a matter of continuing
anxiety. She felt that education and discussion of the kind described and the
conditions for governing release did not constitute rehabilitation in the
normal sense but rather coercion and an infringement of the provisions of the
Covenant in regard to freedom of conscience. In the case of the advance
permission needed for assemblies and demonstrations, she suggested that a
permit should only be required if the assembly was actually to take place in
an unacceptable location. Otherwise, there should be freedom of assembly. In
the context of the control of torture and the allegations made in that
connection, the information provided on the National Security Planning Agency
and the outcome of prosecutions was of great interest. The real problem in
regard to detention was the period allowed for interrogation before charges
were laid. She was aware of the findings of the Constitutional Court but her
understanding was that, as a general rule, detention could last for a full
20 days within the jurisdiction of the National Security Planning Agency plus
30 days within the jurisdiction of the Public Prosecutor. That represented a
very long time before access to the judiciary, not to mention the fact that
the activities of the Agency did not seem to be subject to identifiable
democratic controls or access to the usual organs of recourse. Article 9 (3)
of the Covenant spoke of the duty to bring a detainee to trial "within a
reasonable time". The period she regarded as reasonable was very
significantly shorter than the period which seemed to operate under the
National Security Law.

54. In conclusion, she thanked the Government of the Republic of Korea again
for its very well-prepared initial report and congratulated the delegation on
its excellent contribution to the discussion.

55. Mr. MYULLERSON thanked the delegation for its admirable endeavours to
answer the many questions put by Committee members. He had, however, been
surprised by the sharpness of the responses to some of the questions asked.
He did not think that it was at all the opinion of the Committee that there

were no rights in the Republic of Korea. Many concerns had of course been expressed, but members of the Committee had also spoken of the progress that had been made, especially recently.

56. One of his own concerns was that visits to North Korea could only be undertaken with the permission of the authorities in the Republic of Korea. Such restrictions were not reasonable and not in conformity with the Covenant. Surely such visits would merely contribute to reunification of the Korean peninsula. A truly democratic country might fear the threat from a totalitarian State but should not need to fear the ideas held in such States.

57. His main anxiety was about some of the laws in force in the Republic, especially the National Security Law. Such a law ought to be superfluous since, as Mrs. Higgins had pointed out, ordinary and more specific criminal laws should suffice to deal with offences against national security. The Law was very loosely phrased, using such broad concepts as "sound national spirit", which were open to a variety of interpretations.

58. Again, the delegation had said that propaganda jeopardizing national security was prohibited. Acts could certainly jeopardize security, but it was not clear to him how propaganda could do so. There was a danger that such concepts could be used against those who merely held different views.

59. The number of crimes for which the death penalty could be imposed was still rather high, and he hoped that it would continue to be reduced.

60. With regard to the Committee's attitude to NGO reports, the members were used to drawing on material from a variety of sources in assessing State party reports. They did not, however, take it all at face value and only accepted it when there was supporting evidence from other sources, often in fact asking Government delegations for their comments.

61. In conclusion, he congratulated the Republic of Korea on its accession to the Covenant and its ratification of the Optional Protocol. It had submitted a good report and had engaged in helpful discussion. He hoped that the outcome would be still further improvements in the human rights situation in the Republic. No country offered a safe haven for human rights, and there was always room for improvement.

62. Mr. HERNDL thanked the delegation for its comprehensive report and its replies to the many questions put by members of the Committee, who all welcomed the accession of the Republic to the Covenant, its ratification of the Optional Protocol and its accession to membership of ILO. There had clearly been a fundamental change in the human rights situation in the country with the introduction of its new Constitution.

63. While the political situation in which the Republic found itself must undoubtedly have implications for public order, the importance of such a situation should not be overemphasized, and every effort should be made to manage it by use of the ordinary criminal law, as Mrs. Higgins had urged. Like previous speakers, he had some lingering doubts: was the National Security Law really necessary? And should not an effort be made to reduce the number of crimes for which capital punishment could be imposed? The fact that

there had been 82 executions over a period of 10 years was difficult to reconcile with the spirit of the Covenant. In all countries there was a permanent need to keep police activities under surveillance, and the delegation must be conscious of that need in the Republic of Korea too. The long periods of detention practised under the National Security Law must also be a cause for concern.

64. In conclusion, he emphasized that comments by members of the Committee were always intended to assist Governments in adopting policies to enhance the enjoyment of human rights.

65. Miss CHANET thanked the delegation for its well-constructed report and expressed appreciation of its endeavours to respond to the many questions asked by members of the Committee.

66. It was a matter for concern that, according to NGO reports, a considerable number of political prisoners - whom she would rather call "prisoners of opinion" - were still being held in the Republic. As to the plots to overthrow the Government to which the delegation had referred, the overthrowing of Governments was a legitimate objective of opposition parties and an essential part of the democratic process; it was only reprehensible when violence was used to that end. For her, holding "prisoners of opinion" in detention seemed dangerously like imprisoning the political opposition. Such appalling acts as the destruction of Korean Air flight 858 by terrorists, which had been mentioned in defence of the National Security Law, were utterly deplorable, but many other States had also been victims of terrorism, and such acts did not warrant sweeping limitations of the rights of citizens. The Covenant provided for some flexibility in emergency situations but it should not be so broadly interpreted as to justify restrictions on the basic rights and freedoms of citizens.

67. Nor was she fully satisfied with the information given to members of the Committee on articles 4 and 7 of the National Security Law, which were so vaguely drafted, for example with regard to espionage, as to leave the Government wide discretion in such matters as assessing the damage caused to the State by the divulging of secrets. Citizens appeared to be left in doubt as to whether or not, in engaging in particular actions, they were violating the Law. Such legislation posed problems in relation to articles 15, 18 and 19 of the Covenant.

68. In spite of the explanations given, she continued to be concerned about the number of cases in which the death penalty could still be incurred, whether under the National Security Law or the Criminal Code. For instance, the inclusion of robbery among capital offences certainly seemed to contravene article 6 of the Covenant, which restricted the death sentence to "the most serious crimes". Even if judges in practice refrained from imposing that sentence, it did not appear justified to retain it on the statute-book in so many cases. She associated herself with Mr. Wennergren's remarks about the National Security Planning Agency, and with the disquiet expressed by Mrs. Higgins and Mr. Herndl about the duration of pre-trial detention.

69. In conclusion, she expressed gratification that the human rights situation in the Republic had improved and that the Government was advancing towards a truly democratic system guaranteeing the rights and freedoms of individuals.

0124

70. Mr. ANDO expressed gratitude to the delegation for its painstaking efforts to answer the questions asked by members of the Committee. As previous speakers had said, the primary purpose of the reporting procedure was to permit a constructive dialogue with States and to explore ways in which any human rights problems that existed could be solved. The Committee could be thought of as holding out a helping hand to fellow human beings in difficulty.

71. Despite the clarifications given, he continued to share a number of the concerns expressed by previous speakers. One was the persisting inequality of the sexes. He understood the difficulties posed by Confucian and other historical traditions, but the objective of social policy must be to achieve conformity with the goals of the Covenant. He also felt disquiet over the excessively long periods of pre-trial detention; that was clearly a matter that called for review. As to the treatment of prisoners, he could see no justification for attempting to change their beliefs or convictions by pressure, even in the context of endeavouring to inculcate democratic ideas. Any kind of coercion, whether physical or philosophical, was inadmissible. Moreover, under the right of association, teachers and journalists should be free to join the political party of their choice. Since the Republic of Korea had recently become a member of ILO, it was to be hoped that the many conventions of that organization would provide guidelines for future policy. Despite the explanations given, he was still not convinced that the application of the National Security Law did not impair human rights. Its very vague wording and wide scope, particularly in relation to anti-State activities, constituted a particular danger.

72. While he recognized the difficulties resulting from the existence of North Korea and its policies, which were perhaps not always fully appreciated by those who had not visited the Republic, it was important to realize that changes were occurring, and that what was essential above all else was to persuade others that democracy was preferable to any other political system and to demonstrate it by a conduct of affairs in sharp contrast with that of dictatorships. Like Japan, the Republic of Korea had made great economic progress in a short space of time. Such progress, however, generated its own problems and often brought capital and unions into confrontation. It was essential for both sides to learn from one another so that they could achieve a genuinely free market system working to maximum efficiency. Again like Japan, Korea was a homogeneous society, and in spite of the advantages of such societies, it was particularly difficult for them to learn how other people thought and behaved. The pursuit of human rights was one of the ways of developing tolerance and understanding of those with different ideas and backgrounds. There was no doubt that the Republic had set out on the right road and made a clear break with certain attitudes of the past. He was confident that, when it presented its next report to the Committee, further improvements in the human rights situation would be apparent.

73. Mr. AGUILAR URBINA said the facts that the Republic of Korea had acceded to the Covenant, ratified the Optional Protocol and joined ILO, and that it had sent a high-level delegation to present its report to the Committee all testified to its willingness to advance towards better implementation of human rights. While he was grateful to the delegation for its efforts to respond to questions put by Committee members, he felt some uneasiness about some of the answers and explanations given, which were not quite those expected. He was

0125

particularly concerned about the National Security Law, which seemed to him to reflect practices that pervaded the legislation of the Republic. The definitions used were often so broad as to be hardly definitions at all. The legislation did not concretely define a great number of concepts affecting the enjoyment of human rights - for example, what comprised anti-State organizations under article 2 of the National Security Law and article 37 of the Constitution - and it would be possible to make a virtually endless list of uses in the report itself and in a whole series of laws. Mr. Park had spoken of aspects of the past that had been eliminated, but Mr. Yoo had conceded that vestiges of traditional discrimination against women still remained. Great changes had been and were being made, and the present was a transitional period, and a period of hope. But in such periods it was necessary to win hearts and minds, as Mrs. Higgins had put it. That was the main task facing any democratic system. It was not by such laws as the National Security Law with its broad definitions that such a victory could be won.

74. He was concerned over what had been said about the application of the death penalty. In answer to the claim that there were 50 crimes for which that penalty could be imposed under the National Security Law, it had been stated that in fact there was only one crime - anti-State activities that endangered State security. That answer gave grounds for even graver concern since it appeared, in view of such a breadth of definition, that, instead of 50 crimes more or less specifically defined, there were an infinite number of acts that might be considered crimes that could attract the death penalty. He had similar concerns relating to the inclusion of theft among the crimes for which the death penalty could be imposed. Mr. Yoo had said that it would only be so punished if it had been committed with vile aggravating circumstances, but what such circumstances might be had not been indicated. It was that uncertainty about what was in practice against the law that he regarded as a vestige of the past. He accepted the assurance that such vestiges were disappearing, and he hoped that that process would be completed in the near future. There were still considerable discrepancies between the Covenant and the legislation of the Republic in its present form, and there was a clear need for revision. The Covenant was in general an expression of the democratic system to which the Republic was aspiring. In the National Security Law among others there was a series of limitations relating to anti-State organizations and many references to communism and communists. A joke he had heard recently asked what was the difference between United States and Russian democracy, the answer being that in the former the Communist Party was allowed to exist. The United States Constitution was in fact one that acted as a bulwark to freedom. The United States had, in acceding to the Covenant, made a reservation to article 19, and, unlike most such reservations, it was one that could only arouse respect, namely that, in the United States view, the article placed unwarranted limitations upon the exercise of freedom of expression. The National Security Law, on the other hand, was in his opinion unacceptable and in flagrant contradiction with the Covenant. Another such matter was the re-education to which prisoners were submitted in order to ensure their fitness to re-enter democratic society after their release. Such attempts to change people's ideas and opinions by pressure were clear violations of human rights and were incompatible with article 14 of the Covenant. A much more effective means for the Republic to achieve the objectives it had set itself would be to have no such laws as the

0126

National Security Law and to welcome the fact that prisoners re-entering
society enjoyed full freedom of criticism, for improvements could only be
achieved when people were free to criticize the existing order.

75. Mr. PRADO VALLEJO said he found the dialogue to have been generally
positive, and commended the cooperative attitude displayed by the delegation
of the Republic of Korea, where progress had undoubtedly been made in the
guarantee and exercise of human rights. It seemed clear, none the less, that
there were ingrained habits of thought and deeply-rooted customs to be
overcome before the provisions of the Covenant, and more particularly
article 2, paragraph 2, were fully complied with.

76. He noted with special concern the excessively broad interpretation given
in the Republic to the notion of public emergency. The possibility of
restricting rights by law when that was deemed necessary for "public welfare"
was most disquieting: that was certainly at variance with articles 4 and 9 of
the Covenant.

77. As remarked, the National Security Law seemed to leave the way open for
abuses both in interpretation and application. He referred especially to the
provisions concerning detention, which could be imposed for activities vaguely
qualified as dangerous to national security and the survival of the State, of
the repressive and authoritarian manner in which political prisoners and
prisoners of conscience were considered and treated, even after serving
sentences, and of the unduly lengthy periods during which persons could be
held without trial, as well as the delays which virtually paralysed the
investigation of allegations concerning abuses, including torture, committed
by police and other officials. The number of offences for which the death
penalty could apparently be imposed was also alarming.

78. That being said, he acknowledged the endeavours of the Government in a
situation that still bore the scars of past events. There were welcome signs
of social renewal that could encourage the fuller flourishing of human
rights. It was especially to be hoped that, against the worldwide background
of crumbling dictatorships, especially in the East, further progress would
soon be made in dismantling the barriers that separated the two countries of
the Korean peninsula and in striving towards the unity that was the earnest
desire of all people of goodwill.

79. Thanking the delegation of the Republic of Korea for its detailed replies
to questions, Mr. DIMITRIJEVIC assured its members that in dealing with
reports submitted by States parties, the Committee had always endeavoured to
display an understanding and helpful attitude. He wished to dispel any
suggestion that some of the remarks made had been deliberately negative,
adding that members of the Committee were no more immune than others to
journalistic distortion.

80. It appeared to him that in the structures of government of the Republic
of Korea there remained persistent apprehension concerning a perceived
imminent threat of totalitarianism from outside the country, and that such
apprehension continued to fuel a logic which was at variance with ideas
fundamental to the Covenant. For example, he had been struck by the phrasing
of the third sentence of paragraph 103 of the report, where rights that should

be guaranteed under all circumstances were presented as exceptional, at least where crimes subject to the death penalty were concerned. He earnestly hoped that the apprehension and the consequent logic to which he had alluded would soon be relegated to the past: the ideology once so greatly feared as terribly contagious had lost its virulence, and there now seemed to be very little risk to the Republic of Korea of contamination by ideas.

81. Much concern had been voiced over the issue of legality, the principle of nullum crimen sine lege, nulla poena sine lege, and the provisions of article 15 of the Covenant. Even non-lawyers, considered the law as an essential means of achieving certainty and predictability and of guiding behaviour in society. He had the impression that in the Republic of Korea, the National Security Law failed to provide such orientation; as well as lending itself to various types of abuse in the form of revenge, denunciation, defamation and so on, it perpetuated uncertainty as to what was permissible, anxiety about such matters as the confidentiality of information, and misgivings about what constituted an offence. As a consequence, many people in the Republic, particularly the young, could be at a loss to know what kind of behaviour was actually encouraged, supported or tolerated by the State, and what was considered anti-social or dangerous. Added to that were the disquieting phenomena of indeterminate surveillance of persons who had already been sentenced and punished, the exercise of pressure to recant beliefs, and unwholesome inquiry into what was happening in people's minds.

82. It must be acknowledged that the Republic of Korea had fared better, both socially and economically, than certain other divided countries, and its achievements commanded respect, but surely it could now abandon some of the defensive imperatives of the past and rely more strongly on a more firmly-rooted democracy informed by the law. No nation in the world was completely free of extremist political fringes, whether of the right or of the left, but in democratic societies they were generally rendered impotent by tolerance.

83. In conclusion, he praised the quality and structure of the report presented by the Republic of Korea, which was certainly not unique among those submitted by States parties in being somewhat short on facts. He thanked the delegation and trusted that it would have found the dialogue useful.

84. Mr. SADI noted with satisfaction that as a result of the political decision to introduce human rights in accordance with the Covenant, an embryonic human rights culture now existed in the Republic of Korea. Continuing tension with its northern neighbour was no doubt hampering implementation, and the consequences of that political decision had, perhaps understandably, not yet fully reached down to other parts of the system, notably the police and security services, where a campaign of education was undoubtedly called for. The Committee would certainly wish to see improvements occurring at a faster pace, and hoped that due account would be taken of its views.

85. Mr. NDIAYE said that the Republic of Korea had incontestably made considerable progress - most notably in the economic field, although its achievements in the field of human rights were far from negligible. It was unfortunate that, as a consequence of difficulties with its neighbours,

0128

actions were not always compatible with the provisions of the Covenant. It also appeared that the ancient question quis custodiet ipsos custodes remained relevant in many instances, and should indeed be posed. There was certainly much room for a further extension of nascent liberties. It seemed likely that unification of the two Koreas would eliminate many problems, but in the meantime he would urge the authorities of the Republic to make every effort to return to a system of laws more compatible with the Covenant.

86. He had noted with interest references in the report to the importance of traditional customs; however, he would respectfully suggest that tradition could be synonymous with immobility, and that the more forward-looking approach which was called for might be better served through greater regard to the advantages of written law.

87. The CHAIRMAN commended the delegation of the Republic of Korea on the quality of its report, its open approach to the dialogue, and the clear and comprehensive replies provided to numerous questions.

88. The main conclusion to be drawn from the discussion was that, thanks to the Government's commitment, an enormous number of positive developments had occurred during the past four years, especially but not exclusively as a consequence of the watchful activity of the Constitutional Court. The situation of human rights had changed radically, even if the Constitution for the moment failed to guarantee all the rights set forth in the Covenant.

89. Various concerns had been voiced by Committee members, in connection, inter alia, with the National Security Law, capital punishment, the right of peaceful assembly and other important issues. He felt sure that those concerns had been duly noted by the delegation; in that connection, he pointed out that only the written comments which would be adopted - in accordance with the Committee's new procedure - at the end of the session would constitute its considered views as reflected in the official documents. He was confident that those views would be taken into account during the formulation of new legislation and the revision of existing laws. Further important improvements were to be expected in the years to come, and he wished the Republic of Korea every success in that endeavour.

90. Mr. Soo Gil PARK (Republic of Korea) said that the meeting with the Committee had been a most valuable occasion for an exchange of views on human rights issues, to which the international community was paying growing attention and which seemed to be increasingly considered as outside the exclusive jurisdiction provided for in Article 2, paragraph 7, of the Charter of the United Nations. Those were welcome developments.

91. In the light of certain remarks by members of the Committee, he wished first to quote the adage that while realism without idealism was immorality, idealism without realism was impotence; and then to suggest that specific contexts and circumstances sometimes had to be taken into account in the interpretation and application of the law, including international treaties. He did so particularly because some concern had been voiced in connection with the inculcation during prisoners' education of what was referred to in the Republic as a "sound national spirit". It should be clearly understood that there was absolutely no connection between that notion and the nefarious

0129

ideologies of Nazism and Hitlerism; the concern was simply to ensure that when convicted persons re-entered society they would be imbued with the traditional cultural values unique to their country and thus capable of adapting to and leading a normal life.

92. In a concluding statement, he expressed pride in the fact that the Republic of Korea, for the first time in its history, had taken the significant step of submitting its human rights record to the Committee for collective evaluation through open and constructive dialogue. The outcome of the deliberations had increased the Government's awareness of its responsibilities as an important member of the democratic community, at the same time enhancing the awareness of all citizens of the rights and freedoms guaranteed under both the Covenant and their country's Constitution. The Committee had helped to place the issue of human rights even higher on the domestic agenda.

93. While he welcomed the constructive observations made, there were some points on which he sharply disagreed. Nevertheless, his delegation was happy with the positive assessment of progress since 1988. The positive comments would be an encouragement to renewed efforts in favour of human rights; criticism would act as an accelerator where further improvement was called for. His delegation's appearance before the Committee testified to the Government's commitment and demonstrated its resolve to proceed steadily along the difficult but rewarding path towards the universally desired goals of human rights. No country could claim a blameless record in human rights, and his country was no exception: what was important was the resolute determination to fulfil its commitment under the Covenant.

94. He assured members of the Committee that their comments would be duly conveyed to his Government and that questions which had not been addressed in sufficient detail because of lack of time would be covered in the second periodic report.

95. The CHAIRMAN thanked the delegation of the Republic of Korea and said that consideration of the initial report of the Republic was thus concluded. The second periodic report would be due on 9 April 1996.

The meeting rose at 6.20 p.m.

0130

Laying down the law

By James West

The establishment of an independent judiciary committed to protecting South Koreans' basic constitutional rights was a major demand of the democratisation movement that filled the streets of Seoul in the spring of 1987. In response, future president Roh Tae Woo promised on 29 June 1987 to institute an authentic "rule of law" as a key feature of the county's transition from authoritarian to more democratic rule. One visible step taken to implement this promise was the 1988 revision of the constitution to create a new Constitutional Court.

Great political changes have occurred on the Korean peninsula and throughout the world in the brief interval since the new court started functioning in August 1988.

And though mutual mistrust remains high between the two Koreas over a variety of issues, there is growing recognition that the Constitutional Court may have an increasingly important role in laying legal foundations for a peaceful reunification process over the next decade. Within the context of reunification, decisions rendered by the Constitutional Court acquire additional significance — though their immediate impact on democratisation within South Korea is crucial enough in itself.

President Roh's government avers that the Constitutional Court has already emerged as the authoritative voice of an autonomous judiciary fully committed to democracy and justice under law. A South Korean Government report submitted last summer to the UN Human Rights Committee proclaims that "the Constitutional Court has been performing an important and effective role in checking the abusive acts of government, securing the independence of the judiciary and protecting fundamental rights."

Defenders of this sanguine assessment point to more than 50 challenges to legislation decided by the court since 1989, including some 20 cases in which laws were declared unconstitutional.

Court decisions in the domain of election laws have been widely perceived as progressive and "nonpartisan." For example, legislation was invalidated that had required large sums of money to be deposited by candidates for seats in the National Assembly and local councils. In addition, campaign restrictions that disadvantaged independents were ruled unconstitutional — a decision reflected in the outcome of the March 1992 National Assembly elections in which 21 independents won seats.

Another significant case was a September 1989 ruling in which the court established a constitutional right to information by granting the petition of a citizen denied access to land records in a local government registry office. In February 1992, the court took up the right to information again in a case challenging the Military Secrets Protection Act. Five of the nine justices held that over-broad classification of military information poses a threat to freedom of information, but the statute was upheld on the condition that it be interpreted to minimise encroachments on basic rights.

In June, a civil liberties decision also attracted attention when the Constitutional Court invalidated a legal requirement that firms had to own high-speed printing presses in order to be registered as publishers. Removal of this clause will allow newly established publishers to contract out their printing.

Other important cases, however, have seen the Constitutional Court reject challenges to so-called "evil laws" inherited by Roh's Sixth Republic from the authoritarian Fifth Republic. A provision of the Labour Dispute Adjustment Act that criminalises "third-party intervention" in labour disputes was upheld over a strong dissent by Justice Byun Jeong Soo. The court also upheld laws under which Chonkyojo, a left-of-centre national teachers union, has been outlawed and repressed since late 1989.

Further, efforts to enhance the independence of judicial institutions have encountered tenacious resistance. The annual human-rights report recently published by the US State Department remarks that the court's significance grew in 1991, yet it also notes that "the judiciary remains subject to executive influence in political cases" and that "it appeared that the number of political prisoners and detainees

Roh: legal foundations.

Efforts to enhance the independence of judicial institutions have encountered tenacious resistance

as defined by international human-rights standards remained in the hundreds."

The National Security Act, under which dissidents continue to be imprisoned for opinions and conduct deemed to be pro-communist is an "evil law" South Korean progressives hoped would be invalidated by an independent Constitutional Court. In April 1990, the court acknowledged that the law had become anachronistic and denied legitimate expression. Nevertheless, a majority opinion found the law constitutional on condition of proper interpretation. The decision is viewed as having had little or no real impact on political prosecutions.

In addition, the willingness of executive-branch organs — including prosecutors, the Agency for National Security Planning (ANSP) and the military police — to respect and comply with the court's judgment remains questionable. In cases where the court granted petitions challenging prosecutors' discretionary decisions, its rulings have been circumvented after remand by prosecutors who reached the original result by other discretionary routes. On 20 January, for example, though the court held that the ANSP's practice of taping interviews between political detainees and their lawyers was unconstitutional, The Law Times reported that ANSP officials declined to discontinue the practice.

Only when those who defy or circumvent judicial control incur swift and calculable sanctions will it be meaningful to speak of a rule of law in South Korea. To move towards that day, contempt powers should be conferred on the court so that those tempted to defy its judgments might learn to reflect with care upon the implications of official illegality. ∎

James West *is an American attorney working for a South Korean law firm in Seoul.*

0131

외 무 부

WGVF-0296 920723 1537 WG

번 호 :   년월일 :   시간 :

수 신 : 주 제 네 바   대사

발 신 : 외무부장관(연이)

제 목 : 제45차 인권이사회 관련 보도

　　　제45차 인권이사회에서의 우리 최초보고서 검토와 관련한

국내보도자료를 별첨 송부함. 끝.

　　　　　　　　총 3 매(표지포함)

보 안 통 제	7h
외신과 통 제	

0132

유엔 인권이사회 한국보고서 검토회의

유엔에서는 한국의 인권상황을 어떻게 보고 있는가.

지난 13일부터 사흘간 스위스 제네바의 유엔 인권센터에서 열린 유엔 인권이사회의 한국정부 인권보고서 검토회의 결과를 두고 정부대표로 참석한 법무부와 참관인 자격으로 회의 진행을 지켜본 '민주사회를 위한 변호사 모임'(민변)이 상반되는 평가를 내려 주목되고 있다.

유엔 인권이사회 제45차 회기 중에 열린 이 회의는 90년 국제인권규약에 가입한 한국정부가 이 규약 조항에 따라 지난해 7월 유엔에 낸 한국의 인권상황에 대한 보고서를 검토·평가하는 자리로서, 최초로 국내 인권상황에 대해 정부대표와 국제기구가 공식 대화를 가졌다는 점에서 큰 의미를 지니고 있다.

특히 인권이사회 위원들은 국내에서도 개폐논란이 끊이지 않고 있는 국가보안법에 대해 많

뒤 국가보안법 등을 지적했으며 그것도 법 자체를 비판한 것이 아니라 남용될 소지가 있음을 문제점으로 지적한 것"이라며 "이번 회의는 한국의 인권상황에 대한 국제사회의 인식을 바꿔놓는 전환점이 됐을 것"이라고 밝혔다.

법무부는 회의 내용을 녹음한 테이프를 제네바 대사관에서 건네받아 민변쪽의 평가가 왜곡된 것임을 입증하겠다는 입장이나 민변도 자체 녹음한 테이프를 번역하는 대로 바로 출판해 내용을 널리 알리겠다는 방침이어서 이번 회의에 대한 평가를 놓고 양쪽의 논란이 계속될 전망이다.

◇민변쪽 참관기=민변은 이번 회의에 최영도 대한변협 인권위원장과 함께 천정배, 박원순, 조용환 변호사를 참관인으로 보냈다.

이들에 따르면 회의는 인권이

의장 포카(이탈리아)를 비롯한 몇몇 위원들이 '한국 인권상황이 개선됐다'고 말했으나 이는 다분히 외교적 표현으로 해석되며 위원들의 강조점은 국가보안법과 전향제도의 문제점을 지적하는 데 두어졌다"면서 "각국 정부가 추천한 사람들로 구성된 인권이사회가 이런 입장을 보이는 데 새삼 놀랐다"고 말했다.

◇법무부 입장=법무부는 유국현 인권과장과 검사 2명을 박수길 제네바 대표부 대사와 함께 정부대표로 회의에 보냈다.

법무부에 따르면 이번 회의에 참석한 위원들은 모두 한국의 인권상황 개선을 높이 평가했으며 외교단체가 아닌 유엔 인권이사회의 이런 발언은 결코 외교적 표현이 아니라는 것이다.

법무부는 이의 대표적 예로서 "한국은 특히 88년 이래 많고 중요한 인권보호 분야에서, 획기적인 발전을 이룩했고 헌법재판

보안법·전향제도 강력비판

민변·법무부 평가엇갈려   정부는 상황개선 지적

은 관심을 갖고 문제점을 지적한 것으로 알려졌다.

민변은 20일 발표한 이번 회의의 참관기를 통해 "유엔 인권이사회의 위원들은 극히 이례적일 정도로 한국의 국가보안법과 전향제도를 비판했다"고 밝혔다.

민변에 따르면 18명의 인권이사회 위원 대다수가 한국정부의 보고·답변태도 및 한국의 법제도 가운데 특히 국가보안법과 전향제도를 비판하고 표현의 자유와 사상의 자유가 전적으로 보장돼야 함을 거듭 강조했다는 것이다.

이와 달리 법무부는 이번 회의에서 위원들이 모두 6공이 출범한 88년 이후의 한국 인권상황 개선을 "획기적이고 인상적"이라고 높이 평가했음에도 민변이 이를 무시하고 마치 국가보안법을 성토하는 장이 돼버린 것처럼 주장하는 것은 납득할 수 없다는 입장이다.

법무부는 "위원들은 모두 국내 인권상황의 개선을 인정한

사회 위원들의 질문→정부 답변→위원들의 논평 순으로 진행됐다.

위원들의 질문은 △국제인권규약이 국내법체계에서 어떤 지위 및 효력을 갖는가 △여성에 대한 차별이나 정치적 견해를 이유로 한 차별을 어떻게 금지하고 있는가 △안기부의 구성과 권한 △국내 재판제도 등 전반적인 사항에 걸쳐 1백항이 넘었으나 상당 부분이 국가보안법과 전향제도에 모아졌다는 것이다.

위원들은 정부의 답변을 들은 뒤 최후 논평에서 요르단과 세네갈 대표 2명을 제외하고는 공통으로 한국의 법제도와 인권상황에 문제점이 있으며 한국정부는 이를 해결하기 위해 노력해야 한다고 지적했다는 것이다.

특히 위원들은 국가보안법과 사상전향제도가 한국의 특수한 상황을 고려하더라도 인권규약에 위반된다는 점을 되풀이해 지적했다고 민변은 밝혔다.

천정배 변호사는 "인권이사회

소의 각종 위헌판결과 같은 획기적 변화를 이뤘다"는 포카 의장의 최종 논평을 들었다.

따라서 이번 회의는 그동안 국내 인권문제와 관련한 국제사회의 많은 오해를 불식하고 한국의 인권개선이 국제적으로 공인받게 된 계기로 봐야 한다는 것이다.

법무부는 또 △국가보안법 △사형범위 △집회의 자유 등과 관련해 위원들의 문제 지적이 있었으나 이는 법이나 제도 자체가 인권규약에 위반된다는 취지가 아니라 앞으로 좀더 개선해나가야 할 방향으로 제기된 것으로 봐야 한다고 밝혔다.

유국현 인권과장은 "유엔 인권이사회가 한 나라의 인권상황을 거론하면서 이런 찬사를 보낸 전례가 드물다"면서 "이런 중대한 변화를 간과한 채 문제점이 지적된 부분만 부각시켜 이번 회의를 평가하는 것은 본말이 전도된 태도"라고 말했다.

〈임범 기자〉

0133

한겨레 13면 92.7.24.

"88이후 상당히 개선"

45차 국제人權이사회 평가

이틀간 百51항목 집중 질문
"保安法 문제점 많다" 비판도

「人權청문회」로 불리는 제 45차 국제人權이사회가 13일부터 30일간 스위스 제네바에서 열려 韓國의 인권상황이 세계무대에서 공식적으로 평가받는 기회를 가졌다.

이번 이사회는 우리나라가 90년 7월 국제인권규약에 가입하고 1년뒤 최초로 인권보고서를 제출하고 났던 관계자와 방청인으로 참가했던 대한변협·民辯관계자들의 현장기록을 통해 인권이사회에서 토의된 내용과 우리나라 인권에 대한 국제사회의 평가를 정리해 본다.

특히 이번 인권이사회에 는 한국정부가 공식제출한 인권보고서와 함께 民辯과 KNCC가 공동으로 작성한 반박보고서까지 참고자료로 제출돼 한국의 인권보고에 이어 정부의 개방인권보 ◇이사회=13일 오후3시 5가지나 제기됐다.
◇평가=1시간에 걸친

「人權청문회」로 불리는 제 상황을 일체적으로 살펴보 는 좋은 기회가 됐다는 평 가다.

제네바 인권이사회에 정부대표로 참석했던 법무부다.

의 집중적인 질문이 있었 다. 15일 오후 3시부터 질 문에대한 정부답변이 있었고 1시간에 걸친 각 위원들의 「코멘트(평가)」에 이어 아탈리아 포카의장의 종합평가를 끝으로 폐회됐다.

위원들은 그러나 「한국인권에 대한 신뢰과 의견·생각을 알고자해서는 안되며 이를 개인에게 불이익을 줄수 없다」고 천명, 비전향장기수문제를 직접적으로 지적했다.

그러나 포카의장은 위원들의 의견을 수렴한 종합평가를 통해 『한국 인권상황이 종합적으로 볼 때 상당히 개선됐다』고 전제하고 『한국의 인권상황이 국제사회에서 처음으로 공개토론됨으로써 한국은 인권시비에서 벗어날 수 있게 됐다』고 평가했다.

위원들의 개별평가에서 위원들은 우선 88년이후 한국의 인권상황이 상당히 향상됐다고 될 정도로 모든 것도 문제점이 있다고 구속기간이 50일로 되어 지적했다.

위원들은 『국가가 개인 의 인권을 개선돼 다른 국가의 향상됐다고 평가했다.

국보법에 50개조항에 걸 쳐 사형을 선고할 수 있다고 규정해놓은 것은 국보법의 표명한 위원들은 국보법이 있는 점도 문제점으로 지적했다.

국보법의 이적표현부분도 「사실상의 검열제도」라고 비판했다.

질문에는 총 18명의 위의 인권보고서는 인권에 대한 원중 14명이 참가, 의장을 한 실제상황·장애요인·제외한 13명이 질문에 나 판결절차를 설정지었다는 결섰다. 질문은 주로 국가보 점이 있다』는 전해를 피안법의 인권규약을 위반한 역했다.

위원들은 특히 국가보안 법의 反국가단체의 개념이 모호하고 광범위해 처벌조 도의 문제점등 구체적인 항이 반국가전반에 걸쳐 1백 인권문제전반에 걸쳐 1백 난다고 지적하고, 국보법

〈陳世根기자〉

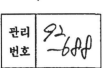

외 무 부

종 별 :

번 호 : GVW-1450   일 시 : 92 0723 1830

수 신 : 장관(연이,기정)

발 신 : 주 제네바 대사

제 목 : 인권 보고서 심의

  1. 아국 인권 보고서 심의 기록이 SUMMARY RECORD 로 작성된바, 이중 의장의 최종 요약 발언 부분을 FAX 편 송부함.(전체 기록은 금 파편 송부하는바, 7.14 일 기록은 현재 불어본만이 작성되어 있어 동 불어본을 송부함.)

  2. 한편 본직은 금 7.23 인권 이사회의장 POCAR 와 위원인 HERNDL 과 오찬을 한바, POCAR 의장은 아국 인권보고서 심의시 아측 보고서와 발언에 북한을 언급하는 부분이 있었던 점과 관련, 당지 북한 대사가 자신에게 공한을 보내어 한국측에 해명을 하도록 하고 위원들에게도 주의를 환기시켜 줄것을 요구하여 왔으나, 자신은 심의의 원만한 진행을 위하여 이를 DISREGARD 하였다고 언급하였음. 끝

  (대사 박수길-국장)

  예고 92.12.31. 까지

국기국   안기부

。ㄱ

7ㄴ

주 제 네 바 대 표 부

2

번호 : GVW(F) - 458

수신 : 장   관(연이)

발신 : 주제네바대사

제목 : 인권보고서 심의

년월일 : 20723   시간 : 1800

보 안	
통 제	

외신관	
통 제	

총   2   매(표지프함)

차관보	이차관보	외정실	관석실	아주국	미주국	구주국	중아국	국기국	경제국	통상국	문화국	의연원	청외대	안기부	공보처	경기원	상공부	재무부	농수부	동자부	과기처
							0														

✓

458-2-1

0136

actions were not always compatible with the provisions of the Covenant. It also appeared that the ancient question *quis custodiet ipsos custodes* remained relevant in many instances, and should indeed be posed. There was certainly much room for a further extension of nascent liberties. It seemed likely that unification of the two Koreas would eliminate many problems, but in the meantime he would urge the authorities of the Republic to make every effort to return to a system of laws more compatible with the Covenant.

86. He had noted with interest references in the report to the importance of traditional customs; however, he would respectfully suggest that tradition could be synonymous with immobility, and that the more forward-looking approach which was called for might be better served through greater regard to the advantages of written law.

87. The CHAIRMAN commended the delegation of the Republic of Korea on the quality of its report, its open approach to the dialogue, and the clear and comprehensive replies provided to numerous questions.

88. The main conclusion to be drawn from the discussion was that, thanks to the Government's commitment, an enormous number of positive developments had occurred during the past four years, especially but not exclusively as a consequence of the watchful activity of the Constitutional Court. The situation of human rights had changed radically, even if the Constitution for the moment failed to guarantee all the rights set forth in the Covenant.

89. Various concerns had been voiced by Committee members, in connection, *inter alia*, with the National Security Law, capital punishment, the right of peaceful assembly and other important issues. He felt sure that those concerns had been duly noted by the delegation; in that connection, he pointed out that only the written comments which would be adopted - in accordance with the Committee's new procedure - at the end of the session would constitute its considered views as reflected in the official documents. He was confident that those views would be taken into account during the formulation of new legislation and the revision of existing laws. Further important improvements were to be expected in the years to come, and he wished the Republic of Korea every success in that endeavour.

90. Mr. Soo Gil PARK (Republic of Korea) said that the meeting with the Committee had been a most valuable occasion for an exchange of views on human rights issues, to which the international community was paying growing attention and which seemed to be increasingly considered as outside the exclusive jurisdiction provided for in Article 2, paragraph 7, of the Charter of the United Nations. Those were welcome developments.

91. In the light of certain remarks by members of the Committee, he wished first to quote the adage that while realism without idealism was immorality, idealism without realism was impotence; and then to suggest that specific contexts and circumstances sometimes had to be taken into account in the interpretation and application of the law, including international treaties. He did so particularly because some concern had been voiced in connection with the inculcation during prisoners' education of what was referred to in the Republic as a "sound national spirit". It should be clearly understood that there was absolutely no connection between that notion and the nefarious

0137

458-2-2

외 무 부

WGVF-0298 920724 1457 FY

번 호 :   년월일 :   시간 :

수 신 : 주 제 네 바   대사

발 신 : 외무부장관(연이   )

제 목 : 제 45차 인권이사회 관련 보도

　　　제 45차 인권이사회에서의 우리 최초보고서 검토와 관련한

국내보도자료를 별첨 송부함. 끝.

　　　　　　　　　　　총 3 매(표지포함)

보 안 통 제	7W
외신과 통 제	

0138

'한국인권' 유엔회의에 대한 엇갈린 평가

한국정부의 인권보고서를 검토한 국제연합 인권이사회의 논의결과를 놓고 이 회의에 참석한 정부대표와 '민주사회를 위한 변호사 모임'(민변) 변호사들이 엇갈린 평가를 내리고 있다는 보도에, 솔직히 말해서 남들 앞에서 알몸을 드러내 보인 듯한 부끄러움이 앞선다. 우리의 인권상황이 국제회의의 도마위에 올려져 논란을 빚었다는 사실만으로도 낯이 뜨거워지는 일이거늘, 그 회의 결과를 놓고 외국인들로부터 칭찬을 들었느니, 야단을 맞았느니 하고 정부와 민간이 다투는 꼴이 되어버린 상황은 누구의 잘잘못을 떠나 참으로 국민된 자존심을 짓밟는 딱한 일이 아닐 수 없다. 민변 변호사들의 주장에 백번 공감하고, 또 그만한 부작용을 무릅쓰고라도 정부의 인권 시각을 따지고 나설 수밖에 없는 그들의 고충을 이해하고 남으면서도 그러한 낭패감만은 어쩔 수 없음을 먼저 집고 넘어가지 않을 수 없다.

물론 오늘의 공방은, 지난해 7월 정부가 국제연합 인권이사회에 '시민적 및 정치적 권리에 관한 국제규약 제40조에 따른 최초보고서'를 제출하고, 지난 5월 민변과 한국기독교교회협의회가 이 보고서에 대한 '반박보고서'를 제출했을 때부터 이미 예견됐던 일이었다. 더 근본적으로는, 국가보안법이나 사상전향 제도, 고문 따위의 반문명적 법과 제도와 관행의 철폐를 줄기차게 요구해온 재야 법조인들과, 분단상황과 안보논리를 내세워 이런 요구를 철저하게 봉쇄해온 정부당국의 인권상황에 대한 해묵은 인식의 거리가 빚은 당연한 결과이기도 하다.

물론 우리의 인권상황에 대해 정부대표와 국제연합의 공식기구가 공개적인 대화를 가진 이번 회의의 의미를 폄하할 이유는 없다. 또 연사흘에 걸쳐 18개국 위원 중 13명이 발언한 것으로 보도된 이번 회의에서, 정부대표가 주장하듯 "6공 출범 이후 한국 인권상황의 개선은 인

상적"이라는 치사도 있었겠고, 민변쪽이 강조하듯 "극히 이례적이라 할 만큼 국가보안법과 전향제도를 비판"하는 논평도 있었을 것이다. 분명한 것은, 그동안 인권상황에 대한 우리 정부와 민간의 인식의 거리가 터무니없이 멀고, 따라서 개선을 위한 의지와 다짐 또한 크게 달랐으니 발언의 강조점이 서로 다르게 들릴 수밖에 없었을 것이라는 점이다.

인권현실에 관한 한 서슴없이 민변의 입장에서는 우리는, 이 자리에서 그동안 끝도 없이 역설해온 보안법이나 전향제도 철폐의 당위성을 되풀이할 생각은 없다. 다만 엊그제 〈한겨레신문〉 15면에 '국가보안법 철폐를 위한 범국민투쟁본부'가 20년∼42년째 복역하고 있는, 그야말로 세계 어느 나라에서도 그 유례를 찾아보기 어려운 장기수 30여명을 포함한 양심수 43명의 이름으로 낸 광고내용을 일깨우는 것으로 대신하고자 한다. 민족의 통일을 가로막는 모든 법과 제도의 청산을 촉구하는 옥중 단식에 들어가면서 낸 이 피맺힌 광고는, 20년 전 7·4 남북공동성명이 발표됐을 때 장기수들의 부풀었던 기대는 무자비한 고문에 의한 전향공작으로 산산조각이 났고, '남북합의서'가 채택된 오늘도 수십년동안 그들을 묶어온 분단의 법과 제도가 아직도 시퍼렇게 살아 8백명을 넘는 양심수를 가둬놓고 있다고 절규하고 있기 때문이다.

굳이 긴 설명을 덧붙이지 않는 것은, 정부가 할 일은 이제 우리의 인권 개선이 국제적으로 공인받게 됐다고 알맹이 없는 자화자찬으로 허세를 부릴 것이 아니라, 그야말로 국제적으로 지적된 법제도와 인권상황의 문제점을 어떻게 하면 하루라도 빨리 해결할 것인가에 머리를 싸매는 일이기 때문이다. "갇힌 자, 가둔 자, 그리고 바라보고만 있는 자, 누구도 자유로울 수 없는 분단의 세상을 끝내자"는 저들의 절규에 이제는 온몸으로 귀 기울여야 한다.

한겨레 2면 92.7.24.

0139

지난 13일부터 15일까지 제네바에있는 유엔인권센터에서는 한국정부가 「市民的 및 政治的 權利에 關한 規約」(이하 規約)」 제40조에 따라 지난91년 7월 유엔사무총장에게 제출한 최초의보고서를 검토하는 인권이사회가 열렸다.

「한국 人權」 뜨거운 질문공세

保安法 언론의 自由등 集中거론
內部비판 허용분위기 긍정평가

동아 9면　92. 7. 24.

0140

	분류번호	보존기간

발 신 전 보

WGV-1111   920727 1847 FY

번   호 : _____   종별 : _____

수   신 : 주   제네바   대사. ♣♣♣♣♣♣

발   신 : 장 관 (연이)

제   목 : 인권이사회의 아국 보고서 심의

제45차 인권이사회 종료 직전 채택예정인 아국 보고서 심의에 대한

이사회 평가(comments) 토의에 ~~관관 관계관이 참석하여 회의경과 및~~ comments

내용을 ~~파악~~, 보고바람. 끝.

(국제기구국장   김재섭)

	보 안 통 제	(서명)

	안 고 재	92 년 7 월 27 일	유엔 2 과	기안자 성명 263중론		과 장 (서명)	심의관 (서명)	국 장 (서명)		차 관 (서명)	장 관 (서명)

외신과통제

0141

외 무 부

110-760 서울 종로구 세종로 77번지 / 전화 (02) 723-8934 / 전송 (02) 723-3505

문서번호 연이 20314-132

시행일자 1992.7.30.

(경유)

수신 조약국장

참조

취급		장 관	
보존			
국 장	전결		
심의관			
과 장			
기안	김종훈		협조

제목 인권규약(B) 최초보고서 심의 후속조치

───────────────────────────────

1. 우리 정부가 제출한 "시민적 정치적 권리에 관한 국제규약" 최초보고서에 대한
    인권이사회의 심의가 92.7.13-7.15간 제네바에서 개최된 바 있습니다.

2. 금번 심의와 관련한 후속조치의 일환으로 규약 3개 조항에 대한 아국 유보의
    철회와 고문방지협약 가입을 적극 검토하는 것이 필요하다고 사료되오니,
    동 문제들에 대하여 심의과정에서 제기된 아래 내용을 참조하시고, 이의 추진에
    필요한 조치를 취하여 주시기 바랍니다.

                    - 아   래 -

가. 규약 3개 조항에 대한 아국 유보의 철회문제

    1) 수석대표인 박수길 대사의 관련 기조발언 내용
        "우리 정부는 이러한 유보가 규약에 구현된 기본원칙에서 벗어나지
        않는 것으로 믿고는 있으나, 유보의 범위를 더욱 축소하는 가능성과
        관련하여 기존의 입장을 재검토하고 있음."

                                        / 계속 /

                                                    0142

2) 인권위원들의 관련 발언내용

  ㅇ 프랑스, 영국, 요르단 위원

    "제23조에 대한 유보 철회를 환영하며, 나머지 조항에 대한 유보도
    빠른 시일내 철회되기를 희망"

  ㅇ 에콰돌 위원

    "3개 조항에 대한 유보, 특히 하급법원에서의 오심 가능성에 비추어
    상소권을 제한한 제14조 5항의 유보는 철회되기를 희망"

3) 인권이사회 평가(comments) 내용

  ㅇ 한국정부가 유보철회 가능성을 검토하고 있다는데에 만족 표명

  ㅇ 정부가 제14조의 유보를 철회할 것을 제의

4) 기타 고려사항

  ㅇ 사이프러스 대표는 정당법에 의하여 일부 교사와 언론인의 정당
    참여가 금지되는 것은 규약 및 한국 헌법에 위배되는 것 같다고
    언급함. 또한 코스타리카 대표도 동 정당법 규정에 대하여 의문을
    제기함.

나. 고문방지협약 가입 문제

  ㅇ 인권신장을 위한 우리 정부의 적극적인 자세를 표명하기 위하여
    향후 계획의 하나로서 협약가입 방침을 밝힌 바 있음.

첨부 : 1. 인권이사회 평가(comments) 내용

     2. 수석대표 기조발언문(국.영문) 1부. 끝.

0143

관리 번호	92 -718

외 무 부

종 별 : 지 급

번 호 : GVW-1479

일 시 : 92 0729 1930

수 신 : 장관(연이, 법무부, 기정)

발 신 : 주 제네바 대사

제 목 : 아국인권 보고서 평가

대: WGV-1111

1. 제 45 차 인권 이사회는 금 7.29(금) 금번 회기중 보고서 심의를 받은 아국등 4 개국에 대한 평가회의를 갖고 아국 보고서에 대한 <u>COMMENTS 를 토의 채택</u>하였는바 금일 회의 결과 비공식 문서 우선 별첨 (FAX) 송부하며 <u>최종 평가서 공식문서</u>는 수일내에 사무국에서 배포할 예정임.

2. 동 아국 인권 보고서 COMMENTS 는 오지리의 HERNDL 위원이 초안을 작성 하였으며, 토의를 통해 일부 문안 수정이 있었는바, 최근의 아국 인권 상황 개선내용을 긍정적으로 평가하는 한편 국가 보안법 문제, 사형제도, 집시법, 규약유보 문제등에 대해서는 비판적인 견해를 피력하고 있음을 참고 바람.

첨부: GVW(F)-468

(대사 박수길-국장)

예고 92.12.31. 까지

국기국   장관   차관   분석관   청와대   안기부   법무부

PAGE 1

92.07.30   03:58

외신 2과 통제관 BZ

0144

주 제 네 바 대 표 부

번 호 : GVW(F) - 468   년월일 : 20724   시간 : 1800

수 신 : 장   관 (연서, 법무부, 기획)

발 신 : 주 제 네 바 대 사

제 목 : 〃첨부〃

총 5 매(표지포함)

보 안 통 제	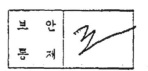
외신과 통 제	

0145

COMMENTS OF THE HUMAN RIGHTS COMMITTEE ON THE

INITIAL REPORT OF THE REPUBLIC OF KOREA 1/

Draft prepared by Mr. Herndl

1. The Committee considered the initial report of the Republic of Korea
(CCPR/C/68/Add.1) at its 1150th, 1151st and 1154th meetings, held on 13, 14
and 15 July 1992, and adopted the following comments:

A. Introduction

2. The Committee expresses its appreciation for the State party's
well-documented report which had been submitted within the specified
time-limit. The report contained detailed information on the laws and
regulations relating to the implementation of the Covenant. However, the
Committee notes that the report does not include sufficient information about
the implementation of the Covenant in practice and about factors and
difficulties which might impede the application of the Covenant. At the same
time the Committee appreciates the clear and comprehensive oral replies and
detailed clarifications given by the delegation.

    1/   Adopted at the forty-fifth session (..... meeting), held on
28 July 1992.

0146

- 2 -

B. Positive aspects

3. The Committee notes with satisfaction that in recent years the Republic of
Korea has become a party to a number of international human rights
instruments, including the Covenant and its Optional Protocol. It has made
the declaration provided for in article 41 of the Covenant, and has joined the
International Labour Organization. The Committee also notes with satisfaction
that currently consideration is being given to the possibility of withdrawing
the Republic of Korea's reservations to the Covenant. Additionally, progress
has been made in regard to the provision of legal aid and towards narrowing
the scope of operation of the National Security Law. Internal political dissent is now more accepted and the Constitutional Court, is playing a
vigorous and important role. , independent organ,

C. Factors and difficulties impeding the application of the Covenant

4. The Committee notes that, the relations between the two Koreas still appear to affect overall human rights situation in the Republic of
Korea. The recent conclusion of the Agreement on Reconciliation,
Non-Agression and Exchanges and Co-operation appears to constitute a positive step
towards the settlement of the situation. According to the authorities, the
Republic of Korea is, however, still coping with a very real threat of
destabilization and military provocation and, therefore, the Government
continues to hold the view that it is essential to retain the National
Security Law in order to protect the security and integrity of its liberal
democratic system.

0147

- 3 -

D.   <u>Principal subjects of concern</u>

5.   The Committee expresses its concern over the fact that the Constitution does not cover all the rights enshrined in the Covenant. Also, the non-discrimination provisions of Article 11 of the Constitution would seem to be rather incomplete as compared with Articles 2 and 26 of the Covenant. These concerns are not allayed by the argument that, pursuant to article 37 of the Constitution, various rights and freedoms not enumerated therein are not to be neglected.

6.   The Committee's main concern relates to the continued operation of the National Security Law. Although the particular ~~international~~ situation in which the Republic of Korea finds itself undoubtedly has implications on public order in the country, its influence ought not to be overestimated. The Committee believes that ordinary laws and specifically applicable criminal laws should be sufficient to deal with offences against national security. Furthermore, some issues addressed by the National Security Law are defined in somewhat vague terms allowing for broad interpretation that may result in prohibiting ~~sanctioning~~ acts that may not be truly dangerous for State security, ~~In that~~

7. ~~context,~~ Concern is expressed regarding the use of excessive force by the police; the extent of the investigatory powers of the National Security Planning Agency; and the implementation of article 12, particularly in so far as visits to the Democratic People's Republic of Korea are concerned. The Committee also considers that the conditions under which prisoners are being re-educated do not constitute rehabilitation in the normal sense of the term and that the amount of coercion utilized in that process could amount to an infringement of the provisions of the Covenant relating to freedom of conscience. The broad definition of State secrets in connection with the definition of espionage is also potentially open to abuse.

.0148

– 4 –

7. The Committee also expresses concern about the still high number of offences liable to the death penalty. In particular, the inclusion of robbery among the offences carrying the death penalty clearly contravenes article 6 of the Covenant. The very long period, allowed for interrogation before charges are brought, seems incompatible with article 9, paragraph 3, of the Covenant. Other areas of concern relate to the persistence of discrimination against women in certain respects; problems relating to article 15 of the Covenant; the high number of prisoners of conscience and the requirement for advance authorization of assemblies and demonstrations.

E. Suggestions and recommendations

8. Taking into account the positive developments regarding respect of human rights that have taken place in the State party over the last years, the Committee recommends that the State party intensify its efforts to bring its legislation more in line with the provisions of the Covenant. To that end, a serious attempt ought to be made to phase out the National Security Law which the Committee perceives as a major obstacle to the full realization of the rights enshrined in the Covenant. Furthermore, measures should be taken to reduce the cases in which the death penalty is applied; to harmonize to a greater extent the Penal Code with the provisions of article 15 of the Covenant; and to reduce further the restrictions on the exercise of the right to peaceful assembly (article 21). Finally, the Committee suggests that the Government actively consider withdrawing its (sweeping) reservation in respect of article 14 and take additional steps with a view to enhancing public awareness of the Covenant in the State party.

0149

관리 번호	92-723

	분류번호	보존기간

발 신 전 보

번 호 : WGV-1135 920730 1443 FY 종별 : 긴 급

수 신 : 주 제네바 대사. [redacted]

발 신 : 장 관 (연이)

제 목 : 아국 인권규약 보고서 심의

대 : GVW-1479

연 : WGV-0305(92.2.22)

1. 대호, 이사회에서 채택한 아국 보고서에 대한 comments중 Para 8의 "상당수의 양심수"(high number of prisoners of conscience) 부분에 대하여는 아래와 같은 사유로 수용하기 어려움.

가. 금번 심의기간중 "political prisoners" 또는 "prisoners of opinion"에 대한 언급은 있었으나 양심수가 많다는데 대한 구체적인 언급이나 우려 표명은 없었음. (단, 교도행정과 관련 "양심수에 대한 차별처우"에 대하여 에콰돌 위원의 발언은 있었음.)

나. 양심수가 많다고 할 경우 우리나라에서 가장 기본적(essential) 권리의 하나인 양심의 자유가 크게 침해되고 있다는 의미가 되므로, 우리의 인권보장 상황에 비추어 사실과 다름. (A.I.와 같은 민간 기구가 양심수 문제를 언급하는 것과 공식 인권협약 기구가 이를 언급하는 것은 다르며, 정부는 A.I.에 대해서도 꾸준히 항의를 해오고 있음.)

/ 계속 /

보안 통제	(서명)

앙 고 재	92년 7월 30일	유엔 2과	기안자 성명		과 장	심의관	국 장		차 관	장 관
			(서명)		(서명)	(서명)	전결			(서명)

외신과통제

0150

2. 상기를 고려, 귀관에서 인권이사회측에 적절한 방법으로 이의 시정을
   요청하고, 필요하다면 추후 서면으로 우리 입장을 통보하여, 동 입장이
   이사회 보고서에 반영되도록 요청바람.

3. 참고로 "양심수"라는 표현에 대한 국내적 민감성 등을 고려할 때,
   본부로서는 상기 정치범 또는 양심수 문제에 대하여 이사회가 굳이
   언급하고자 할 경우에는 "prisoners of conscience" 보다는 comments
   초안상의 표현대로 "political prisoners"로 표현하는 것이 금번 심의
   내용에 비추어 보다 낫다고 봄. ("political prisoner" 문제에 대해서는
   우리측이 답변을 통해 이미 입장을 밝힌 바도 있으나, "prisoners of
   conscience"에 대해서는 우리의 입장을 밝힐 기회도 없었음을 참고바람.)

4. 양심수의 개념 등과 관련, 연호 설명을 참조바람. 끝.

(국제기구국장 김재섭)

0151

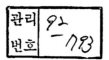

외 무 부

110-760 서울 종로구 세종로 77번지 / 전화 (02) 723-8934 / 전송 (02) 723-3505

문서번호 연이 20314-1986
시행일자 1992.7.31.

수신 법무부장관
참조

취급		차 관	장 관
보존			
국 장			
심의관		제1차관보	
과 장			
기안	김종훈		협조

제목 인권규약(B) 최초보고서 심의 후속조치

　　　1. 우리 정부가 제출한 "시민적.정치적 권리에 관한 국제규약" 최초보고서에
대한 인권이사회의 심의가 92.7.13-7.15간 제네바에서 개최된 바 있습니다.

　　　2. 금번 보고서 심의를 통하여 인권위원들이 제기하고, 인권이사회가 채택한
우리나라의 인권관련 법령 및 제도에 관한 평가와 제의 내용을 별첨과 같이 통보
하오니, 귀부에서 추진하는 각종 형사관련 법령의 제정 및 개정, 각종 사법행정의
개선작업에 참고 ~~또는 반영~~하여 주시기 바랍니다.

　　　3. 또한 보고서 심의결과에 관한 대통령 보고내용을 별첨 송부하오니 참고
하시기 바랍니다.

첨부 : 1. 우리나라의 인권관련 법령 및 제도에 관한 인권이사회와 인권위원들의
　　　　　 평가와 제의 1부
　　　　2. 보고서 심의결과에 관한 대통령 보고내용 1부. 끝.

0152

우리나라의 인권관련 법령 및 제도에 관한
인권이사회와 인권위원들의 평가와 제의

1. 규약 3개 조항에 대한 우리나라 유보의 철회문제

가. 인권이사회의 평가

○ 한국정부가 유보 철회의 가능성을 검토하고 있다는데에 만족을 표명함.

○ 정부가 제14조의 유보를 철회할 것을 제의함.

나. 인권위원들의 평가

○ 제23조에 대한 유보 철회를 환영하며, 나머지 조항에 대한 유보도 빠른 시일내에 철회되기를 희망함.

○ 특히 하급법원에서의 오심 가능성에 비추어 상소권을 제한한 제14조 5항의 유보는 철회되어야 함.

2. 고문방지협약의 가입 추진

○ 인권신장을 위한 우리 정부의 적극적인 자세를 표명하기 위하여 수석 대표 기조발언을 통하여 향후 계획의 하나로서 고문방지협약에 대한 가입방침을 밝힘.

 - 인권위원들은 동 내용을 평가함.

0153

1

3. 국가보안법 관련사항

가. 인권이사회의 평가

- ○ 국가보안법의 단계적 폐지를 위한 정부의 노력 필요
- ○ 일반 법률 및 특정한 형사관련 법률로도 국가안보 침해 사범에 대한 처리가 충분함.
- ○ 법의 일부 내용이 다소 모호하게 규정되어 있어 광범위한 해석이 가능함에 따라 국가안보에 위해가 되지 않는 행위를 제한할 우려가 있음.
- ○ 간첩의 정의와 관련, 국가비밀의 광범위한 정의에 따른 남용 우려

나. 인권위원들의 평가

- ○ 법 제15조상의 반국가단체의 정의가 모호하여 죄형법정주의의 저촉이 우려
- ○ 신법의 형량이 가벼울 경우 소급효가 인정되어야 한다는 원칙에 비추어 개정 국가보안법 부칙 규정은 헌법 및 규약 위반으로 평가
- ○ 법 제3조 규정은 동일 범죄에 대하여 형량의 범위가 너무 광범위함.

4. 사형제도

가. 인권이사회의 평가

- ○ 법률상 사형대상 범죄의 숫자를 줄이기 위한 조치 필요. 특히 강도 행위에 대한 사형가능 규정은 규약 제6조에 명백히 위반

2

0154

5. 사법 경찰관에 대한 교육

가. 인권위원들의 평가

   ○ 고문방지를 위하여 사법 경찰관을 대상으로 하는 교육과정에 인권 관련 국제협약 내용도 포함할 것을 희망

6. 구속제도

가. 인권이사회의 평가

   ○ 재판전 장기간의 구속이 허용되는 것은 규약 제9조와 양립하지 않음.

나. 인권위원들의 평가

   ○ 국가보안법상 범죄와 일반범죄간의 최장 구속기간 차별의 필요성에 의문

   ○ 영장없이 체포할 수 있는 경우가 과다함.

7. 재소자 인권보장

가. 인권이사회의 평가

   ○ 수형자에 대한 재교육의 내용이 일반적 의미의 교화와 상충되며, 이 과정에서의 강제성이 규약상 양심의 자유 규정에 저촉될 수 있다고 판단됨.
     - 사상전향 강요의 문제

나. 인권위원들의 평가

○ 재소자 접견권 및 접견시 비밀보장 필요

8. 거주.이전의 자유

가. 인권이사회의 평가

○ 북한 방문문제와 관련한 규약 제12조의 이행문제

9. 죄형법정주의

가. 인권이사회의 평가

○ 형법이 죄형법정주의 등을 규정한 규약 제15조에 가능한 부합되도록 조치를 취하여야 함.

나. 인권위원들의 평가

○ 헌법재판소법 제47조 2항에서 형벌법규에 대하여만 예외적으로 위헌결정의 소급효를 인정한 것의 문제

10. 보안관찰법

가. 인권위원들의 평가

○ 보안관찰법은 국가보안법 관련 출소자에 대하여 2년으로부터 무기한 감시가 가능하며, 정부 비판자의 비폭력적 시위 참여를 금지하는데 악용될 우려가 있음.

11. 표현의 자유

가. 인권이사회의 평가

ㅇ 정치적 견해 때문에 투옥된 인사들이 상존하는 것에 대하여 우려 표명

* 상기 문안은 "상당수의 정치범에 대하여 우려 표명"이라는 표현을 이사회가 평가에서 채택한데 대하여, 박수길 주제네바 대사가 의장 및 인권위원들과 개별적으로 교섭하여 회의 최종일 보고서 채택시 변경시킨 것이며, 기채택된 문안이 당사국의 요청으로 변경된 것은 인권이사회에서 전례가 없음.

12. 집회 및 결사의 자유

가. 인권이사회의 평가

ㅇ 집회 및 결사에 관한 사전허가 요구에 우려를 표명하며, 평화적 집회의 권리행사에 대한 제한을 더욱 축소할 것을 요청함.

13. 여타 정부기관 관련 문제

가. 인권이사회의 평가

ㅇ 경찰의 과도한 무력사용에 우려를 표명함.
ㅇ 국가안전기획부의 수사권의 범위에 우려를 표명함.

0157

5

長 官 報 告 事 項

報 告 畢

1992. 7. 31.
國 際 機 構 局
國際聯合 2課 (43)

題 目 : 人權規約 報告書 審議 관련 人權理事會의 綜合 評價

7.31. 閉會한 第45次 人權理事會는 우리 人權報告書 審議와 관련한 理事會의 綜合評價(comments)를 採擇한 바, 關聯內容을 아래 報告드립니다.

1. 綜合評價의 性格

○ 審議時 委員들의 質疑 및 個別 評價內容을 綜合, 書面으로 作成한 것으로서 人權理事會 報告書에 포함, 今番 유엔總會에 報告

○ (ⅰ) 序論 : 報告書 體制 및 答辯內容 評價, (ⅱ) 肯定的 側面, (ⅲ) 規約 履行의 障碍要因, (ⅳ) 憂慮事項, (ⅴ) 提案 및 勸告事項으로 構成

2. 勸告事項 內容

○ 最近의 肯定的 人權發展을 考慮, 國內法의 規約과의 合致 努力 勸告

○ 國家保安法의 段階的 廢止(phase out)를 위한 각별한 措置 必要

○ 死刑範圍의 縮小, 刑法上 罪刑法定主義 保障 强化, 平和的 集會에 대한 制約 縮小 措置

○ 우리나라가 행한 留保의 撤回(특히 上訴權 保障 條項)를 勸告

0158

3. 特記事項

o 當初 綜合評價 內容에 "상당수의 良心囚(High number of prisoners of conscience)에 대한 憂慮"라는 表現이 있었는 바, 이에 대하여 7.30. 駐제네바 大使는 本部指示에 따라, 審議內容에 비추어 同 表現의 不當性을 指摘하고, 이의 是正을 理事會 議長 및 人權委員들에게 强力 要請

o 이에 따라 7.31. 最終會議에서 "政治的 見解 때문에 投獄中인 人士들의 常存에 憂慮"로 修正, 採擇되었으며, 理事會 報告書에도 同 文案이 反映됨.

o 人權理事會에서 採擇된 綜合評價 文案이 再論되어 修正된 것은 前例없는 措置
  * 同件은 法務部와도 協議되었음.

4. 觀 察

o 今番 綜合評價는 報告書 審議時 政府立場 說明과 人權委員들의 論評 內容을 均衡있게 反映하였으며, 改善하여야 할 事項에 대하여도 法的, 制度的 側面에서 客觀的으로 記述

5. 措置事項

o 理事會 勸告內容 및 기타 審議內容이 人權關聯 法令改正 및 政策立案時 反映되도록 法務部에 要請(92.8.1. 公文 發送)

o 留保撤回 및 拷問防止協約 加入 推進(條約局 措置中)

6. 言論對策

o 해당 없음. 끝.

0159

長官報告事項

報告畢

1992. 7. 31.
國際機構局
國際聯合2課(43)

題 目 : 人權規約 報告書 審議 관련 人權理事會의 綜合 評價

7.31. 閉會한 第45次 人權理事會는 우리 人權報告書 審議와 관련한
理事會의 綜合評價(comments)를 採擇한 바, 關聯內容을 아래 報告드립니다.

---

1. 綜合評價의 性格

o 審議時 委員들의 質疑 및 個別 評價內容을 綜合, 書面으로 作成한 것으로서
  人權理事會 報告書에 포함, 유엔總會에 報告

o (i) 序論 : 報告書 體制 및 答辯內容 評價, (ii) 肯定的 側面, (iii) 規約
  履行의 障碍要因, (iv) 憂慮事項, (v) 提案 및 勸告事項으로 構成

2. 綜合評價中 勸告事項 內容

o 最近의 肯定的 人權發展을 考慮, 國內法의 規約과의 合致 努力 勸告

o 國家保安法의 段階的 廢止(phase out)를 위한 각별한 措置 必要

o 死刑範圍의 縮小, 刑法上 罪刑法定主義 保障 强化, 平和的 集會에 대한
  制約 縮小 措置

o 우리나라가 행한 留保의 撤回(특히 上訴權 保障 條項)를 勸告

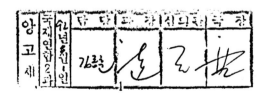

0160

3. 特記事項

ㅇ 當初 綜合評價 內容에 "상당수의 良心囚(High number of prisoners of conscience)에 대한 憂慮"라는 表現이 있었던 바, 이에 대하여 7.30. 駐제네바 大使는 本部指示에 따라, 審議內容에 비추어 同 表現의 不當性을 指摘하고, 이의 是正을 理事會 議長 및 人權委員들에게 强力 要請

ㅇ 이에 따라 7.31. 最終會議에서 "政治的 見解 때문에 投獄中인 人士들의 常存에 憂慮"로 修正, 採擇되었으며, 理事會 報告書에도 同 文案이 反映됨.

ㅇ 人權理事會에서 採擇된 綜合評價 文案이 再論되어 修正된 것은 前例 없는 措置
   * 同件은 法務部와도 協議되었음.

4. 觀 察

ㅇ 今番 綜合評價는 報告書 審議時 政府立場 說明과 人權委員들의 論評 內容을 均衡있게 反映하였으며, 改善하여야 할 事項에 대하여도 法的, 制度的 側面에서 客觀的으로 記述

5. 措置事項

ㅇ 理事會 勸告內容 및 기타 審議內容이 人權關聯 法令改正 및 政策立案時 反映되도록 法務部에 要請(92.8.1. 公文 發送)

ㅇ 留保撤回 및 拷問防止協約 加入 推進(條約局 措置中)

6. 言論對策

ㅇ 해당 없음. 끝.

0161

1

원 본

외 무 부

종   별 : 지 급

번   호 : GVW-1483

일   시 : 92 0730 2000

수   신 : 장관(연이)

발   신 : 주 제네바 대사

제   목 : 아국인권 보고서 심의

대: WGV-1135

1. 대호관련 본직은 금 7.30 인권이사회 POKAR 의장, HERNDL 위원, HIGGINS위원, AGUILLAR 위원, DMITRIJEVIC 위원등을 만나 "많은 수의 양심수가 있다"는 식의 표현이 사실과 다를뿐만 아니라, 한국 국내적으로 논란을 야기시키고 일방에 편을 드는 결과를 초래할 것이므로 객관적이고 불편 부당하여야 할 인권 이사회로서 삼가야 할 언급이라고 지적하였음. 또한 본직은 인권이사회의 이러한 표현이 일국의 국내정치에 이용되는 위험한 선례가 될것임을 지적하고 인권이사회 권위와 공정성을 위해서도 동 표현이 반드시 수정되어야 함을 강조하였음.

2. 이에 POKAR 의장을 비롯한 대부분 위원들은 상당한 이해를 표하면서도, 일단 이사회가 채택한 문안을 바꾸기가 어렵다고 전제하고, 동 표현이 각 언어로DRAFT 되는 과정에서 부정확하게 쓰여진 점이 있지 않았나 하는 측면에서 (DRAFTING CHANGE 의 일환으로서) 문제를 제기, 최종회의일인 명일 전체보고 채택과정에서 이를 수정하는 방식을 신중 고려하여 보겠다는 반응을 보였음.

3. 본직은 HIGH NUMBER 와 양심수 표현 모두에 문제가 있다고 재강조하여 두었는바, 만일 수정이 불가능할 경우 상기 표현의 문제점을 지적하는 강력한 입장을 문서로 작성, 의장에게 추후 송부하는 방안도 검토코자함.

4. 한편 본직은 PARCOR 의장에게 동 이사회의 전례에도 불구하고 문제의 중요성에 비추어 본직으로 하여금 동 이사회에서 직접 공식적으로 문제를 제기 정정을 요청할수 있는 기회를 부여할 것을 요청해 두었음도 참고로 첨언함. 끝

(대사 박수길-국장)

예고: 92.12.31. 까지

국기국   장관   차관   1차보   분석관   정와대   안기부

PAGE 1

92.07.31   04:01

외신 2과 통제관 EC

0162

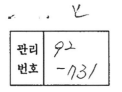

외 무 부

관리 번호 : 92 -731

종   별 : 지급
번   호 : GVW-1494   일   시 : 92 0731 1830
수   신 : 장관(연이, 법무부, 기정동문)
발   신 : 주 제네바 대사
제   목 : 인권 보고서 심의

연 : GVW-1483

1. 연호 45 차 인권이사회는 금 7.31(금) 최종일 회의를 열고 UN 총회에 보고하는 DRAFT ANNUAL REPORT 를 심의하였는바, 본직의 회의 참석을 확인한 의장이 제일먼저 한국관계 REPORT 안(ADD. 14. 별첨)을 상정하였으며, 곧 HERNDL 위원이 한국관계" COMMENTS"의 작성자로서 한국인권 보고서 심의 과정에서 실제 언급된 사실과 상이한 내용이 "REPORT" 및 "COMMENTS"에 포함되어있음을 언급, 문제된 표현(THE HIGH NUMBEF OF PRISONERS OF CONSICENCE)을 실제 토의과정에 비추어 ' THE CONTINUED EXISTENCE OF PERSONS IMPRISONED ON THE GROUND OF POLITICAL OPINION ' 으로 수정할 것을 제의하고 지난 7.27 채택된 COMMENTS OF THE COMMITTEE 부분도 이에 따라 그대로 반영수정할 것을 아울러 요청하자, SADI 위원, DIMITRIJEVIC 위원등이 지지하여 의장은 이를 즉각 채택함.

2. 상기 수정안 채택은 작일 및 금일에걸쳐 본직이 의장을 비롯한 대부분의위원을 접촉하여, 인권이사회가 규약 당사국의 국내 정치적인 논쟁에 이용되는선례는 극히 바람직하지 못하다는 점을 강조, HIGH NUMBER 와 양심수 표현 모두 삭제를 요청한데 대해 의장 및 대부분 위원들이 이를 수용한 결과임.(특히 의장은 기채택된 보고서를 당사국 대표와 만나 재론하는 전례가 없었음을 지적하면서도 시종 아국입장을 이해하고 동정하는 태도 견지)

3. 금일 채택된 DRAFT ANNUAL REPORT 의 아국 보고서 심의관계문서는 RAPPORTEUR 가 아국 인권보고서 심의과정을 SUMMARY RECORD 에 기초, 작성한 것으로서 지난 7.27 채택된 COMMITTEE CONNMENT 와는 별개이나, 뒷부분 CONCLUDING OBSERVATION 부분은 HERNDL 위원의 COMMENT DRAFT 와 상당부분이 같으며, 금일 회의시에는 동 REPORT 의 동일 부분을 수정하면서 지난 7.27 이미 채택한 COMMENTS의 표현까지 소급제기,

---

국기국   장관   차관   1차보   분석관   정와대   안기부   법무부

시민적.정치적 권리에 관한 국제규약(B규약) 한국 최초 인권보고서 제출 및 심의, 1991-92. 전5권 (V.5 1992.7.10-10월) 169

REPORT 와 COMMENTS 의 내용을 함께 수정하는 형식을 취하였음.

   4. 한편 사무국 WONG 담당관에 따르면, 금일 공식 회의 종료후 인권이사회 위원들은 비공개 회의를 갖고, 아국 보고서 평가 수정과 관련, 인권이사회 COMMENT 작업 문서 (DRAFT) 가 심의 채택후 공표되기전에는 비공개 문서임에도 불구하고 당사국에 유출되어 기채택된 문안을 변경하는 상황이 발생할 사실이 전례가없을 뿐아니라 위원들을 상당히 당혹케 하였다는 취지의 의견 교환이 있었다함을 참고로 보고함.

   첨부: 아국관련 보고서 (CCPR/C/45/CRP. 1/ADD.14)
   (WGV(F)-472)
   (대사 박수길-국장)
   예고 92.12.31. 까지

2. 人權理事十 우리 人權報告書 審議結果 報告書 採擇

○ 7.31 閉會된 제45차 人權理事會는 제6共和國 출범 이후 民主化 進展과 人權伸張을 위한 우리政府의 제반 努力을 높이 評價하면서, 아래 內容의 勸告가 포함된 報告書를 採擇함.

- 최근의 肯定的 人權發展을 고려, 國內法을 人權規約에 보다 합치시키기도록 努力

- 특히 國家保安法의 段階的 廢止를 위한 措置 및 人權規約 加入時 우리나라가 행한 留保의 撤回

0165

주 제 네 바 대 표 부

〈지급〉

번호 : GVW(P) - 492   연월일 : 20231   시간 : 1800

수신 : 장 관 (단기, 민원국, 기연동향)

발신 : 주제네바대사

제목 : ` 천역 `

총 16 매 드립드림

<table>
<tr><td>분
류</td><td>산정</td><td>⼻</td></tr>
<tr><td>외신관제
통 제</td><td></td></tr>
</table>

492-164

0166

INTERNATIONAL COVENANT
ON CIVIL AND POLITICAL
RIGHTS

For participants only

CCPR/C/45/CRP.1/Add.14
27 July 1992

ENGLISH
Original: FRENCH/ENGLISH

HUMAN RIGHTS COMMITTEE
Forty-fifth session
Agenda item 5

DRAFT ANNUAL REPORT OF THE HUMAN RIGHTS COMMITTEE
TO THE GENERAL ASSEMBLY THROUGH THE ECONOMIC AND
SOCIAL COUNCIL UNDER ARTICLE 45 OF THE COVENANT
AND ARTICLE 6 OF THE OPTIONAL PROTOCOL

Rapporteur: Mr. Nisuke Ando

CONTENTS

GE.92-16597/4731B

0167

472-16-2

Republic of Korea

1.   The Committee considered the initial report of the Republic of Korea (CCPR/C/68/Add.1) at its 1150th, 1151st and 1154th meetings, held on 13, 14 and 15 July 1992 (CCPR/C/SR.1150, SR.1151 and SR.1154).

2.   The report was introduced by the representative of the State party who explained that, subsequent to the revision of the Constitution on 29 October 1987, institutional measures had been taken to embody genuinely democratic principles and to enhance the protection of human rights. The Constitution, based on the 29 June 1987 Declaration for Democracy, represented a turning- point in the struggle for democracy in the Republic of Korea and provided for the election of the President of the Republic by direct popular vote. It had strengthened the power of the National Assembly vis-à-vis the administration and improved the procedure for appointing judges. A Constitutional Court had been established to review the constitutionality of laws and rule on petitions by individuals seeking redress of human rights infringements. Improvements had also been made in the penal administration by the institution of legal aid programmes and the abolition of the death penalty for 15 types of crime. Furthermore, amendments to the Penal Code and the Code of Penal Procedure to reinforce the principle of nullum crimen sine lege were being finalized.

3.   Accession to the Covenant had played an important role in the overall strengthening of human rights and fundamental freedoms in the Republic of Korea. International human rights instruments had been translated and published into the Korean language, and measures had been taken to publicize the Covenant among law enforcement officials. Provisions of the Covenant had already been applied by the Constitutional Court and the Government was currently undertaking a review of its position regarding the reservations it had made in acceding to the Covenant. The admission of the Republic of Korea to membership of the United Nations in September 1991 had given additional momentum to the Government's efforts to promote human rights in accordance with the Charter. Furthermore, in becoming a full-fledged member of the International Labour Organisation in December 1991, the Republic of Korea had strongly endorsed international endeavours to ensure the protection of fundamental trade union rights and was currently considering acceding to various ILO Conventions.

0168

4.   The representative of the State party further emphasized that one of the most important factors affecting the implementation of the Covenant in the Republic of Korea was the tense situation resulting from the division of the Korean peninsula. It was not until 1991, following the end of the cold war, that the two sides succeeded in engaging in a serious dialogue and began to seek a way to reunify the nation peacefully. The Agreement on Reconciliation, Non-Aggression and Exchanges and Cooperation had subsequently been concluded in February 1991 and had led to a series of regular consultations that were expected to narrow the gap between the two Koreas in every field. Nevertheless, it was only natural that a country which had been nearly overthrown by invasion should feel unable to relax its guard against further aggression or subversion of its liberal democratic system. Accordingly, the National Security Law had been adopted and continued to operate to protect the security and the integrity of the system. In spite of the call in some quarters for its abolition, it was the national consensus that the National Security Law should be maintained until the signature of a peace agreement between the two Koreas. In the meantime, however, the Government remained determined to eliminate any infringement of human rights resulting from the application of the Law beyond restrictions permitted by the Constitution and the Covenant.

5.   With reference to article 1 of the Covenant, members of the Committee sought clarification of the position of the Republic of Korea, given the movement towards reunification, regarding the right of peoples to self-determination as well as their entitlement to democracy and to choose their own economic, social, political and cultural system.

6.   With regard to the constitutional and legal framework within which the Covenant was implemented, members of the Committee wished to receive further information on the status of the Covenant in domestic law. Observing that the Covenant had the same force as any ordinary domestic law, members wondered how a conflict between provisions of the Covenant and subsequent domestic legislation would be resolved. It was inquired whether provisions of the Covenant had ever been invoked before the courts and whether a national institution had been established to deal with matters relating to human rights. More generally, with regard to remedies available to individuals, it was asked what effect petitions filed by individuals would have, whether an

0169

472-16-4

appeal could be lodged against a decision handed down as a result of a
petition, what was the procedure for bringing a case before the Supreme Court
and whether there were administrative courts. Clarification was requested of
the meaning of article 37 of the Constitution according to which freedoms and
the rights of citizens would not be neglected on the grounds that they were
not enumerated in the Constitution. Information was requested on the manner
in which the Korean population would be informed of the dialogue entered into
by Korean authorities with the Committee and how, in the future, the
Government would implement any decisions made about it by the Committee in
pursuance of the Optional Protocol.

7.   Necessary additional information was requested on the National Security
Law, in particular as far as restrictions or limitations to articles 18, 18
and 19 of the Covenant were concerned. There was concern that, under that
Law, it was possible to arrest anyone found in conversation with
North Koreans, that political prisoners who had left prison after serving
their sentences, were still required to report to the police every three
months, and that under its provisions even peaceful demonstrations could be
forbidden. Further information was also requested on the meaning of the term
"espionage" and on the extent to which the Supreme Court was empowered to
decide on the legality of the provisions of the National Security Law.

8.   As to the prohibition of discrimination on various grounds, clarification
was requested of the absence in article 11 of the Constitution of some grounds
of discrimination enumerated in article 2, paragraph 1, of the Covenant,
particularly race, religion and political opinion. Information was also
sought on any remaining de facto discrimination against women existing in the
Republic of Korea, in particular regarding property rights, and about measures
taken to eliminate them, as well as on the meaning of the term "reasonable
cultural discrimination" used in the report. It was inquired whether the
procurement of women for prostitution was a criminal offence in the
Republic of Korea. Clarification was further requested of provisions of
domestic law prohibiting foreigners from holding public office.

9.   With regard to article 4 of the Covenant, members of the Committee wished
to receive clarification of legal provisions relating to a public emergency,
in particular those relating to the powers of the President under those

472-16-5

0170

circumstances, and their conformity with the Covenant. Further information was also requested about the constitutional or statutory basis for ensuring conformity with article 4, paragraph 2, of the Covenant.

10. In connection with article 6 of the Covenant, the recent limitation of the categories of crimes subject to the death penalty was welcomed. Clarification of the crimes still carrying the death penalty, particularly under the National Security Law, was, however, requested and, in particular, it was inquired whether the death sentence could still be imposed for robbery. Noting that under national legislation, widely varying penalties, which could range from five years' imprisonment to death could be applied for practically the same offences, it was pointed out that the Committee had always clearly stated that under the provisions of the Covenant, the death penalty could be imposed only for the most odious and serious crimes. Information was requested on instructions given to members of the police in connection with the use of force during public demonstrations, the method used to carry out the death penalty and on the legal provisions concerning abortion. Clarification was also requested of the statement in the report that the rights of people suffering from certain categories of communicable diseases could be limited.

11. With reference to articles 7, 8, 9 and 10 of the Covenant, members of the Committee wished to know whether any statement or confession made as a result of torture could be invoked as evidence in court proceedings, and whether there had been any complaints of torture of prisoners or detainees and, if so, whether there had been any convictions on such charges. Clarification was requested with regard to a number of individual cases, as well as of how many officials had been found guilty of such violations, the sentences they had received and of whether persons who may have been sentenced in the past on the grounds of confessions obtained under such circumstances would benefit from the positive developments occurring in the Republic of Korea. It was also inquired how quickly after arrest a person's family was informed; what regulations governed solitary confinement; what the role of the national security agency with regard to article 9 of the Covenant was; and at what age criminal law was applicable. Clarification was also requested of the compatibility with the Covenant of the very long period of pre-trial detention, in particular under the National Security Law.

12.   Clarification was requested with regard to the legal provisions governing the remedy of habeas corpus or any other similar remedy and concerning provisions which stated that an inmate was permitted to see other persons only "when deemed necessary". It was also inquired whether the provisions under which the treatment of prisoners was designed to reform and educate them to help them to reintegrate into society by inculcating in them a sound national spirit were in accordance with the provisions of the Covenant. As for article 8 of the Covenant further details were requested about the provisions of the Criminal Code which provided for penal servitude "with a certain amount of labour".

13.   Members of the Committee wished to receive further information on the implementation of article 14 of the Covenant and on the structure of the judiciary, including the legal and administrative provisions governing tenure, dismissal and disciplining of members of the judiciary. It was inquired how the independence and impartiality of the judiciary was guaranteed; whether there was any free legal aid and advisory scheme and, if so, how it operated; and whether prosecutors were subject to executive or to judicial authority. Also, members of the Committee wished to know the exact nature of the role of the prosecutor, about the guarantees of his independence, and the responsibilities entrusted to the human rights consultation centres established by him. Clarification was requested of the compatibility with the Covenant of the restrictions mentioned in the report to the right of the person deprived of his liberty to communicate with a lawyer; and of the meaning of the reservation made by the Government relating to appeals against military trials under extraordinary laws. Information was also requested on the implementation of article 15 of the Covenant and in particular the retroactive effect of a decision of unconstitutionality.

14.   With reference to articles 12 and 13 of the Covenant, clarification was requested of de facto and _de jure_ restrictions or limitations on freedom of movement as far as visits to the Democratic People's Republic of Korea were concerned; about the compatibility with the Covenant of certain provisions of the Social Surveillance Act, under which anyone suspected of offences under the National Security Law could be kept under surveillance for up to two years; and of the Resident Registration Law. It was asked what "preventive restrictions" could be imposed on freedom of movement under article 12 of the

472-16-7

0172

178   한국 인권문제 시민적·정치적 권리 국제규약 인권보고서 3

Constitution; and what legal provisions governed the admission or expulsion of
"boat people" in the country. Information was also requested on what stage
had been reached in negotiations being held to solve the serious problem of
the separation of families and to bring about their reunion.

15. In connection with articles 17, 18 and 19 of the Covenant, it was asked
whether attempts had ever been made to force people to recant their beliefs;
whether efforts to promote anti-communism were still made despite the changes
that had taken place in the world; whether conscientious objection was
permitted under the law; and whether there were any political prisoners. It
was inquired whether the condition whereby such prisoners could, apparently,
be released only if they renounced their opinions and beliefs was compatible
with the Covenant. Clarification was also requested of the meaning of a
sentence in the report that the purposes of the Broadcasting Act was to help
the formation of public opinion.

16. With regard to articles 21 and 22 of the Covenant, members of the
Committee wished to receive information on the alleged dissolution of certain
private university or school teachers' unions. It was asked why an
authorization had to be obtained in advance in order to organize meetings or
demonstrations and in how many cases such an authorization was refused and for
what reasons.

17. In connection with article 24 of the Covenant, additional information was
requested on the exact definition of "juveniles" as well as on measures taken
to prevent the employment of children at an age when they should be enrolled
in compulsory education.

18. With reference to article 25 of the Covenant, members of the Committee
wished to know why certain teachers and journalists were prohibited from
becoming founders or members of a political party.

19. Regarding article 27 of the Covenant, members of the Committee wished to
receive additional information on the situation and composition of religious
and other minorities in the country.

20. In his reply, the representative of the State party recalled that
relations between the two Koreas were among the most important factors
affecting the human rights situation in his country. The adoption of the
Agreement on Reconciliation, Non-Agression and Exchanges and Cooperation as
well as the Joint Declaration on the Denuclearization of the Korean Peninsula
had raised hopes of a dialogue between the two sides. In May 1992, three

0173

bodies had been established to work on a basic agreement governing unification. The two sides' differences on the nuclear issue had, however, hindered progress in the negotiations. According to his Government, the reunification of the peninsula had to be based on the principles of self-determination, peace and democracy. The other side took a different approach to that issue and it was therefore difficult to predict the outcome of the current dialogue. It was, however, to be hoped that an agreement would soon be reached on family reunion since, at present, separated family members were still not allowed to telephone or write to one another.

21. The Republic of Korea was still coping with a very real threat of destabilization and military provocation and, until the other side stopped using terrorism as an instrument of its foreign policy, his country was bound to retain the National Security Law. That law was strictly applied and interpreted in accordance with the Constitution and the Covenant and was only used to counter subversive acts which endangered national security and the democratic order. The substance of a decision of the Constitutional Court of April 1990 which had, inter alia, defined activities "endangering national security and survival" as well as the "basic liberal democratic order" had been incorporated into the National Security Law. It was, therefore, not possible to be convicted under that Law simply for expressing communist ideas or for having a positive attitude towards the Democratic People's Republic of Korea, provided that those sentiments did not lead to the commission of explicit acts. The concept of espionage covered only information which might jeopardize national security, and it was not invoked unless there had clearly been an attempt to pass information with the knowledge that that information would endanger the Republic of Korea. People had been convicted under the National Security Law if they had attempted or advocated the overthrow of the Government by violent means, and in all cases, defendants had enjoyed the full constitutional safeguard which ensured a fair trial. The amendment to the National Security Law was, however, not retroactive and the old law still applied to acts which had taken place before the amendment.

22. Referring to questions relating to the status of the Covenant, the representative of the State party explained that under article 6 of the Constitution the Covenant had the same effect as domestic law. Guarantees contained in the Covenant could, however, not be overturned by subsequent domestic legislation due to the Republic of Korea's commitment to human rights

472-16-P

and the increasing public awareness of the Covenant. Furthermore, since most
of the rights enshrined in the Covenant were also embodied in the
Constitution, any conflicting domestic legislation would be deemed
unconstitutional. If an individual claimed that his rights under the Covenant
had been infringed, the court would normally rule on the basis of domestic
legislation; in the rare cases where that was not possible, the Covenant could
be invoked directly before the courts. Furthermore, according to his
Government, all the rights enshrined in the Covenant were covered by
article 37 of the Constitution and, therefore, could not be neglected.
Complaints lodged by a petitioner would be dealt with by the relevant
administrative agency and, if the petitioner was not satisfied with the
result, he was automatically entitled to lodge a complaint with the courts.
Moreover, individuals were free to activate the procedures outlined in the
Optional Protocol and in case the Committee adopted views concerning the
Republic of Korea, the Government would make every effort to reflect them in
its future legislation.

23. With regard to questions relating to equality and non-discrimination, the
representative of the State party stated that the list laid down in article 11
of the Constitution was a purely indicative one and other grounds of
discrimination, such as political opinion, were not excluded. The term
"reasonable cultural discrimination" intended to cover differentiation based
upon a person's educational accomplishments. Although foreigners were not
guaranteed the right to hold public office, the Government did employ
foreigners on a contractual basis. Despite the advances in women's status,
most female workers were still in low-paid jobs and there were few women in
senior academic posts. Furthermore, there were not enough State child-care
facilities for low income families and traditional discrimination against
women still lingered on. The Government had endeavoured to eliminate
traditional stereotypes, promote women's participation in social and economic
activities and increase welfare facilities. The Government was also
considering an amendment to a provision of the Nationality Act which provided
that women were obliged to take their husband's nationality on marriage and to
be naturalized if the husband was naturalized.

24. Regarding article 4 of the Covenant, the representative of the State
party stated that, under article 37 of the Constitution and in conformity with
article 4, paragraph 2, of the Covenant, it was not permissible to restrict

the "essential aspect" of a freedom or right. Under article 76 of the Constitution, the President could issue an emergency order in times of insurgency, external threat, natural calamity or serious financial or economic crisis. If the National Assembly subsequently found that the emergency order was not justified it would be revoked forthwith.

25. With reference to article 6 of the Covenant, the representative of the State party stated that, in addition to the offences covered by the National Security Law, 15 crimes were subject to the death penalty. The death sentence could be imposed in cases of robbery committed with vile aggravating circumstances. The Government had already considerably reduced the number of capital offences and intended to progress further in that direction. The National Security Law dealt with only one generic crime - anti-State activities which endangered national security - and many offences referred to in the law, such as murder for the purposes of insurrection, were also covered by the Criminal Code. Under the Penal Administration Act, the death penalty was carried out by hanging. Although abortion was penalized under the Criminal Code, the Maternal and Child Health Act permitted exceptions in cases of rape, incest and threat to the health of the mother. The reference in the report to abortions for eugenic reasons covered cases where the foetus was severely deformed.

26. Regarding article 7 of the Covenant, the representative of the State party emphasized that the courts would not accept a confession unless it could be proved beyond reasonable doubt that it had been made voluntarily. Referring to specific cases mentioned by some members of the Committee, he explained that the conviction of Mr. Kim Rae Park had been based on objective evidence and not on a confession extracted under torture, as had been alleged. His sentence had been reduced for good behaviour and he had been released on probation on 25 May 1991. Following an investigation into the unnatural death of Mr. Jong Chul Park in January 1987, five police officers had been convicted and sentenced to prison terms of between 3 and 10 years. Additionally, six other officers had been sentenced to prison for 2-10 years, 14 had received suspended sentences and 9 more cases were awaiting trial. Places of detention were inspected regularly by prosecutors and the Ministry of Justice and any complaints of inhumane treatment were investigated by the prosecutor's office. Concerning long-term prisoners

0176

convicted of attempts to overthrow the Government by violence, the representative said that the Government could not afford to release them unless it was sure that their release would not jeopardize national security.

37. Responding to questions raised in connection with articles 9, 10 and 11 of the Covenant, the representative of the State party said that detention pending trial could not exceed six months and the court had to render its judgement during that period or release the suspect. There were no exceptions to a suspect's right to communicate with counsel and the Constitutional Court had decided, in January 1992, that article 62 of the Penal Administration Act was unconstitutional because it prohibited a detainee from meeting his attorney without being accompanied by a prison officer. The purpose of the correctional system was the prevention of further crimes and the rehabilitation of prisoners. To accomplish the latter, inmates received correctional education aimed at cultivating sound civic values with a view to preventing the recurrence of crimes. Inmates incarcerated under the National Security Law also participated in correctional education programmes, including exchange of views about competing ideologies, the goal being that a prisoner's re-entry into society should not pose a problem to the country. Inmates whose beliefs, translated into action, might pose a threat to the country were not eligible for parole. The inculcation during prisoners' education of what was referred to in the Republic of Korea as a "sound national spirit" aimed at ensuring that convicted persons when re-entering society would be imbued with traditional cultural values unique to their country and thus be capable of adapting to a normal life.

28. Referring to questions relating to article 14 of the Covenant, the representative of the State party said that prosecutors were officials of the executive branch, coming under the authority of the Ministry of Justice, and were guaranteed independence by the Prosecution Organization Act. They could not be suspended, except by impeachment or conviction for certain crimes, and their salary levels were guaranteed. The National Security Planning Agency gathered domestic security information about communist and subversive activities and conducted investigations in a limited number of cases, including alleged violations of the National Security Law. Judges served for 10 years, and could be reappointed for further terms; they could not be dismissed except by impeachment or conviction for certain crimes and their political activities were restricted. The Constitutional Court ruled on the

0177

K 72-18-12

constitutionality of laws, impeachment cases, the dissolution of political
parties and conflicts of jurisdiction. The Military Court Act specified the
procedures to be applied by military justice and guaranteed the fundamental
rights of the defendant in the same way as the civil courts' Code of Criminal
Procedure, the only exception being the right to appeal. Military justice
could apply to civilians who committed such crimes as military espionage,
supply of contaminated food to soldiers, and unlawful activities in respect of
prisoners of war and sentries under martial law. In the latter connection,
the term "extraordinary law" mentioned in the report refered to martial law as
declared in states of siege or on the outbreak of war.

29. With reference to articles 12 and 13 of the Covenant, the representative
of the State party explained that, since the hope of peaceful reunification
had yet to be fulfilled, some restrictions were placed on travel to the
Democratic People's Republic of Korea, in acordance with article 12,
paragraph 3, of the Covenant, which provided for restrictions on the freedom
of movement for reasons of national security. The Government was working with
UNHCR to provide humanitarian assistance to boat people until they could be
resettled in the country of their ultimate destination or a third country
willing to accept them. So far, about 1,220 boat people had been resettled in
third countries after arriving in the Republic of Korea and 155 were still
residing in a temporary accomodation camp.

30. In response to questions relating to articles 17, 18 and 19 of the
Covenant, the representative of the State party emphasized that the Republic
of Korea did not practise censorship. The writings of Marx, Lenin and other
communist works were, for instance, freely available in bookstores and
university libraries. Propaganda that could destabilize the country was,
however, restricted under the National Security Law and the publication,
copying, transportation or dissemination of propaganda for the purpose of
jeopardizing national security was forbidden. The Performance Act, the Movies
Act and the Act concerning Records and Video Materials imposed, in accordance
with article 19 of the Covenant, very limited restrictions on movies, records
and tapes for the purpose of maintaining public order and morality.

31. With regard to articles 21, 22 and 25 of the Covenant, the representative
of the State party stated that, on receivng notice of an assembly or
demonstration, the police examined it to see whether the gathering would occur
at a prohibited time and place and whether it would disrupt traffic. If the

0178

demonstration had the potential to create violence or posed a clear threat to public order and safety, a prohibition order was issued, nullification of which could be sought in the courts. A recently established Assembly and Demonstration Consideration Committee had issued objective standards for limiting prohibitions of assemblies, with a view to a better protection of human rights. Teachers and journalists were prohibited from joining certain political parties so as to preserve their strict impartiality in party politics. Under article 8 of the Constitution, if the purpose or activities of a political party were contrary to the fundamental democratic order, the Government could bring an action for its dissolution before the Constitutional Court.

32. Regarding article 24 of the Covenant, the representative of the State party stated that the Government was making every effort to prevent the employment of children in bars or in the entertainment business.

33. In connection with article 27 of the Covenant, the representative of the State party emphasized that the Republic of Korea was a homogenous nation with a distinct population sharing a common language and culture. There were, however, approximatively 51,000 residents of foreign origin, of whom 23,500 were Chinese. All of them enjoyed fundamental human rights in every field, pursuant to the Constitution and the Covenant.

Concluding observations

34. Members of the Committee thanked the representative of the State party for his co-operation in presenting the report and for having endeavoured to respond to the many questions asked by members. The report, which had been submitted within the specified period, contained detailed information on the laws and regulations relating to the implementation of the Covenant. It, however, lacked information about the implementation of the Covenant in practice and about factors and difficulties impeding the application of the Covenant.

35. Members noted with satisfaction that the Republic of Korea had acceded to a number of international human rights instruments, including the Covenant and its Optional Protocol, and had joined the International Labour Organisation. Members were also pleased to note that consideration was being given to the possibility of withdrawing the Republic of Korea's reservations to the Covenant. Furthermore, progress had been made in regard to legal aid and

0179

472-16-14

towards narrowing the scope of operation of the National Security Law.
Internal dissent was now possible and the Constitutional Court was playing a
vigorous and independent role.

36. At the same time, it was noted that some of the concerns expressed by
members of the Committee had not been fully allayed. The Constitution itself
did not cover all the rights enshrined in the Covenant and the argument that,
under article 37 of the Constitution, various rights and freedoms not
enumerated in the Constitution were not to be neglected, was not deemed
satisfactory. Deep concern was expressed over the continued operation of the
National Security Law. Although the political situation in which the Republic
of Korea found itself undoubtedly had implications on public order in the
country, the importance of such a situation ought not be overemphasised. It
was thus felt that ordinary laws and specifically applicable criminal laws
should be sufficient to deal with offences against national security. It was
noted with concern that some issues addressed by the National Security Law
were defined in somewhat vague terms, which seemed to allow for broad
interpretation and result in sanctions for acts that might not be truly
dangerous for the State. Furthermore, a broad definition of State secrets in
connection with the definition of espionage was potentially open to abuse.

37. Members also expressed concern in respect of the persisting areas of
discrimination against women; the still high number of offences liable to the
death penalty; the inclusion of robbery among the offences carrying the death
penalty, which seemed to clearly contravene article 6 of the Covenant; the use
of excessive force by the police; the excessively long periods of pre-trial
detention; the extent of the investigatoy powers of the National Security
Planning Agency; the implementation of article 12, particularly as concerned
visits to the Democratic People's Republic of Korea, problems relating to
article 15 of the Covenant; the high number of political prisoners; and the
request of an advance authorization for assemblies and demonstrations. It was
also considered that the conditions under which prisoners were being
re-educated did not constitute rehabilitation in the normal sense but rather
coercion and an infringement of the provisions of the Covenant relating to
freedom of conscience.

38. The representative of the State party assured the members of the
Committee that the comments that had been made would be transmitted to his
Government and stressed the importance his country attached to the dialogue

0180

with the Committee. The outcome of the consideration of the report by the Committee had increased the Government's awareness of its responsibilities under the Covenant. Positive comments made by members would be an encouragement to renewed efforts in favour of human rights while criticisms would act as an accelerator where further improvement was called for.

39. In concluding the consideration of the initial report of the Republic of Korea, the Chairman thanked the delegation for its clear and comprehensive replies to the questions asked by members of the Committee. He expressed the hope that all the Committee's comments would be transmitted to the competent bodies and taken into account during the formulation of new legislation and the revision of existing laws.

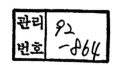

관리 92
번호 -864
주 제 네 바 대 표 부

20. Route de Pre-Bois, POB 566   /   (022) 791-0111   /   (022) 791-0525(FAX)

문서번호 제네(정) 2031-30

시행일자 1992. 8. 14

선결			지시	
접	일자시간	PM 6.20	결재	
수	번호	3477	공람	
	처리과			
	담당자			

수신 장 관

참조 국제기구국장, 법무부장관

제목: 인권보고서 평가 최종본

92 8. 14

연 : GVW-1494

    지난 7. 29 및 31 인권이사회에서 채택된 아국 인권 보고서에 대한 이사회
평가 최종본 별첨 송부하며 동 최종본은 사무국에서 조만간 공한으로 아국 정부
(외무부장관앞)에 공식 송부할 예정입니다.

    첨부 : 상기 문서 1부. 끝.

                    주 제 네 바 대   자

HUMAN RIGHTS COMMITTEE
Forty-fifth session

COMMENTS OF THE HUMAN RIGHTS COMMITTEE ON THE
INITIAL REPORT OF THE REPUBLIC OF KOREA 1/

1. The Committee considered the initial report of the Republic of Korea
(CCPR/C/68/Add.1) at its 1150th, 1151st and 1154th meetings, held on 13, 14
and 15 July 1992, and adopted the following comments:

A. Introduction

2. The Committee expresses its appreciation for the State party's
well-documented report which had been submitted within the specified
time-limit. The report contained detailed information on the laws and
regulations relating to the implementation of the Covenant. However, the
Committee notes that the report does not include sufficient information about
the implementation of the Covenant in practice and about factors and
difficulties which might impede the application of the Covenant. At the same
time the Committee appreciates the clear and comprehensive oral replies and
detailed clarifications given by the delegation.

B. Positive aspects

3. The Committee notes with satisfaction that in recent years the Republic of
Korea has become a party to a number of international human rights
instruments, including the Covenant and its Optional Protocol, and that it has
made the declaration provided for in article 41 of the Covenant. It has also
joined the International Labour Organisation. The Committee also notes with
satisfaction that currently consideration is being given to the possibility of
withdrawing the Republic of Korea's reservations to the Covenant.
Additionally, progress has been made in regard to the provision of legal aid
and towards narrowing the scope of operation of the National Security Law.
Internal political dissent is now more accepted. The Constitutional Court, an
independent organ, is playing a vigorous and important role.

_____

1/ Adopted at the forty-fifth session (1173rd meeting), held on
29 July 1992.

M/CCPR/92/36/Rev.1
GE.92-16975/4909H

0183

C. <u>Factors and difficulties impeding the application of the Covenant</u>

4.   The Committee notes that the relations between the two Koreas still appear to be an important factor affecting the human rights situation in the Republic of Korea. The recent conclusion of the Agreement on Reconciliation, Non-Aggression and Exchanges and Co-operation appears to constitute a positive step. According to the authorities, the Republic of Korea is, however, still coping with a very real threat of destabilization and military provocation and, therefore, the Government continues to hold the view that it is essential to retain the National Security Law in order to protect the security and integrity of its liberal democratic system.

D. <u>Principal subjects of concern</u>

5.   The Committee expresses its concern over the fact that the Constitution does not incorporate all the rights enshrined in the Covenant. Also, the non-discrimination provisions of article 11 of the Constitution would seem to be rather incomplete as compared with articles 2 and 26 of the Covenant. These concerns are not allayed by the argument that, pursuant to article 37 of the Constitution, various rights and freedoms not enumerated therein are not to be neglected.

6.   The Committee's main concern relates to the continued operation of the National Security Law. Although the particular situation in which the Republic of Korea finds itself has implications on public order in the country, its influence ought not to be overestimated. The Committee believes that ordinary laws and specifically applicable criminal laws should be sufficient to deal with offences against national security. Furthermore, some issues addressed by the National Security Law are defined in somewhat vague terms, allowing for broad interpretation that may result in sanctioning acts that may not be truly dangerous for State security and responses unauthorized by the Covenant.

7.   The Committee wishes to express its concern regarding the use of excessive force by the police; the extent of the investigatory powers of the National Security Planning Agency; and the implementation of article 12, particularly in so far as visits to the Democratic People's Republic of Korea are concerned. The Committee also considers that the conditions under which prisoners are being re-educated do not constitute rehabilitation in the normal sense of the term and that the amount of coercion utilized in that process

0184

could amount to an infringement of the provisions of the Covenant relating to freedom of conscience. The broad definition of State secrets in connection with the definition of espionage is also potentially open to abuse.

8. The Committee also expresses concern about the still high number of offences liable to the death penalty. In particular, the inclusion of robbery among the offences carrying the death penalty clearly contravenes article 6 of the Covenant. The very long period, allowed for interrogation before charges are brought, is incompatible with article 9, paragraph 3, of the Covenant. Other areas of concern relate to the continued imprisonment of persons on grounds of their political opinion; the persistence of discrimination against women in certain respects; problems relating to the principle of the lawfulness of the penalties covered by article 15 of the Covenant; and the requirement for advance authorization of assemblies and demonstrations.

E. Suggestions and recommendations

9. Taking into account the positive developments regarding respect of human rights that have taken place in the State party over the last years, the Committee recommends that the State party intensify its efforts to bring its legislation more in line with the provisions of the Covenant. To that end, a serious attempt ought to be made to phase out the National Security Law which the Committee perceives as a major obstacle to the full realization of the rights enshrined in the Covenant and, in the meanwhile, not to derogate from certain basic rights. Furthermore, measures should be taken to reduce the cases in which the death penalty is applied; to harmonize to a greater extent the Penal Code with the provisions of article 15 of the Covenant; and to reduce further the restrictions on the exercise of the right to peaceful assembly (article 21). Finally, the Committee suggests that the Government actively consider withdrawing its sweeping reservation in respect of article 14 and take additional steps with a view to enhancing public awareness of the Covenant and the Optional Protocol in the State party.

- - - - -

0185

UNITED NATIONS

CCPR

International covenant on civil and political rights

Distr.
GENERAL

CCPR/C/78
27 May 1992 .

Original: ENGLISH

HUMAN RIGHTS COMMITTEE
Forty-fifth session
Geneva, 13-31 July 1992

PROVISIONAL AGENDA AND ANNOTATIONS

Note by the Secretary-General

1.   The forty-fifth session of the Human Rights Committee will be held at the United Nations Office at Geneva from 13 to 31 July 1992. The first meeting will be convened on Monday, 13 July 1992 at 10.30 a.m.

2.   In accordance with rule 6 of the rules of procedure, the Secretary-General has prepared, in consultation with the Chairman of the Committee, the attached provisional agenda for the forty-fifth session. Annotations to the provisional agenda are also attached.

3.   Pursuant to rule 33 of the rules of procedure, the meetings of the Committee will be held in public unless the Committee decides otherwise or it appears from the relevant provisions of the Covenant or the Optional Protocol that the meetings should be held in private.

4.   The attention of the States parties is drawn, in particular, to the annotations to item 4 which contain the tentative timetable for the consideration of reports at the forty-fifth session. In accordance with rule 68 of the rules of procedure, representatives of States parties may be present at the meetings of the Committee when their reports are examined.

5.   At its forty-fourth session, the Committee decided that two working groups, established under rules 62 and 89 of its rules of procedure, should meet for a period of one week prior to its forty-fifth session. The working groups are scheduled to meet at the United Nations Office at Geneva from 6 to 10 July 1992.

GE.92-15839/4108H

0186

PROVISIONAL AGENDA

1. Adoption of the agenda

2. Organizational and other matters

3. Submission of reports by States parties under article 40 of the Covenant

4. Consideration of reports submitted by States parties under article 40 of the Covenant

5. Consideration of communications under the Optional Protocol to the Covenant

6. Preparatory activities relating to the World Conference on Human Rights

7. Annual report of the Committee to the General Assembly through the Economic and Social Council under article 45 of the Covenant and article 6 of the Optional Protocol

ANNOTATIONS

1.   Adoption of the agenda

Under rule 8 of the rules of procedure, the first item on the provisional agenda for any session shall be the adoption of the agenda. In accordance with rule 9, during a session, the Committee may revise the agenda and may, as appropriate, defer or delete items; only urgent and important items may be added to the agenda.

2.   Organizational and other matters

Under this item, the Committee will consider its programme of work for the session. In this connection, it may be noted that the Committee decided at its forty-fourth session to set up, in addition to the pre-sessional working group on communications, a working group under article 40 of the Covenant to prepare concise lists of issues concerning second and third periodic reports scheduled for consideration at the forty-fifth session; to further consider an issue relating to article 14, paragraphs 5 and 7 of the Covenant raised by a State party during the consideration of its report at the forty-third session and to give further consideration to draft general comments relating to articles 18 and 25 of the Covenant.

0187

3. Submission of reports by States parties under article 40 of the Covenant

Reports received

In addition to the reports which are scheduled for consideration by the Committee at its forty-fifth session (see the timetable for consideration of reports under item 4 below), the Secretary-General has received the reports of the following States parties:

Niger	Initial report due in 1987	(CCPR/C/45/Add.4)
Iran (Islamic Republic of)	Second periodic report due in 1983	(CCPR/C/28/Add.14)
Venezuela	Second periodic report due in 1985	(CCPR/C/57/Add.14)
United Republic of Tanzania	Second periodic report due in 1986	(CCPR/C/42/Add.12)
Egypt	Second periodic report due in 1988	(CCPR/C/51/Add.5)
Guinea	Second periodic report due in 1989	(CCPR/C/57/Add.2)
Luxembourg	Second periodic report due in 1989	(CCPR/C/57/Add.4)
Afghanistan	Second periodic report due in 1989	(CCPR/C/57/Add.5)
Uruguay	Third periodic report due in 1990	(CCPR/C/64/Add.4)
Senegal	Third periodic report due in 1990	(CCPR/C/64/Add.3)
Hungary	Third periodic report due in 1990	(CCPR/C/64/Add.7)
Japan	Third periodic report due in 1991	(CCPR/C/70/Add.1)
Norway	Third periodic report due in 1991	(CCPR/C/70/Add.2)

The Secretary-General has also received supplementary reports from Kenya and the Gambia which the Committee will consider together with those States parties' second periodic reports.

Reports due

The situation with regard to the submission of reports by States parties under article 40 of the Covenant is as follows:

States parties whose reports were due by the closing date of the forty-fourth session (10 April 1992) but have not yet been received

Initial reports

State party	Date due	Number of reminders sent
Gabon	20 April 1984	16
Equatorial Guinea	24 December 1988	7
Ireland	7 March 1991	3
Somalia	23 April 1991	2
Malta	12 December 1991	1

0188

Second periodic reports

Libyan Arab Jamahiriya	4 February 1983	18
Bulgaria	28 April 1984	17
Cyprus	18 August 1984	17
Syrian Arab Republic	18 August 1984	17
New Zealand - Cook Islands	27 March 1985	6
Gambia	21 June 1985	15
Suriname	2 August 1985	14
Lebanon	21 March 1986	14
Kenya	11 April 1986	13
Mali	11 April 1986	13
Jamaica	1 August 1986	11
Netherlands-Antilles	31 October 1986	5
Guyana	10 April 1987	11
Iceland	30 October 1987	10
Democratic People's Republic of Korea	13 December 1987	9
El Salvador	31 December 1988	7
Central African Republic	9 April 1989	6
Gabon a/	20 April 1989	6
Congo	4 January 1990	5
Zambia	9 July 1990	4
Bolivia	13 July 1990	4
Togo	23 August 1990	4
Cameroon	26 September 1990	4
Viet Nam	31 July 1991	2
Saint Vincent and the Grenadines	31 October 1991	2
San Marino	17 January 1992	1

Third periodic reports

Iran (Islamic Republic of)	21 March 1988	-
Libyan Arab Jamahiriya b/	4 February 1988	9
Lebanon b/	21 March 1988	9
Bulgaria b/	28 April 1989	6
Romania	28 April 1989	6
Cyprus b/	18 August 1989	6
Syrian Arab Republic b/	18 August 1989	6
Trinidad and Tobago	20 March 1990	5
New Zealand	27 March 1990	5
Gambia b/	21 June 1990	4
Mauritius	18 July 1990	4
Suriname b/	2 August 1990	4
Denmark	1 November 1990	4
Italy	1 November 1990	4
Venezuela	1 November 1990	-

0189

El Salvador b/	28 February 1991	3
Barbados	11 April 1991	3
Kenya b/	11 April 1991	3
Mali b/	11 April 1991	3
United Republic of Tanzania	11 April 1991	-
Nicaragua	11 June 1991	2
Zaire	31 July 1991	2
Jamaica b/	1 August 1991	2
Portugal	1 August 1991	2
Costa Rica	1 August 1991	2
Sri Lanka	10 September 1991	2
Netherlands	31 October 1991	2
Dominican Republic	31 October 1991	2
Australia	12 November 1991	1
Jordan	22 January 1992	1
France	3 February 1992	1
India	31 March 1992	1
Panama	31 March 1992	1
Guyana b/	10 April 1992	1
Rwanda	10 April 1992	1

States parties whose reports are to be submitted between the closing date of the Committee's forty-fourth session (10 April 1992) and the closing date of its forty-fifth session (31 July 1992)

Initial reports

State party	Date due
Haiti	5 May 1992

Second periodic reports

Niger	6 June 1992
Sudan	17 June 1992

Third periodic reports

Mexico	22 June 1992
Madagascar	31 July 1992

4. **Consideration of reports submitted by States parties under article 40 of the Covenant**

A tentative timetable for the consideration of reports at the forty-fifth session, prepared in consultation with the Chairman and subject to approval by the Committee, is given below:

0190

Timetable for consideration of reports of States parties

Republic of Korea (initial report)	CCPR/C/68/Add.1	Monday, p.m. Wednesday, p.m.	13 July 1992 15 July 1992
Belarus (third periodic)	CCPR/C/52/Add.8	Tuesday, a.m./p.m. Wednesday, a.m.	14 July 1992 15 July 1992
Mongolia (third periodic)	CCPR/C/64/Add.2	Thursday, p.m. Friday, a.m./p.m.	16 July 1992 17 July 1992
Peru c/ (second periodic)	CCPR/C/51/Add.4	Monday, a.m.	20 July 1992
Burundi (initial report)	CCPR/C/68/Add.2	Tuesday, a.m. Thursday, a.m.	21 July 1992 23 July 1992

In accordance with rule 68 of the rules of procedure, the Secretary-General has informed the States parties concerned of the tentative dates on which their respective reports are scheduled for consideration by the Committee at its forty-fifth session.

Under this item, the Committee will also consider any draft general comment that may be submitted to it by its working group.

5. **Consideration of communications under the Optional Protocol to the Covenant**

In accordance with the provisions of chapter XVII of the rules of procedure, the Committee will consider under this item communications which are or appear to be submitted to it under the Optional Protocol.

One hundred and forty-eight communications are pending before the Committee from earlier sessions. Taking into account the deadlines established by the Committee for submission of further information from the parties, 49 cases (earlier declared admissible) may be considered for the adoption of final views and 99 cases may be considered for a decision on admissibility. In addition, the Committee will have before it summaries of a number of recently registered communications and summaries of new communications registered after its last session, together with an indication of any action which may have been taken by the Special Rapporteur for new communications.

In accordance with article 5, paragraph 3, of the Optional Protocol and rule 82 of the rules of procedure, this agenda item will be considered in closed meetings.

0191

6. <u>Preparatory activities relating to the World Conference on
Human Rights</u>

Under this item, the Committe will consider any further contributions it may wish to make to the preparatory process. It will have before it the report of the second meeting of the Preparatory Committee (A/CONF.157/PC/37 and Corr.1).

7. <u>Annual report of the Committee to the General Assembly through the
Economic and Social Council under article 45 of the Covenant and
article 6 of the Optional Protocol</u>

Under article 45 of the Covenant, the Committee is to submit to the General Assembly, through the Economic and Social Council, an annual report on its activities. Article 6 of the Optional Protocol provides that the Committee shall include in its annual report a summary of its activities under the Protocol.

At its fifth session, the Committee decided that, beginning with 1979, it would adopt its annual report at the end of its second annual (summer) session, for appropriate transmission to the General Assembly. Accordingly, the annual report of the Committee in 1992 will cover the activities of the Committee at its forty-third (October/November 1991), forty-fourth and forty-fifth sessions.

Notes

<u>a</u>/ The State party's initial report has not yet been received.

<u>b</u>/ The State party's second periodic report has not yet been received.

<u>c</u>/ The Committee began consideration of the second periodic report of Peru at its 1133rd to 1136th meetings (forty-fourth session) and decided to revert to it at the forty-fifth session. The Committee also decided to request the Government of Peru to submit a supplementary report relating to events occurring subsequent to the consideration of the report, in particular in respect of the application of articles 4, 6, 7, 9, 19 and 25 of the Covenant, for discussion by the Committee during its forty-fifth session.

0192

PRESS RELEASE

KOREAN OVERSEAS INFORMATION SERVICE

Foreign News Division
Seoul, Korea
Phone: 720-4728, 2396
FAX: 733-2237

~~August 18, 1992~~

KPS · · · The International Community Appreciates
ROK Endeavors to Protect Human Rights

The Human Rights Committee of the United Nations met in Geneva from July 13 to 15, 1992 to study in depth the first report that the Republic of Korea Government filed in July 1991 under the International Covenant on Civic and Political Rights. A ROK Government delegation participated in the meeting, which was attended by 14 of the 18 duly seated members of the committee.

The committee members reviewed the report as a whole and asked detailed and wide-ranging questions about the ROK's statutes intended to guarantee human rights and how they are enforced. Their queries were focused on such topics as possible impediments to human rights protection stemming from the division and confrontation on the Korean Peninsula; measures to ensure domestic compliance with the International Covenant on Civic and Political Rights; steps to uphold due process of law in administering criminal justice; certain sensitive provisions of the National Security Law and the manner of their enforcement; the ROK's capital punishment provisions; the degree of the independence of the judiciary; the ROK's preparedness to withdraw its reservations to the Covenant; and measures to ensure equal rights to women.

In evaluating the ROK report, the committee arrived at the positive conclusion that since the advent of the Sixth Republic,

0193

the ROK Government has pursued open-ended and active policies to guarantee human rights. In particular, it cited as examples of this the extensive revisions to the Constitution and other laws and regulations with the aim of promoting human rights and the creation of the Constitution Court to prevent abuse of power, among other things. It also noted that the ROK has become party to two relevant international conventions to reinforce guarantees for human rights. The committee also expressed the view that the ROK delegates to the meeting gave earnest answers to its questions.

The committee's review of human rights reports from parties to the International Covenant on Civil and Political Rights is aimed not at discussing the human rights situation in the reporting countries: it is intended to determine whether or not their legislative, administrative and law-enforcement measures are suitable for ensuring compliance with the covenant. To that end, the committee studies not only reports from the governments concerned but also other reference material. In this sense, the committee's deliberation of reports from parties to the pact is usually termed "constructive dialogue" between it and the delegations from the reporting governments.

The Human Rights Committee, an authoritative U.N. agency, has just objectively examined and assessed for the first time the ROK's institutional devices for guaranteeing human rights and the state of their administration in reviewing the ROK report on human rights. The Government considers this of great significance because it is giving an added impetus to the promotion of human rights in this nation. In its further efforts to protect human rights, the Government will take into full consideration both the assessments that the committee has made and the questions it has raised.

The chief ROK delegate to the committee meeting, Park Soo-

∂

0194

gil, who is the ROK ambassador to Geneva, delivered a speech before the committee on July 13, explaining the highlights of the ROK report and democratic development and concomitant improvements in the human rights situation since the birth of the Sixth Republic. He elaborated on the ROK's newly-adopted direct presidential election system, measures taken to enhance the independence of the judiciary, the establishment of the Constitution Court, the sweeping revisions to the Constitution and other relevant laws and regulations to promote human rights, the reductions in the range of application of the death penalty and the reintroduction of local autonomy.

Ambassador Park told the committee that since it filed the July 1991 report, the ROK has continued efforts to extend human rights by joining the International Labor Organization, ratifying the U.N. Convention on Child Rights and seeking to become a party to the convention on refugees and the protocol therefor. As for the future course of action by the ROK in the human rights field, he explained that the ROK is considering becoming a party to the convention on the prevention of torture. The ROK Government, he said, is also working on legislative proposals to revise the Criminal Law, the Criminal Procedures Act and labor-related laws. In that way, he added, the ROK will continue its endeavors to promote and protect human rights in every respect.

Ambassador Park noted that the tension and confrontation stemming from the division of the Korean Peninsula is among the major factors affecting the ROK's compliance with the Covenant. He said the basic position of the ROK Government is to actively pursue South-North dialogue aimed at achieving peace and unification, while effectively countering subversive groups in the South that pose a threat to freedom and democracy. He added this is why the National Security Law and other similar laws must be maintained at this stage.

Committee members made comments and asked questions

0195

regarding the ROK report and the ambassador's explanation on the afternoon of July 13 and on the morning of July 14. They favorably evaluated democratic development and improvements in the human rights situation in the ROK explained in the ROK report and Park's address and made the following final comments:

1. Since the advent of the Sixth Republic in February 1988, remarkable progress has been made in democratization and the improvement of the human rights situation. The efforts of the ROK Government toward those ends are appreciated.

2. The ROK Government report is written in detail, faithfully following the criteria and guidelines set forth in the Covenant. Both its substance and format are excellent. In particular, it covers all statutes and government measures relating to human rights in the same sequence as the clauses of the Covenant.

0196

/0

도마오른 한국人權

유엔회의 참관 千正培변호사

"국가보안법등 냉혹한 평가에 놀라"

「국가보안법은 모든 종류의 인권침해를 일으킬 수 있었던 「북한을 빌미로 국제인권규약의 실천을 유보할수 없다」 상황은 범하는데 긴장은 정부당국자의 마음 속에 있는것 같다」

7월13~15일 스위스 제네바의 유엔인권센터에서 유엔인권 이사회 한국인권보고서 검토회의가 열렸을때 각국의 인권위원들이 지적한 내용이다.

방청자격으로 회의를 참관하고온 대한변협인권위원 千正培변호사(38·사진)는 요즘 회의녹음테이프를 번역하고 자료집을 발간하는 일을 하고있다.

千변호사는 우리나라의 인권상황에 대한 국제사회의 평가에 놀랐다고 한다. 이번 이사회는 90년7월 국제인권규약에 가입한뒤 지난해7월 유엔에 제출한 한국정부의 인권보고서를 검토·평가하기 위해 열린것.

18명의 인권위원이 1백50여항목을 질문한뒤 정부답변을 듣는 식으로 진행된 회의에서는 국가보안법·사상전향제도등 정치적 의사표현의 자유를 억압하는 법과 제도가 도마에 올랐다.

「진보적 인권단체가 개최한 회의도 아니고 각국 정부가 추천한 사람들로 구성된 인권이사회가 정부대표와 공식대화를 나눈 자리였는데도 우리의 인권상황에 심각한 우려를 표명하는 것을 보고 놀랐습니다」

千변호사는 자료집발간이 끝나면 인권규약 위반사항을 시정해 주도록 법무부에 요청할 계획이다.

72년 木浦高를 나와 서울大법대에 수석입학한 千변호사는 졸업과 동시에 사법시험에 합격, 군법무관을 거쳐 81년 변호사개업을 했다.

처음엔 검사가 되려했으나 10·26과 5·17을 거치면서 정부의 임명장을 받기 싫어 변호사가 됐다. 千변호사는 「국제정세와 남북관계가 상당히 개선된만큼 정부의 제권리를 국제적 수준이 되게 해야 한다」고 말했다.

[高在鶴기자]

한국일보 '92.8.1.

외   무   부

110-760 서울 종로구 세종로 77번지 / 전화 (02) 723-8934 / 전송 (02) 723-3505

문서번호 연이 20314-

시행일자 1992.9.14.

취급		차 관	장 관
보존		전결	秋
국 장	쁠		
심의관	틀	제1차관보	
과 장	츨		
기안	김종훈		협조

수신 보   고

참조

제목 우리나라 인권규약 최초보고서 검토 관련 인권이사회 회의참가 보고서

　　　우리나라의 인권규약(B) 최초보고서를 검토한 제45차 인권이사회 회의

(92.7.13-7.15, 제네바) 참가 보고서를 별첨과 같이 보고드립니다.

첨부 : 동 보고서 1부. 끝.

0198

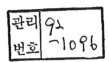

외 무 부

110-760 서울 종로구 세종로 77번지 / 전화 (02) 723-8934 / 전송 (02) 723-3505

문서번호 연이 20314-166

시행일자 1992.9.30.

수신 장관, 차관, 제1,2차관보,
각 실.국장

취급		장 관
보존		
국 장	전결	
심의관		
과 장		
기안	함상욱	협조

제목 인권이사회 참가 보고서 송부

    제45차 인권이사회 참가 보고서를 별첨 송부하니 귀업무에 참고하시기

바랍니다.

첨부 : 제45차 인권이사회 참가 보고서 1부. 끝.

예고 : 첨부물 분리시 일반

0199

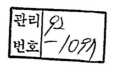

외 무 부

110-760 서울 종로구 세종로 77번지 / 전화 (02) 723-8934 / 전송 (02) 723-3505

문서번호 연이 20314- 161

시행일자 1992.9.30.

수신 연구원장, 연구실장,
     교수부장, 각 연구부장,
     연구위원실

취급		장 관
보존		
국 장	전결	
심의관		
과 장		
기안	함상욱	협조

제목 인권이사회 참가 보고서 송부

     제45차 인권이사회 참가 보고서를 별첨 송부하니 귀업무에 참고하시기
바랍니다.

첨부 : 제45차 인권이사회 참가 보고서 1부. 끝.

예고 : 첨부물 분리시 일반

0200

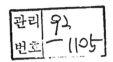

외 무 부

110-760 서울 종로구 세종로 77번지 / 전화 (02) 723-8934 / 전송 (02) 723-3505

문서번호 연이 20314-2487

시행일자 1992.9.30.

취급		장 관	
보존			
국 장	전결		
심의관			
과 장			
기안	함상욱		협조

수신 법무부장관,
      국가안전기획부장

제목 인권이사회 참가 보고서 송부

　　　제45차 인권이사회 참가 보고서를 별첨 송부하니 귀업무에 참고하시기
바랍니다.

첨부 : 제45차 인권이사회 참가 보고서 2부. 끝.

예고 : 첨부물 분리시 일반

0201

외 무 부

110-760 서울 종로구 세종로 77번지 / 전화 (02) 723-8934 / 전송 (02) 723-3505

문서번호 연이 20314-2489

시행일자 1992.9.30.

취급		장 관
보존		
국 장	전결	
심의관		
과 장		
기안	함상욱	협조

수신 수신처 참조

제목 인권이사회 참가 보고서 송부

　　　제45차 인권이사회 참가 보고서를 별첨 송부하니 귀업무에 참고하시기
바랍니다.

첨부 : 제45차 인권이사회 참가 보고서 1부. 끝.

애고 : 첨부물 분리시 일반

수신처 : 주 카이로, 홍콩, 뉴욕, 시드니, 라성, 마이애미, 보스톤, 상항,
　　　　　시애틀, 시카고, 아가나. 아틀란타, 앵커리지, 호놀루루, 휴스턴,
　　　　　몬트리올, 밴쿠우버, 토론토, 백림, 프랑크푸르트, 함부르크 총영사

0202

외 무 부

110-760 서울 종로구 세종로 77번지 / 전화 (02) 723-8934 / 전송 (02) 723-3505

문서번호 연이 20314-2484

시행일자 1992.9.30.

수신 수신처 참조

취급		장 관	
보존			
국 장	전결	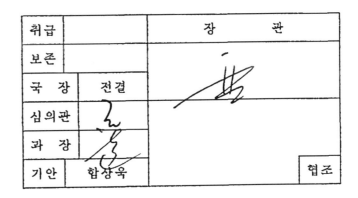	
심의관			
과 장			
기안	함상욱		협조

재목 인권이사회 참가 보고서 송부

제45차 인권이사회 참가 보고서를 별첨 송부하니 귀업무에 참고하시기

바랍니다.

첨부 : 제45차 인권이사회 참가 보고서 1부. 끝.

예고 : 첨부물 분리시 일반

수신처 : 대통령비서실장(비서실장, 외교안보수석보좌관, 정책조사보좌관,
   정책자료실), 국무총리비서실장(정무비서실장, 행정조정실장),
   통일원장관, 내무부장관, 국방부장관, 국회사무처, 법원행정처,
   헌법재판소장, 교육부장관, 보건사회부장관, 노동부장관, 문화부장관,
   공보처장관, 법제처장, 정무 제1장관, 정무 제2장관 , **경찰청장**

0203

외 무 부

110-760 서울 종로구 세종로 77번지 / 전화 (02) 723-8934 / 전송 (02) 723-3505

문서번호 연이 20314-2490

시행일자 1992.9.30.

수신 주유엔대사, 주제네바대사

취급		장 관		
보존				
국 장	전결			
심의관				
과 장				
기안	함상욱			협조

제목 인권이사회 참가 보고서 송부

    제45차 인권이사회 참가 보고서를 별첨 송부하니 귀업무에 참고하시기

바랍니다.

첨부 : 제45차 인권이사회 참가 보고서 2부. 끝.

예고 : 첨부물 분리시 일반

0204

외 무 부

110-760 서울 종로구 세종로 77번지 / 전화 (02) 723-8934 / 전송 (02) 723-3505

문서번호 연이 20314-249

시행일자 1992.9.30.

수신 전재외공관장
      (총영사관 및 주제내바,
      주유엔대표부 제외)

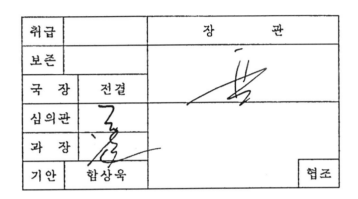

취급		장 관		
보존				
국 장	전결			
심의관				
과 장				
기안	함상욱			협조

제목 인권이사회 참가 보고서 송부

　　　제45차 인권이사회 참가 보고서를 별첨 송부하니 귀업무에 참고하시기

바랍니다.

첨부 : 제45차 인권이사회 참가 보고서 1부. 끝.

예고 : 첨부물 분리시 일반

0205

주 제 네 바 대 표 부

20, Route de Pre-Bois, POB 566 / (022) 791-0111 / (022) 791-0525(FAX)

문서번호 : 제네(정)2031-P47

시행일자 : 1992.10.29.

수신 : 장 관

참조 : 국제기구국장

선결				지시		
접수	일자시간			결재	대 사	
	번호	62172			차석대사	
처리자				공람	참사관	
담당자					서기관	

제목 : 92년도 국별인권보고서 심의평가(CCPR)

    아국등 인권이사회의 92년도 시민적 정치적 권리규약 국별 보고서 심의
평가서를 별첨 송부합니다.

첨부 :   1. 한국(CCPR/C/Add.6)

    2. 알제리 (Add.1)

    3. 벨기에(Add.3)   92. 10. 2 9

    4. 유고(Add.4)

    5. 벨라루스(Add.5)

    6. 몽고(Add.7)

    7. 페루(Add.8)

주 제 네 바 대

0206

UNITED
NATIONS

**International covenant
on civil and
political rights**

CCPR

Distr.
GENERAL

CCPR/C/79/Add.6
25 September 1992

Original: ENGLISH

HUMAN RIGHTS COMMITTEE

CONSIDERATION OF REPORTS SUBMITTED BY STATES PARTIES
UNDER ARTICLE 40 OF THE COVENANT

<u>Comments of the Human Rights Committee</u>

REPUBLIC OF KOREA

1.   The Committee considered the initial report of the Republic of Korea
(CCPR/C/68/Add.1) at its 1150th, 1151st and 1154th meetings, held on 13, 14 and
15 July 1992, and adopted* the following comments:

A.   <u>Introduction</u>

2.   The Committee expresses its appreciation for the State party's
well-documented report which had been submitted within the specified time-limit.
The report contained detailed information on the laws and regulations relating to
the implementation of the Covenant. However, the Committee notes that the report
does not include sufficient information about the implementation of the Covenant in
practice and about factors and difficulties which might impede the application of
the Covenant. At the same time the Committee appreciates the clear and
comprehensive oral replies and detailed clarifications given by the delegation.

---

    * At the forty-fifth session (1173rd meeting), held on 29 July 1992.

GE.92-17652 (E)

B.   Positive aspects

3.   The Committee notes with satisfaction that in recent years the Republic of Korea has become a party to a number of international human rights instruments, including the Covenant and its Optional Protocol, and that it has made the declaration provided for in article 41 of the Covenant. It has also joined the International Labour Organisation. The Committee also notes with satisfaction that currently consideration is being given to the possibility of withdrawing the Republic of Korea's reservations to the Covenant. Additionally, progress has been made in regard to the provision of legal aid and towards narrowing the scope of operation of the National Security Law. Internal political dissent is now more accepted. The Constitutional Court, an independent organ, is playing a vigorous and important role.

C.   Factors and difficulties impeding the application of the Covenant

4.   The Committee notes that the relations between the two Koreas still appear to be an important factor affecting the human rights situation in the Republic of Korea. The recent conclusion of the Agreement on Reconciliation, Non-Aggression and Exchanges and Co-operation appears to constitute a positive step. According to the authorities, the Republic of Korea is, however, still coping with a very real threat of destabilization and military provocation and, therefore, the Government continues to hold the view that it is essential to retain the National Security Law in order to protect the security and integrity of its liberal democratic system.

D.   Principal subjects of concern

5.   The Committee expresses its concern over the fact that the Constitution does not incorporate all the rights enshrined in the Covenant. Also, the non-discrimination provisions of article 11 of the Constitution would seem to be rather incomplete as compared with articles 2 and 26 of the Covenant. These concerns are not allayed by the argument that, pursuant to article 37 of the Constitution, various rights and freedoms not enumerated therein are not to be neglected.

6.   The Committee's main concern relates to the continued operation of the National Security Law. Although the particular situation in which the Republic of Korea finds itself has implications on public order in the country, its influence ought not to be overestimated. The Committee believes that ordinary laws and specifically applicable criminal laws should be sufficient to deal with offences against national security. Furthermore, some issues addressed by the National Security Law are defined in somewhat vague terms, allowing for broad interpretation that may result in sanctioning acts that may not be truly dangerous for State security and responses unauthorized by the Covenant.

7.   The Committee wishes to express its concern regarding the use of excessive force by the police; the extent of the investigatory powers of the National Security Planning Agency; and the implementation of article 12, particularly in so far as visits to the Democratic People's Republic of Korea are concerned. The Committee also considers that the conditions under which prisoners are being

0208

re-educated do not constitute rehabilitation in the normal sense of the term and that the amount of coercion utilized in that process could amount to an infringement of the provisions of the Covenant relating to freedom of conscience. The broad definition of State secrets in connection with the definition of espionage is also potentially open to abuse.

8.   The Committee also expresses concern about the still high number of offences liable to the death penalty. In particular, the inclusion of robbery among the offences carrying the death penalty clearly contravenes article 6 of the Covenant. The very long period, allowed for interrogation before charges are brought, is incompatible with article 9, paragraph 3, of the Covenant. Other areas of concern relate to the continued imprisonment of persons on grounds of their political opinion; the persistence of discrimination against women in certain respects; problems relating to the principle of the lawfulness of the penalties covered by article 15 of the Covenant; and the requirement for advance authorization of assemblies and demonstrations.

E.   Suggestions and recommendations

9.   Taking into account the positive developments regarding respect of human rights that have taken place in the State party over the last years, the Committee recommends that the State party intensify its efforts to bring its legislation more in line with the provisions of the Covenant. To that end, a serious attempt ought to be made to phase out the National Security Law which the Committee perceives as a major obstacle to the full realization of the rights enshrined in the Covenant and, in the meanwhile, not to derogate from certain basic rights. Furthermore, measures should be taken to reduce the cases in which the death penalty is applied; to harmonize to a greater extent the Penal Code with the provisions of article 15 of the Covenant; and to reduce further the restrictions on the exercise of the right to peaceful assembly (art. 21). Finally, the Committee suggests that the Government actively consider withdrawing its sweeping reservation in respect of article 14 and take additional steps with a view to enhancing public awareness of the Covenant and the Optional Protocol in the State party.

- - - - -

0209

International covenant
on civil and
political rights

Distr.
GENERAL

CCPR/C/79/Add.1
25 September 1992

Original: ENGLISH

HUMAN RIGHTS COMMITTEE

CONSIDERATION OF REPORTS SUBMITTED BY STATES PARTIES
UNDER ARTICLE 40 OF THE COVENANT

<u>Comments of the Human Rights Committee</u>

ALGERIA

1.   The Committee considered the initial report of Algeria
(CCPR/C/62/Add.1) at its 1125th and 1128th meetings, held on 25 and
27 March 1992, and adopted* the following comments:

A.   <u>Introduction</u>

2.   The Committee notes that the dialogue with the Algerian delegation was
particularly constructive, because the delegation endeavoured to answer
members' questions candidly without trying to conceal the difficulties. It
thanks the State party through the latter's representative for its good
report, which was submitted within the specified period. The report
contains detailed information on the laws and regulations relating to the
application of the provisions of the Covenant. The Committee regrets,
however, that the report includes little information concerning the actual
application of human rights standards. It also regrets the failure of the
report to indicate the factors and difficulties which are impeding the
application of those standards. Lastly, it notes with regret that the
report, having been submitted on 5 April 1991, could make no reference to
the states of emergency, notification of which reached the Secretary-
General on 19 June and 13 February 1992 respectively.

---

    * At the 1147th meeting, held on 9 April 1992.

GE.92-17627 (E)

0210

B.   Positive aspects

3.   The Committee notes with satisfaction that Algeria has ratified or acceded to a number of international human rights instruments, in particular the Covenant and the first Optional Protocol thereto, and has made the declaration provided for in article 41 of the Covenant.   In addition, Algeria has included in its Constitution various provisions relating to human rights and has amended a number of legislative texts in order to reflect international human rights standards.   The Committee also notes with satisfaction the establishment of a Ministry of Human Rights later replaced by a national human rights monitoring body.

C.   Factors and difficulties impeding the application of the Covenant

4.   The Committee notes that at the time of the submission of the report, Algeria was in a process of transition to democracy.   Since that time, Algeria has been faced with substantial difficulties which have brought this process to a standstill.   The Algerian authorities therefore considered such ways and means as seemed to them appropriate in order to prevent forces that they considered hostile to democracy from taking advantage of democratic procedure in order to harm democracy.   Among the measures adopted in this respect are the proclamation of the two states of emergency and the interruption of the electoral process.

D.   Principal subjects of concern

5.   The Committee expresses its concern regarding the suspension of the democratic process and, in general, regarding the blocking of democratic mechanisms.   It is concerned about the high number of arrests (8,800) and the abusive use of firearms by members of the police in order to disperse demonstrations.   The Committee expresses doubts about respect for due process, especially before military tribunals, about the real possibilities for implementing the right to a fair trial, about the numerous cases of torture and ill-treatment which have been brought to its attention, and about the restrictions on rights to freedom of opinion and expression and freedom of the press.   The Committee further considers that, in the light of the provision of article 6 requiring States parties which have not abolished the death penalty to reserve it for the most serious crimes, it is contrary to the Covenant to impose the death penalty for crimes which are of an economic nature.

6.   The Committee also regrets the many cases of discrimination against women and the non-recognition of minorities, especially the Berbers.

0211

E.   Suggestions and recommendation

7.   The Committee recommends that Algeria put an end as promptly as possible to the exceptional situation which prevails within its borders and allow all the democratic mechanisms to resume their functioning under fair and free conditions. It draws the attention of the State party to the fact that the Covenant does not permit derogation from certain rights even in times of emergency and that, therefore, any excesses relating to, inter alia, the right to life, torture and the right to freedom of conscience and expression are violations of the Covenant which should not be allowed to continue. The Committee hopes that the State party will make an evaluation of the application of the provisions of the Covenant after the report was written and would like to be kept informed of any charges in the situation and of all future developments.

0212

CCPR

**International covenant
on civil and
political rights**

Distr.
GENERAL

CCPR/C/79/Add.3
25 September 1992

Original: ENGLISH

HUMAN RIGHTS COMMITTEE

CONSIDERATION OF REPORTS SUBMITTED BY STATES PARTIES
UNDER ARTICLE 40 OF THE COVENANT

Comments of the Human Rights Committee

BELGIUM

1.   The Committee considered the second periodic report of Belgium
(CCPR/C/57/Add.3) at its 1142th and 1143rd meetings, held on 7 April 1992, and
adopted* the following comments:

A.   Introduction

2.   The Committee commends the State party on its excellent report which
contains detailed information on law and practice relating to the implementation
of the Covenant's provisions subsequent to the consideration of the initial
report. The Committee appreciates the comprehensiveness of the report which is
in conformity with the Committee's guidelines. In particular, the Committee is
grateful for both the oral and written responses provided by the State party
representative. The Committee also appreciates the high competence of the
delegation and considers that the dialogue with the State party was fruitful and
constructive.

_____

*   At the 1148th meeting, held on 10 April 1992.

GE.92-17637 (E)

0213

B.   Positive aspects

3.   The Committee notes with satisfaction the changes in law and in practice during the period under review, in particular, the several decisions of the Court of Cassation affirming the applicability of certain provisions of the Covenant; the law on economic reorientation prohibiting any discrimination based on sex; the law abolishing all discrimination between children born in and out of wedlock; the draft law permitting immediate communication between the accused and his lawyer; the bill proposing to abolish the death penalty; and the planned accession to the Second Optional Protocol to the Covenant.

C.   Factors and difficulties impeding the application of the Covenant

4.   The Committee notes some of the major difficulties experienced by Belgium; such as, the centrifugal character of Belgian federalism, the bipolar nature of the legal system, and the language differences among the population. The complexity of the Belgian legal framework seems to have impeded a direct reference to the Covenant to a certain extent.

D.   Principal subjects of concern

5.   Although noting the direct applicability of several provisions of the Covenant which form part of Belgian domestic law, the Committee is concerned about the difference between civil rights enjoyed by citizens and those enjoyed by aliens, which may lead to discrimination against aliens. Other areas of concern include the scope of interpretation given to article 6 of the Covenant; the adequacy of monitoring pre-trial detention as well as the impartiality of the authorities who examine those arrested; the adequacy of remedies for wrongful detention; the adequacy of information on freedom of expression especially in relation to television broadcasting; and arrangements as to freedom of assembly in open air.

E.   Suggestions and Recommendations

6.   The Committee recommends to the State party more adequately to reflect in internal administrative practice the provisions of the Covenant which are not reflected in the European Convention for the Protection of Human Rights and Fundamental Freedoms (e.g. arts. 25, 26 and 27); and to ensure that the laws regarding restrictions on freedom of expression and assembly are compatible with those provided for in the Covenant. The Committee also recommends that the State party further improve the effectiveness of the protection granted to minority rights at the communal level. The Committee further recommends that the State party reconsider its reservations so as to withdraw as many as possible.

0214

CCPR

International covenant
on civil and
political rights

Distr.
GENERAL

CCPR/C/79/Add.4
25 September 1992

Original: ENGLISH

HUMAN RIGHTS COMMITTEE

CONSIDERATION OF REPORTS SUBMITTED BY STATES PARTIES
UNDER ARTICLE 40 OF THE COVENANT

<u>Comments of the Human Rights Committee</u>

YUGOSLAVIA

1.   The Committee considered the third periodic report of Yugoslavia
(CCPR/C/52/Add.9) at its 1144th, 1145th, 1146th and 1147th meetings, on
8 and 9 April 1992, and adopted* the following comments.

A.   <u>Introduction and positive developments</u>

2.   The Committee thanks the State party through its representative for the
report it submitted, albeit late, in response to the decision adopted by
the Committee on 4 November 1991. The Committee appreciates the fact that
despite the serious events that have occurred in the country, the federal
Government has been able to cooperate with the Committee and to present and
discuss its report. The Committee takes note of the information contained
in the report on the present constitutional and legal situation. It
nevertheless regrets the fact that the report does not cover the whole
period since 30 May 1983, the date of the submission of the second periodic
report, and that it does not deal fully enough with the problems
encountered by the State party in applying the provisions of the Covenant
in practice. However, the oral dialogue established in the Committee meant
that it was to some extent possible to obtain additional information on the
obstacles to effective application of the Covenant and to highlight certain
efforts being made to improve the legal and regulatory framework within
which the Covenant was being applied. The Committee noted that a
commission had been set up to inquire into allegations of genocide and
violation of human rights during the armed conflicts.

----

    * At the 1148th meeting, held on 10 April 1992.

GE.92-17642 (E)

0215

B. Factors and difficulties hindering implementation of the Covenant

3. The Committee noted that difficulties had arisen in the province of Kosovo, which had led to the proclamation of several successive states of emergency. More recently, the uncontrolled break-up of the State party's institutions has degenerated into violent inter-ethnic conflicts, leading to widespread violations of most of the human rights safeguarded by the Covenant. As a result of this state of affairs, a peace-keeping operation has been set up under the cease-fire negotiated under the auspices of the United Nations.

C. Issues of particular concern

4. The Committee notes that as things stand, the present crisis prevents it from supervising the application of the Covenant throughout the territory of the State party; because of the federal State's loss of control in a growing number of republics, little information has been communicated to the Committee on the application of the Covenant in those areas. The Committee stresses the importance of continuing to implement the Covenant in those republics. With reference to article 1 of the Covenant, the Committee regrets the fact that there was no procedure under domestic law for implementation of the right to secede recognized in the federal Constitution, which would have enabled the crisis to be settled peacefully. The Committee also regrets the fact that under the state of emergency proclaimed in the province of Kosovo, excessive steps have been taken to limit the rights and freedoms guaranteed by the Covenant.

5. The Committee expresses its gravest concern with regard to the atrocities committed during the inter-ethnic conflicts. It is disturbed by the many violations of human rights protected by the Covenant, especially those referred to in article 4, paragraph 2, of the Covenant, which are to be safeguarded whatever the circumstances (right to life and prohibition of torture in particular). The Committee greatly regrets the many cases of summary or arbitrary execution, forced or involuntary disappearance, torture, rape and pillage committed by members of the federal army. Paramilitary groups and militias have also been guilty of similar abuses. The Committee regrets the extremely low number of inquiries into these violations, the failure to take measures to punish the guilty and prevent any recurrence of such acts, and the consequent impunity of those responsible.

6. The Committee also expresses its concern over conditions in detention centres, the situation of the civilian population, particularly women, children and the elderly, in areas of conflict, and the situation of displaced persons. The Committee also regrets the extent of the restrictions and limitations placed on the exercise of the freedom of movement, the right to protection of privacy, freedom of religion, expression, assembly and association and the right to take part in the conduct of public affairs.

0216

7. The Committee also expresses its concern over the deterioration in the situation of ethnic, religious and linguistic minorities, particularly those of Albanian and Hungarian origin, and the population groups which have become de facto minorities as a result of recent inter-ethnic conflicts.

D. Suggestions and recommendations

8. In view of the serious situation prevailing in the State party, the Committee recommends the Government to take all necessary measures to stop violations of human rights, particularly those relating to the right to life and the prohibition of torture. These measures should include re-establishment of control over the army, dissolution of paramilitary militias and groups, punishment of those guilty of violations and adoption of measures to prevent a recurrence of such abuses. The Committee also recommends full application of article 27 of the Covenant, which recognizes the right of persons belonging to ethnic, religious or linguistic minorities to enjoy their own culture, to profess and practise their own religion and to use their own language.

0217

**UNITED
NATIONS**

**International covenant
on civil and
political rights**

CCPR

Distr.
GENERAL

CCPR/C/79/Add.5
25 September 1992

Original: ENGLISH

HUMAN RIGHTS COMMITTEE

CONSIDERATION OF REPORTS SUBMITTED BY STATES PARTIES
UNDER ARTICLE 40 OF THE COVENANT

Comments of the Human Rights Committee

BELARUS

1.   The Committee considered the third periodic report of Belarus
(CCPR/C/52/Add.8) at its 1151st, 1152nd and 1153rd meetings, held on 14 and
15 July 1992, and adopted* the following comments:

A.   Introduction

2.   The Committee expresses its appreciation to the State party for its
report and for engaging through a high-ranking delegation in a constructive
and frank dialogue with the Committee. The wealth of additional information
provided in the introductory statement and in the replies given by the
delegation of Belarus to the questions raised by the Committee and by
individual members has allowed the Committee to have a clearer picture of the
overall situation in the country at a turning point in its history as it makes
the transition toward multi-party democracy. The report, and the additional
information that was subsequently provided, have enabled the Committee to
obtain a comprehensive view of the State party's compliance with the
obligations undertaken under the International Covenant on Civil and Political
Rights and human rights standards set forth therein.

---

*   At the 1172nd meeting, held on 29 July 1992.

GE.92-17647/1149K (E)

0218

B. Positive aspects

3.   The Committee notes with satisfaction that there has been clear progress
in securing civil and political rights in Belarus since the consideration of
the second periodic report, and especially since the submission of the third
periodic report in July 1990. It is particularly noteworthy that the reforms
in Belarus are being handled in a manner that allows a propitious social and
political environment for the further protection and promotion of human rights.

4.   The Committee also notes with satisfaction that recently enacted laws,
notably the Law on Citizenship, are of a liberal character, demonstrating the
Government's intention to restructure society in accordance with basic
democratic principles. Existing laws, for example those relating to national
minorities, are also generally being applied in a manner compatible with the
Covenant. Additionally, it welcomes the readiness of the Government of
Belarus to make use of the experiences of established democracies with respect
to the promotion and protection of human rights.

C.   Factors and difficulties impeding the implementation of the Covenant

5.   The Committee notes that the heritage of the negative aspects of the past
could not be rectified overnight and that much remains to be done to make
irreversible the process of introducing multi-party democracy and
strengthening the rule of law. The Committee also notes that Belarus
continues to face various problems during the present period of transition
that make the task of implementing civil and political rights particularly
difficult. In this connection, it also notes that the Government's efforts in
restructuring the existing legal system have at times been hampered by certain
lacunae in national legislation as well as by continuing resort to legislation
of the former regime.

D.   Principal subjects of concern

6.   The Committee expresses concern about the fact that certain drafts,
pending before the legislature, are not fully in conformity with the
provisions of the Covenant, particularly in respect of freedom of movement.
Problems in this regard relate in particular to grounds on which passports may
be issued, and to clauses dealing with exit visas, particularly in respect of
holders of State secrets - which are incompatible with article 12,
paragraph 3, of the Covenant. The Committee is also concerned as to the
planned retention of the internal residence permit ("propiska") system. The
retention of the death penalty for many offences, even though limited in
application, is also of concern to the Committee. The retention of the
classification of persons belonging to any religion, in particular the Jewish
faith, as a distinct nationality is also without justification. In many areas
not covered by new legislation, much depends on the good will of the
authorities, with the danger still present that the latter would be unduly
influenced by certain attitudes inherited from the past.

E.   Suggestions and recommendations

7.   The Committee considers it to be particularly important that constitutional and legislative reforms should be expedited and that they should be in full conformity with the existing international standards enshrined in the International Covenant on Civil and Political Rights.   In drafting new legislation affecting human rights special attention should be paid to the establishment of effective judicial guarantees for the safeguard of civil and political rights.   Attention should be paid in all legislation to ensure that any limitations on human rights are in strict conformity with the limitations to those rights permitted in the Covenant.   Existing provisions limiting or restricting freedom of movement, including the requirement for exit visas and the clause relating to holders of State secrets, should be eliminated from pending legislation to bring it fully into conformity with article 12, paragraph 3, of the Covenant.

0220

**International covenant
on civil and
political rights**

Distr.
GENERAL

CCPR/C/79/Add.7
25 September 1992

Original: ENGLISH

HUMAN RIGHTS COMMITTEE

CONSIDERATION OF REPORTS SUBMITTED BY STATES PARTIES
UNDER ARTICLE 40 OF THE COVENANT

<u>Comments of the Human Rights Committee</u>

MONGOLIA

1.   The Committee considered the third periodic report of Mongolia
(CCPR/C/64/Add.2) at its 1155th to 1157th meetings, held on 16 and 17 July 1992,
and adopted* the following comments:

A.   <u>Introduction</u>

2.   The Committee expresses its satisfaction for the timely submission of the
third periodic report of Mongolia, which followed the Committee's guidelines and
which contained valuable information on the situation in Mongolia at the present
time. The Committee appreciates, in particular, the high-level representation
sent to discuss the report, which served as an indication of the importance
attached by the Government of Mongolia to its obligations under the Covenant.
Although its dialogue with the delegation was a useful one, the Committee
regrets that insufficient information was provided, both in the report and in
the answers supplied by the delegation, concerning key elements in the relevant
legislation currently being considered in Parliament. Numerous draft laws and
decrees were cited during the course of the consideration of the report but the
lack of information as to their content impaired the Committee's ability to
assess their potential impact.

---

*At the 1173rd meeting, held on 29 July 1992.

GE.92-17657 (E)

0221

B.   Positive aspects

3.   The Committee notes with satisfaction the significant progress made, since
the consideration of Mongolia's second periodic report, toward establishing and
developing a legal order and democratic institutions which would promote the
protection of human rights.   The new Constitution has been drafted in the spirit
of the Covenant and an extensive reform of the civil, criminal and penal codes
is foreseen.   Similarly, the Committee is encouraged by the indications of the
delegation that many of the restrictive practices of the past are no longer in
force.   The Committee notes with particular satisfaction the recent accession of
Mongolia to the Optional Protocol.   Taken together, these notable developments
indicate that the Government of Mongolia takes very seriously its obligations
under the Covenant and is moving toward establishing a firmer legal basis for
the realization of the rights contained therein.

C.   Factors and difficulties impeding the application of the Covenant

4.   The Committee notes that widespread economic dislocations of resources
accompanying the transitions presently under way in the country have hindered
the full application of the Covenant and the establishment of a new system of
well-functioning democratic institutions and procedures.   For example, the lack
of adequately trained staff in the Mongolian legal service has adversely
affected efforts to reform the judiciary.

D.   Principal subjects of concern

5.   The Committee expresses its concern over the unclear position of the
Covenant in Mongolian law.   Measures undertaken so far to give effect to the
Covenant have not gone far enough in providing judicial guarantees for each
right recognized in the Covenant or toward ensuring that the Covenant can be
invoked by individuals in a court of law.   Similarly, the Committee is concerned
about the continuing applicability of old laws and procedures which have not yet
been revoked or replaced by new legislation providing guarantees and, in
particular, establishing recourse procedures.   In regard to a number of
fundamental rights recognized in the Covenant, some requirements and limitations
presently in force in Mongolian law are so broad and numerous as severely to
restrict the effective exercise of such rights in actual practice.   This is
true, for example, in regard to the criteria for declaring a state of emergency;
the criteria for refusing an application for an exit visa or passport; the
requirement of prior permission for the holding of public meetings and the
criteria for refusing such meetings; and the requirement that political parties
be registered and the criteria for refusing registration.   Additionally, the
absence of adequate mechanisms to appeal against administrative decisions
creates an uncertainty as to whether such fundamental rights as freedom of
association, freedom of assembly and freedom of movement are fully enjoyed in
actual practice.   The Committee also expresses its concern over the exercise and
application of the death penalty in Mongolia.   Grounds for invoking the death
penalty are currently too broad to be in conformity with article 6 of the
Covenant and the number of execution of capital punishments is alarmingly high.

E.   Suggestions and recommendations

6.   The Committee recommends that the State party should ensure that the
provisions of the Covenant be fully incorporated into domestic law and able to
be invoked in a court of law.   The review presently in progress of current and

0222

proposed legislation, policies and administrative procedures should be based on the Covenant and other international human rights instruments in order to ensure that forthcoming changes will accord with the obligations of the State party under these instruments. In regard to the declaration of a state of emergency, the State party should ensure that applicable legislation is in conformity with the Covenant, particularly in regard to paragraph 2 of article 4. The Committee also emphasizes that the texts of the Covenant and the Optional Protocol should be widely publicized in order that the general public, the judiciary and the relevant agencies of the Government are made aware of the rights enshrined in the provisions of these instruments. Adequate training in human rights norms should be provided for attorneys and members of the judiciary as well as for police, prison and other security officials. In undertaking the implementation of these recommendations, the Committee suggests that the State party further avail itself of the Advisory Services and Technical Assistance Programme of the Centre for Human Rights.

0223

**International covenant
on civil and
political rights**

Distr.
GENERAL

CCPR/C/79/Add.8
25 September 1992

Original: ENGLISH

HUMAN RIGHTS COMMITTEE

CONSIDERATION OF REPORTS SUBMITTED BY STATES PARTIES
UNDER ARTICLE 40 OF THE COVENANT

<u>Comments of the Human Rights Committee</u>

PERU

1.   The Human Rights Committee began the consideration of the second periodic
report of Peru (CCPR/C/51/Add.4) at its 1133rd to 1136th meetings (forty-fourth
session), held on 31 March and 1-2 April 1992 (CCPR/C/SR.1133-1136). The Committee
decided, at the request of the Government of Peru, not to conclude the
consideration of that report until its forty-fifth session, and to take into
account the additional information offered by the State party and that was to be
supplied in response to the unanswered queries and concerns of Committee members.

2.   Subsequently, after it had become aware of the events that had occurred in
Peru on 5 April 1992 and which affected human rights, the Committee decided, at its
1148th meeting, held on 10 April 1992, to request that a supplementary report
dealing with those events should also be submitted to it for consideration
(together with the additional information) at its forty-fifth session.
Accordingly, having taken into account the consideration of Peru's second periodic
report (CCPR/C/51/Add.4) during its 1133rd to 1136th meetings, and having noted the
additional information provided by the Government of Peru (CCPR/C/51/Add.5) and
having considered the supplementary report on the effects of the 5 April incidents
on the implementation of articles 4, 6, 7, 9, 19, and 25 of the Covenant
(CCPR/C/51/Add.6) at its 1158th to 1160th meetings, held on 20 and 21 July 1992
(CCPR/C/SR.1158-1160), the Committee adopts* the following comments:

_____

    *   At the 1175th meeting, held on 30 July 1992.

GE.92-17662 (E)

0224

A.   Introduction

3.   The Committee expresses its appreciation for the Government of Peru's cooperation in continuing the dialogue during the consideration of the State party's second periodic report, and especially for providing the additional information on the report as offered by the delegation and complying with the Committee's requests for a supplementary report relating to the situation in Peru after 5 April 1992. While the representatives of the State party have made a commendable effort to answer the numerous queries raised by members, the Committee regrets that its concerns have not been adequately addressed and that most of the questions were not answered satisfactorily, both in the oral presentations and in the addendum to the report. It notes with disappointment that the delegation's offer, made at the Committee's forty-fourth session, for some of the answers to be given in writing had not been acted upon. It also regrets that the State party did not provide information on problems relating to the Covenant's application as a consequence of the events of 5 April 1992, as was requested by the Committee. As a result, the Committee has found it difficult to form a comprehensive view of the human rights situation in Peru during the interval under review and, in particular, the period after 5 April 1992.

B.   Positive aspects

4.   The Committee welcomes the enactment, both prior to and after 5 April 1992, of legislation concerning procedures for registering complaints about extrajudicial detention and torture, and allowing prosecutors to visit and monitor detention centres. The Committee also welcomes the legislative expression of culpability for all persons, including State officers, who engage in terrorism, arbitrary and excessive use of force, or cause disappearances. The Committee also regards as an important feature the creation of a new register on detainees and the envisaged change in the composition of the National Council for Human Rights, in order that members of different Government agencies whose activities affect the realm of human rights be represented therein. The Committee notes also the recent strong statements addressed to the army and police by the President of Peru concerning the importance of human rights.

C.   Factors and difficulties impeding the application of the Covenant

5.   The Committee finds little information in the report itself, relating to the period prior to 5 April 1992 and notes the Peruvian Government's view that much of the system existing before that date suffered from serious and profound flaws and needed reconstruction. Developments after 5 April 1992, when the Executive Branch seized all powers of the Peruvian State and constituted the Government of Emergency and National Reconstruction, have also not been encouraging. The Committee considers that the internal disorder and lawlessness in Peru, both before and after 5 April 1992, have obstructed the Covenant's effectiveness and, in some cases, rendered it inapplicable.

6.   In this connection, the Committee observes that during all the period under examination the assumption of power by military forces in the areas declared to be under a state of emergency has rendered the implementation of certain rights and

freedoms guaranteed under the Covenant ineffective. The acceptance by the Government of civilian vigilante groups that have full army support, notably the peasants' patrols (rondas campesinas) has worsened the situation, and it is clear that the Government is not in a position to rectify various abuses, including excessive and indiscriminate retaliatory responses to terrorist acts.

7.   It remains to be seen if the changes brought about by the Government of Emergency and National Reconstruction will assist in the restoration of internal law and order in Peru. At the present time there is no evidence that this is the case. The concentration of all power in the hands of the Executive, the unilateral changes by the Government of Emergency and National Reconstruction in the Judiciary, and the serious disruptions caused to the legal system have, in the Committee's opinion, impeded the application of the Covenant in Peru.

D.   Principal subjects of concern

8.   The Committee expresses its deep concern about the terrorism which appears to form part of the daily life in Peru. The Committee condemns the atrocities perpetrated by insurgent groups, and is particularly disturbed by the scale of terrorist violence, which shows no consideration for the most basic human rights. Nevertheless, the Committee also censures excessive force and violence used by the military, the para-military, the police, and armed civilian groups. It is troubled by the great number of complaints of extrajudicial executions and disappearances attributed to the security forces. In this respect, the Committee is deeply concerned with the absence of civilian control over the military and para-military groups, especially in the zones under their control, which in some cases amounts to impunity. In particular, the Committee regrets that they can be tried for acts of violence only under military law. The Committee considers that combating terrorism with arbitrary and excessive State violence cannot be justified under any circumstances.

9.   The Committee also expresses concern about the circumstances relating to the events of 5 April 1992. The terms of Decree-Law 25418, which transformed the Executive into a Government of Emergency and National Reconstruction and dissolved other constitutional powers, has effectively suspended important parts of the Constitution and rendered the State of law uncertain; it has left the legal system and the Judiciary in disarray; it has also resulted in the de facto suspension of habeas corpus and amparo, and in the retroactive application of new legislation, especially that drawn up for specific cases.

10. The Committee has serious concerns about the application of the state of emergency in Peru. No formal notice of derogation relating to this period has been received by the Secretary-General. Procedural requirements have not been complied with. Although the Peruvian delegation told the Committee that no non-derogable right under article 4 had been derogated from, the Committee was not informed which articles of either the Covenant or the Constitution were regarded as suspended.

11. The temporary detention on 5 April 1992 of opposition leaders, mainly politicians, labour leaders and journalists, is also a cause for concern and the Committee does not find the reasons for such detentions convincing. Nor can the

0226

unavailability of certain rights to those and other persons, resulting from the events of 5 April 1992, be legally justified.

12.   The Committee also observes with concern that large numbers of persons are held for prolonged periods before trial in police cells, including women with their children.   This cannot be considered compatible with the rights guaranteed under article 9 of the Covenant.

13.   A further matter of concern related to follow-up action taken pursuant to the views adopted by the Committee under the Optional Protocol with regard to Peru, namely communications Nos. 202 (1986) and 203 (1986).   The Committee regrets that no response has been received, despite the request by its Rapporteur on follow-up and repeated queries raised during the dialogue.

E.   Suggestions and recommendations

14.   The Committee notes the intention of the Government of Peru to restore democracy and the rule of law.   However, it considers that especially during the current period, in which the totality of the State's powers lie in the Executive, the Government must pay due attention to the implementation of the rights and freedoms guaranteed under the Covenant.   In the event that emergency circumstances warrant derogation from such rights, they should be strictly confined to the limitations specified under article 4, and other States parties and the Committee should be duly notified of the facts and details of such derogations.   The Committee hopes that the re-establishment of the democratic system will take place as soon as possible.   As elections for a Constituent Assembly have been scheduled for 22 November 1992, the Committee looks forward to seeing full implementation of the rights and freedoms under the Covenant in the near future.

0227

외교문서 비밀해제: 한국 인권문제 8

한국 인권문제 시민적 · 정치적 권리 국제규약 인권보고서 3

초판인쇄 2024년 03월 15일
초판발행 2024년 03월 15일

지은이 한국학술정보(주)
펴낸이 채종준
펴낸곳 한국학술정보(주)
주 소 경기도 파주시 회동길 230(문발동)
전 화 031-908-3181(대표)
팩 스 031-908-3189
홈페이지 http://ebook.kstudy.com
E-mail 출판사업부 publish@kstudy.com
등 록 제일산-115호(2000. 6. 19)

ISBN 979-11-7217-062-2 94340
        979-11-7217-054-7 94340 (set)